The Other Way

The Other Way

A Book of Experiences in Meditation
Based on the *I Ching*

Carol K. Anthony

Anthony Publishing Company
Stow, Massachusetts U.S.A.

Anthony Publishing Company
206 Gleasondale Road, Stow, Massachusetts 01775, U. S. A.

Library of Congress Card Number 89-81483
ISBN-0-9603832-5-5

Printed in the United States of America
Cover by John Holden and Leslie Iverson (Iverson Design)

Contents

Contents

Introduction

When in 1979 I was preparing to publish my first book, *A Guide to the I Ching*, I was aware that it was the first of three books I might write on the *I Ching*, the ancient Chinese oracle. The second book, *The Philosophy of the I Ching*, was published in 1981. This is the third book, relating many of the experiences I had in meditation which gave rise to the other two books, but it is also about the ongoing inner life that one discovers through having such experiences. It is composed of some 250 of more than 300 meditations which occurred over 17 years, from 1972 to the present, 1990.

The meditation technique I describe was taught me by the *I Ching*. As I have explained elsewhere, this technique differs from any of which I am aware.

Many of the concepts mentioned in this book are unique to the *I Ching* and its particular psychology. For example, the human personality is divided into what the *I Ching* calls the Superior Man, the Inferior Man, and the Inferiors. Seen in meditation they are one's essential self, one's ego (or self-image), and one's body self.

The concept of the ego referred to in this book differs from that described by Freud and Jung. The ego is experienced in meditation as a false self, entering our personality surreptitiously, perhaps the way viruses disguise themselves as normal cells so that they are accepted by the body. Through clever rationales, the ego convinces our essential self that it is better-endowed to lead our personality. Once installed as leader of the self, it thrusts the essential self aside in a dominating way, asserting itself as "I." Only during shock and adversity is it discredited, though only temporarily. It is then, however, that we are able to discover the subtle flatteries by which we have allowed it to become dominant. Only then do we discover the necessity to liberate our essential self from the ego's tyranny and deceptions.

Throughout this book I have used terms such as the

Unknown, the Universal Teacher, Sage, and Higher Power interchangeably as different aspects of the Creative Force, or God. I have done so because, as the reader will see, no one term serves to describe adequately all the ways in which this force manifests itself in meditation.

I wish to thank those to whom I am most endebted in producing this book. I am particularly grateful to Pierre Seronde for his editorial assistance, Ethan Anthony for his critique, and John Holden and Leslie Iverson, of Iverson Design, for designing and preparing the cover.

Carol K. Anthony

1.

Meditation as the Other Way

Recently, while I was searching for a title for this book, a good friend began meditating to treat her "incurable" cancer. She had been given six months to live, and she had remarked to me, "For me there is no other way left." This is a book about the other way provided by meditation.

When I had begun to meditate eighteen years ago, I had had done so as a last resort to resolve difficult emotional problems. I had not been desperately ill like my friend, but I was exhausted from emotional stress, and headed towards death through my despair and hopelessness. The cause was the breakup of my marriage after 19 years. I had seen no options, either to repair my marriage, or to be released from the consequences of divorce. In my despair I called to "whatever powers there be," for help.

Although I did not recognize it at the time, help came within a day, brought by my friend Faith—in the form of the *I Ching*, the ancient Chinese oracle consulted through tossing coins. What, I thought, could something so bizarre as that do for me? Only the credibility and sincere good wishes of my friend made me open my mind enough to think, somewhat disparagingly, "Well, why not at least look at it."

Its messages were repetitive, saying to me over and over: "Meditate, quiet the thinking of the heart." Its insistence on this one point made me decide to attempt meditation.

I had no particular resistance to meditating. In fact, I had been impressed when some years earlier my voice teacher had told me she had overworked. To recover from exhaustion she had learned the Transcendental Meditation technique from her daughter. After she began meditating, she said she could handle anything that came. I had always been impressed by her energy and resilience. Even now, at age 84, she still has a full roster of voice students. Knowing that meditation had served her so well, I was interested to try it.

In addition to counseling me to meditate, the *I Ching* spoke to something within me that had been neglected. It seemed to nourish and strengthen me so that almost immediately I began to feel better, not quite so hopeless, not quite so desperate. It was as if its words and images fanned oxygen over the dim coals of my life force. Gradually, they lighted and began to burn again, even though there had been no changes in my outward circumstances.

Thus in the quiet of my room, with the *I Ching* as guide, I embarked on the inner journey. In doing so I was pulled back from a brink and made to revitalize and heal myself. This new direction brought me in contact with something that can only be discovered and understood within—the mysterious and wonderful Presence I call the Sage, the invisible inner teacher.

About the Meditation Process

We tend to think of meditation only as a form of contemplation. That is, after all, the definition of the word. If, however, we dare go deeper into the inner darkness, we discover an inner world that is no less real than the outer one. Different from our outer-world reality, however, is the fact that our experiences of the inner world lead to utter clarity. We are presented with incontrovertible truths. While our outer world experiences lead us to know we exist, we do not know why. We suspect that we have a purpose, but we do not know what it is. In the inner world such matters are resolved, without question. Thus, the inner world, reached though meditation, is a place of insight.

Of course not all insight comes by way of meditation. Sometimes insight comes of itself, while we are driving a car, or walking along. Many people have found routes to insight which do not require meditating. The poet invokes his muse. The inventor discovers an empty space in his mind through which his invention comes. Athletes put themselves into certain inner spaces that enable them to play far beyond what they consider to be their "normal" capacity. Actors and musicians find a special place of concentration in which they are so detached that while performing they seem to be watching themselves and their audiences at the same time. All these people have found the same inner place—a place of intense creativity in which they feel themselves to be but vehicles for what is happening. I daresay that every great breakthrough in human knowledge and understanding is due to someone's having found it within himself.

The fact remains, however, that having found our way there, we still may lose it and wonder, for years, how to return. I hope the experiences I relate in this book will demonstrate to anyone who is interested, how to find this way.

To arrive at this special place within ourselves it is necessary to achieve a finely-tuned inner balance. Then the insight breaks through like lightning. Inner balance creates a sort of lightning rod within ourselves, drawing the insight to us. The insight usually occurs after we have been intensely interested in understanding a problem, or after we have struggled conscientiously to realize the right way to go or the right thing to do. Then, when we have given up on it, let it go in the recognition that we do not have the ability make it come, we become a receiver in the way a radio receives radio waves. Just as there is something "out there" (a radio transmitter) to communicate with the radio, there is something "in there," that communicates with us when we have made ourselves appropriately receptive. That which communicates is complete in its knowing—without limits. Moreover, "it" seems to know what we need—the precise "next step" in our learning process, or the precisely appropriate response to our situation. In the case of the performer, his physical motions become perfect to his task. Ironically, our ability to make ourselves into a lightning rod occurs only when, through making a conscious effort, we become free of conscious effort. Accomplishing this is the function of the meditation technique.

Despite the fact that a host of techniques for meditating exists, none, to my knowledge, lead to the type of experi-

3

ences described in this book. When I first began having them I thought, "So this is why people are so enthusiastic about meditating!" Then I discovered that none of the books I found on the different styles of meditation even mentioned such experiences. Moreover, it is probable that most techniques would prevent them. Zen meditation aims at achieving an empty state of mind, but keeping all thought dispersed might prevent the breakthrough of insight. People who have practiced techniques which use mantras or involve staring at candles tell me they seem to have had experiences, but of being unable to remember them afterwards. Guided Meditation, by which a group leader provides a scenario and then leaves the meditator to finish the scene, or action, may lead to the meditator's perceiving the images of which I speak, but because the guide acts as an interpreter, the insight might get lost. The problem with most techniques is that the meditator controls the process.

The inner chamber of the mind in which insights occur can be reached only when we have stripped ourselves of all aspects of self, and after we have relinquished all control. Asking to be shown the way, and to understand, we present ourselves simply and humbly before the Inner Teacher. All mental supervision conflicts with this principle. We must be willing to relinquish control.

What we experience in meditation is not the product of our imagination, or reasoning, but something that appears of its own accord. It does not necessarily occur with every effort to meditate. We can in no way force it to happen. When it comes, we have the distinct feeling it comes from something beyond us, as a gift. Only afterwards might we allow our intellect or ego to assign an identity or rationale to explain it.

To achieve the state of balance required of meditation, it is necessary to do a few physical exercises to free our bodies of restless energy; then we follow mental procedures that will empty our minds of all fantasy and thought. By following these procedures, which I shall describe more fully elsewhere, we detach from our preoccupation with external affairs, and from consciousness of our body self. We do this through dealing with the contents of consciousness rather than through suppressing, or bypassing them. Thus, wher we say, "I can't meditate, there's too much agitation," that thought becomes the subject and work of meditation.

Although we work towards an ideal of balance and detachment, we do not allow that, or any, goal to dominate us. We deal only with that which shows itself. Then our eyes are freed to look inward, and our ears are freed to hear thoughts which come from the Cosmos. So long as our inner space is filled with clutter, there is no room to receive thoughts which come from beyond ourselves. Humility, determination, and patience with ourselves create this space.

The most notable characteristics of these unusual experiences are: (1) the sheer genius of the thoughts that come in the form of insights, (2) their beauty of expression in terms of form, and (3) the deep knowledge we have that we are only participating in the event, either as a receiver or as a performer, (4) that the thing given is a gift, and (5) that it "happens" to us. In no way can we make it happen; we can only put ourselves in proximity to it so that it can happen. Then, when it happens, we recognize that the experience is subtle and rare. We know at once that others can understand it only if it has happened to them.

The most dramatic meditations occur when we feel driven to understand, or desperate to know which way to go. At such moments we profoundly realize the impotence of all our contrived, ego-centered efforts, and we perceive our great need for help from a source beyond ourselves. Being cognizant of our insufficiency, we attain the deep sincerity and modesty that brings a response.

An essential part of our preparation, therefore, involves acquiring the humility to ask to be shown, and to understand. When our asking comes from the deepest essence of ourself, and not from our ego-self-image, we find ourselves in the presence of the Teacher. (Here ego means the contrived self that we want to be, rather than the unadorned self we really are. Note that the ego asks for specific kinds of help—money to get by, justice to punish the wicked, specific remedies to correct situations; the essential self asks for unqualified help to come in whatever form the Higher

Power sees fit to provide.)

Detachment is in itself a higher mental plane that makes insights possible. Detachment from private, personal interest, from the body self, and from the emotions, enables us to look within. In the case of performers, they are able to draw from this inner resource when their motives are not to shine personally, but to express the essence of the work they are performing. They fulfill what Lao Tzu described in the saying, "The Master Potter leaves no trace [of himself]." This is not to say that selfish interests do not later intrude, or that the ego will not re-emerge to claim itself as the inventor, creator, or great performer, for it is the nature of the ego to do so. But so long as the ego remains as the controller, or is the driving force, the inner resource cannot be tapped.

Because of my meditations I gradually lost all doubt about the existence of this unseen Teacher, or Sage, which teaches through meditations, dreams, and insights, and through the oracle of the *I Ching*.

This Sage grants an abundance of gifts to those who place themselves in proximity to learn. The only requirement is a deep humility and desire to understand. More than one of my experiences pointed out the unwillingness of the Sage to interfere directly in our lives. Only occasionally, when we are in the great danger of doubt, or are paralyzed by fear, might the Sage interfere. Sometimes this interference comes by way of vivid and inexplicable dreams, sometimes by being struck with a powerful insight; sometimes we hear a calm but firm and authoritative voice. Mostly, however, we must seek out the Sage through finding the correct attitude.

Since my technique for meditating was learned from the *I Ching*, I cannot say that the *I Ching* is not also an essential accompaniment to meditating this way. It is my experience that in our inner darkness we need a lantern. The *I Ching* is just such a lantern, for we find, in consulting it, that our inmost thoughts are uncovered and brought to consciousness. An infallible mirror to our egos, it keeps us from the dangers of self-delusion. In my experience, the *I Ching* reading and the meditation accompany one another. When I did not understand an *I Ching* metaphor, it was revealed to me during meditation.

To prepare for meditating I do deep breathing, as in Yoga; I use images to cleanse my mind and heart, as in Guided Meditation; I empty myself of all thought, as in Zen. These activities lead to the inner chamber. There we must wait for entry to the inner world. We only listen and watch. What we see or hear is either self-explanatory, explained by a voice, simply understood, or left with us as a puzzle to contemplate.

Undoubtedly, some people think meditation is self-hypnosis. The meditation I practice, however, is not self-hypnosis. Nor is the meditation state a trance. We are in a state of mental absorption that is nearly identical to reading a novel. It is as if we were in an inner theater watching the inner screen. We are pulled away from this scene by the doorbell or telephone as much as we are interrupted while reading a novel. Having been pulled away, we may return by adjusting our attitude, getting back into the theater, and allowing things to proceed again.

Sometimes what we see in meditation is like a movie. At other times it may be like a still life. Sometimes we merely hear sounds. Some meditations seem minuscule and almost insignificant, while others are big and full of meaning. The following, one of my early meditations, exemplifies the nebulous way meditations often begin.

The Inner House   early 1972

The experience began when I perceived a small bit of light coming through a doorway. As my eyes adjusted to the dim light I saw I was in a log hut which had no windows or floor, only a doorway. The interior was dirty, the walls covered with cobwebs, and the floor with rubbish—tin cans, discarded glass containers, and stones. All was untidy and uncomfortable. It was obvious the hut had not been tended in a long time, if ever.

Then I found myself wondering what this scene meant. No sooner had I mentally asked the question than I became aware that this hut was a reflection of my inner self—dirty, unkempt, neglected. The clutter represented mental trash in the form of worries, wants, and fantasies which I had allowed to accumulate, and had never discarded. The neglect was a statement that I never looked inside myself, or tended my inner condition. The whole was a statement that I needed to visit my inner space often and keep it clean.

Then I noticed that there was a broom against the wall. Obviously, I was meant to sweep out the trash and cobwebs, which I did. For a moment there was some question about what to do with the rubbish, but I decided that now was not the time to answer that. It was important only to sweep everything out of the interior. After this inner cleansing I felt remarkably free for many days.

This hut appeared in many more meditations in which I regularly cleaned it. During this time I found that it was much easier to let thoughts into my mind than to clean them out. Some kinds of thoughts, such as desires, and their attendant frustrations, required vigorous scrubbing. I consequently became more aware of the nature of the thoughts I allowed in, and more conscientious to keep them pure and good. Gradually, my hut improved. It soon had a floor, then windows. It became lighter inside. A year later it had changed to a neat Swiss chalet and its previously undistinguished location had become a pleasant Alpine meadow.

2.

The Meditation Process

Over many years I have obtained the best meditation results when I consulted the *I Ching* each night just before going to sleep, then meditated just after awaking.

Sometimes this has required getting up before others were awake so that my surroundings were quiet. Sometimes it has required letting others know that I might be doing this so that they would not disturb me until I was through. If circumstances made this impossible, I meditated each night before sleeping.

The total time I meditate is between 20 and 40 minutes. My three-part routine is composed of a preparatory period, a cleansing period, and an empty, waiting period. It is during the third period that insights may occur.

The first two parts of this routine require effort, but the third is free of effort. Occasionally, however, without having done any preparation, I will have an insight upon sitting down.

Before sitting down I do some stretching and limbering exercises, then sit cross-legged. I try to make my position as erect, balanced, and relaxed as possible without leaning on anything.

Once seated I try to relax every part of my body. I mentally inspect to see if my stomach, legs, feet, shoulders, and facial muscles are relaxed. Then I breathe in and out slowly and deeply about six times. Generally, my eyes are closed, and I look straight ahead. I then pay attention to how my body feels, to see if areas of pain, stiffness, or discomfort exist? If so, I sympathize with any part of my body which does not feel well. If there is pain, I visualize it, then shine a mental light on it. Then I do whatever else comes to mind to do.

Next, I ask my body's cooperation and patience while I meditate. I speak of the body as a being separate from myself because, in meditation, body elements are heard

9

and seen as separate from the essential self. When I first saw them in meditation they appeared as little people with childlike voices and attitudes. They constantly called attention to bodily concerns in phrases such as "I am hungry!" "I am tired!" "I am uncomfortable!" or, "Why are we doing this?"

When I first became aware of them, the little people were extremely vocal and undisciplined, and to achieve inner quiet, it was necessary to make them leave my inner space. Now they are more disciplined and I may even ask them to join me in meditating, or I may visualize them sitting in a position similar to mine. If any still resist, I make them leave my inner space.

Before my "first" meditation I had what I now think of as a semi-meditation. I say semi-meditation only because I was not conscious of its being a meditation. At the time I thought I must be conjuring up images, although later I realized that it was truly an insight.

The Vertebrae   early 1972

I first saw this image while meditating at night just before sleep, and after having consulted the *I Ching*. I had received *Keeping Still* (Hex. 52), which counsels you to achieve inner quiet through bringing "the nerves of the backbone to a standstill." I was wondering what this meant when I suddenly saw an image of my backbone. Curiously, it was in front of me, as if I were behind myself. Moreover, the image was of a cut-away section of the vertebrae such as you might see in an anatomy textbook. The entire spinal cord was exposed to view, along with the auxiliary nerves radiating outward to the arms, chest, and legs. Although it was black, a multitude of tiny lights blinked within it as if thoughts were busily passing from one cell to another in quick succession. Then I noticed that these lights were timed to the speed of my thoughts. As my thoughts speeded, they speeded; as my thoughts slowed, they slowed. Hundreds of lights, representing hundreds of thoughts and impulses, were traveling down from the brain to the body, while similar numbers of sensations, wants, and feelings

10

were traveling from the body back to the brain. In noticing how fast they were traveling, I recalled what I had read about Alpha and Beta waves, and that various stages of consciousness have different electroencephalogram readings. For instance, "normal" consciousness has a reading of 36 cycles per second, contemplation 12 to 8 cps, meditation 8-5 cps, and sleep 5-0 cps. I could see that my thoughts were now traveling full speed, for I could hear them prattling away as if hundreds of people were whispering. It came to me to shine a light on the entire spinal cord. Immediately, I had a flashlight in my hand and played the light up and down over the spinal cord. As I did this, the activity of the lights (along with the whispering voices) slowed, grew dimmer, and finally stopped. When they were extinguished I felt totally at peace.

From that time to this, when normal procedures fail to slow down my mental activity, I shine a light on my imaginary spinal cord, which I continue to envision in front of me. This is a most helpful image for reducing the restlessness that builds up between meditation sessions.

The second phase of meditation is that of inner cleansing, through emptying my heart of emotions and my mind of thoughts, so that I become totally neutral inside. Inner neutrality is essential for reaching the state which leads to insight.

Sometimes, during this phase of meditation I will be reminded of things I need to remember—appointments, people coming to dinner, or bills I need to pay, therefore, I keep a notebook handy to jot down memos to myself.

I begin this phase by examining my feelings. I inspect to see whether I feel either positive or negative about anything. Am I feeling enthusiastic, or gleeful about something good about to happen? Am I attached to hopes of success, or eagerly looking forward? Am I looking backward on anything in a self-congratulatory way? Do I desire anything? Or, am I down on the world? Do I feel hopeless about anything? Am I angry at an injustice, or am I impatient, or restless? Have I any gripes, or am I holding any grudges? Do I have a pet hate list? Am I indulging petty likes and dislikes in regard to anyone or anything? Am I dreading something coming up?

As attitudes, ideas, and images come to mind during this process, I bring them to full conscious attention, then do with them whatever it seems appropriate to do. For example I let go of anger, gripes, and grudges instead of holding them to me as my sacred right. I put hurt pride on an inner altar (see below), along with all petty likes and dislikes which I hold in the defence that "it is my human nature" to have them. I turn over to the Cosmos all hopes and desires, and their attendant frustrations. If I notice that I am focussing on future rewards, I remove my gaze from what "will be" and bring it back to the present. If I allow my gaze to drift to the side, to dwell on what others are doing, I pull my attention back to my own path. To shift this focus it is often necessary consciously to give others the same space to learn from their mistakes that I would want them to give me. If I find myself dwelling on the past, by remembering mistreatments and disappointments, I bury these as if they were rotting corpses lying around, so that I no longer carry them with me and allow them to intrude in my present life.

Next, I may examine whether my attitude is being influenced by any pacts I may have made in the past, or by any preconceived ideas or prohibitions that may act as defenses and barriers to the Unknown. I ask of God (the Unknown, the Higher Power) that I be freed of any false idea which blocks me from seeing things in their true light. The neutrality I seek is the neutrality of an open-mind.

Usually, in going through such a check-list, some negative memory, egotistical feeling, or reservation of attitude will come to mind. For example, I might have said to myself, "If am required to do something I dislike, I will abandon this path." Such hedging is a suspicion by our ego of the Higher Power; this isolates us from its help, and is unworthy. Perceiving such things, I put them on a visualized inner altar as an item of sacrifice. No sooner are they placed there than they disappear.

Although I have suggested a variety of things to do with inferior thoughts which inhabit the mind—letting go, burying, etc., I highly recommend the visualized inner altar I saw in meditation years ago, which I continue to use to this day. If the beginning meditator will place just about anything and everything he finds in his mind upon it, he will discover its truly magical powers to clean out his inner space, and to correct and heal himself.

The Bin, or Altar of Sacrifice   early 1974

Early in my meditative life, I was often counseled by the *I Ching* to sacrifice a particular attitude or habit of mind—the most common one being anger. Sacrifice is called for because anger is usually justified, and something we think we have a right to feel. Anger, however, is harmful both to the one who clings to it, and to the situation he would like to change. Sacrificing anger advances the general good.

While meditating, I was contemplating the need to sacrifice my anger. One element within me wanted to hold onto it, the other to let go. Then I was concerned to know just how I could sacrifice my anger. Then I saw myself placing it on an altar of sacrifice. Immediately, it disappeared, having become a delicious morsel for God.

No sooner had I done this than I began to think of all the other negative things I could let go of, which would be delicious morsels to present to God. Suddenly the small altar I saw became a great stainless steel bin, large enough to hold vast amounts of inner trash—wants, comforts, just causes for anger, and similar mental elements that make perseverance difficult. As soon as I put these thoughts and attitudes in the bin, they were cleaned entirely out of my mind and whisked away. The bin remained gleaming and empty.

Gradually, over many years, the altar has become smaller again. In addition to problem attitudes, I put on it all my concerns. If I observe something incorrect, I acknowledge it to be incorrect, then place it upon the inner altar for correction. This may only mean that I attain a more correct view of the thing I observe. My willingness to sacrifice my emotional reaction to a problem always leads to its correction.

To complete my inner cleansing I pull down the Cosmic Vacuum Cleaner—another gift I received in meditation—and vacuum out my mind. This frees me of any other petty trash that exists in my inner space—jingles, silly thoughts, or even the restless sort of static that sometimes lingers. The beginning meditator will find that he need only consider these images for them to become available for his use.

The Cosmic Vacuum Cleaner (and Breaking the Inner Mirror) about 1973

During a meditation I heard my inner voice saying flattering things others "must" be saying about me. Then I noticed that as these thoughts were being expressed, I was preening before an inner mirror. I immediately realized that this inner mirror had no place in my inner space, so I dashed it on the ground, only to notice with alarm that now instead of one mirror, hundreds of tiny mirrors were all reflecting vain thoughts at once. I began cleaning them up but they were sharp and pieces of glass jabbed my fingers. In exasperation I asked for help and then noticed that a long vacuum hose came down from above with which I could vacuum up the broken glass. From that time to this I have made much use of this device. One need only pull down this tube, which is about the size of an elephant's trunk, but with the drawing power of a small tornado, to have it whisk anything away.

As the next meditation shows, sometimes we see no objects to vacuum up, but there exists, after we have freed ourselves of bad feelings, a gaseous residue which must also be vacuumed up.

Getting Rid of the Bad Air about 1972

In this meditation I saw myself sitting in a darkened theater, as if waiting for the curtain to rise. I noticed the air seemed to be stagnant and unpleasant. Suddenly a breeze floated through the auditorium, carrying away the bad air.

I was made aware that stale air accompanies bad thoughts. This bad air must be cleared away, along with the bad thoughts. Now, as part of meditation, I vacuum up not only my thoughts but their accompanying stagnant air.

Finally, after completing these physical and mental preparations, I may reflect on any *I Ching* counsel I have received which I do not understand, and ask for help to understand it. Then I let go of everything that concerns me, even those things about which I most feel the need for guidance. Letting go means I turn them over to the Higher Power by putting them on the inner altar.

Letting go of everything helps us to attain acceptance, the perfect state of being that leads to meditations. By acceptance I do not mean we agree with anything or everything that has been happening to us in our external lives. Rather, we put these things aside. We cease resisting them and withdraw our inner connection to them. This is to suspend any inner disbelief that we will be able to deal with them.

Sometimes we think we must keep our eye on a situation to keep it from getting out of control. This idea is simply our fear perpetuating inner conflict, for no matter how much we stare at a problem, it will not be influenced by our gaze. Continuing to stare at it keeps us engaged with it. Meditation shows that we can influence a situation for the good only when we disengage from it, and regain objectivity and inner independence.

Acceptance is surrender. By this I mean we accept our need for help from the Higher Power. By Higher Power I mean that which we do *not* know rather than what we already believe. Our beliefs often serve as barricades against the Unknown, and prevent insights. They also restrict the way the Higher Power can relate to us, for wherever we structure, we also barricade. It is as if we distrust God, and say, in effect, "I am not willing to give you free rein. You can only come to me if you are willing to come in the garb of my belief." Beliefs prevent us from having the truly open mind which is necessary to total acceptance.

Finally, acceptance requires that we forgive everyone

and everything, including the Cosmos and ourselves. Forgiveness, after all, is the ultimate acceptance, for while it comes from the deepest and purest part of ourselves, it involves a great decrease in the importance of the self, a relinquishing of vanity and pride. Thus it is also a moment of great humility, the humility that allows us to enter the inner chamber of meditation where insights occur.

The third period of meditation begins once we have attained neutrality and acceptance, and involves waiting yet a little longer in the empty space. Then we sit, free of all effort, striving, and expectation, ready for what comes. We simply listen and watch, "tuned in" to the Cosmos the way a radio telescope passively, but attentively, "listens" for sounds coming from the Universe.

Thoughts and impulses may come. I listen and look at them, for they are the work of meditation. We may ask why we are seeing these things. Then we wait for the answer.

A meditation may be visual or auditory, big and dramatic, or minuscule, or almost inaudible. If we expect that something will be visual, we might miss it because it is only audible, or vice versa. We need not fear that the experience will require us to do anything. Usually we watch ourselves do things, as if we are members of an audience; what we do is being presented for our learning. There can be no bad experiences—all are there to make us think and enlarge our view. Although we may feel a feeling, we observe ourselves having that feeling. We observe its effect on us and on the situation presented. For example, in one meditation I felt a number of feelings which made streams of tears run down my eyes, but throughout this meditation I was somehow removed from it all. In an objective way I felt sympathy with myself, and understood why those feelings made me cry.

We need to realize that because the meditation-state is a finely-tuned inner balance, this balance is easily disturbed. The ego sleeps lightly and may reawaken at any time to sit on the sideline, as it were, and watch what is going on. For this reason it is important to allow the meditation to complete itself. Sometimes the profundity of the thoughts and experiences is such that our ego may rush

16

in to say, "At last—so this is enlightenment!" When we allow this to happen we interrupt the meditation so that our understanding of it remains incomplete. Some meditations are composed of images, followed by a pause, then an explanation. If we are patient we will sense when the meditation has completed itself. It is as if someone says, "Now it's over, you can go."

It is helpful if afterwards we write down everything we experience. Like dreams, meditations tend to evaporate from consciousness. Then we are left wondering what the realization was that helped us understand our circumstance.

If, after 30 or 40 minutes we have not yet had a meditation, we should get up and go on our way. If we have had a meditation but not yet received an explanation after waiting 10 minutes, we should cease meditating and allow the answer to come on its own, when it will. I had a number of meditations for which I never had explanations. In the meantime we should cease thinking of it and trust that in some way, perhaps subconsciously, it will be used to develop our understanding.

We should not regard it as a failure if we do not have a meditation. Although that is our goal, the nature of meditating requires us to be free of wanting and expectation. Wanting and expectation mean the ego is active, thus preventing meditation. If nothing happens we should remember that the meditation process is the important thing. If we concentrate only on the process, the goal will follow.

Of the three-part routine of meditating, I feel the first two parts to be the most important. Thus, if I have only 10 minutes to meditate, I am content to do only this part. Insights from meditations are simply a bonus, for I know that if I never do anything other than cleanse and purify myself, I will have improved my health and life through attaining inner harmony.

The following meditation was the first in which I recognized that something truly unique had happened. I relate it here to show that meditation involves not only yourself, but also the Higher Power, Sage, or Creative Force.

The Light Meditation   1972

This experience happened one morning between sleeping and waking, when I was not actively connected to any thought process. Suddenly and almost shockingly an intense light flooded into my barely-opened eyes. I was instantly on guard, as if to shut the light out as some "foreign thing." Then I heard a voice speaking in a gentle but commanding tone, "Allow this to happen." The voice was so authoritative that all my resistance faded, to allow the light to pour in through my eyes. I began to experience the most soothing effect, and I soon felt full of light. I felt exhilarated for days afterwards. From that time on I began to have the experiences related in this book, and to recognize that particularly vivid dreams are similarly meaningful.

I was not to realize the full meaning of this experience until about a year later, when I had the following meditation.

Opening the Inner Eye   1973

I saw a team of surgeons unwrapping bandages from the eyes of a man on an operating table. As he sat up, opened his eyes and blinked, I recognized my husband. I realized that he had undergone an operation on his eyes to enable him to see, but for now, and until his eyes had adjusted to the new environment, he could only see light.

My husband had also meditated that morning. When he finished he told me with amazement that the "strangest thing had happened." An intense light, he said, had poured into his eyes. He, too, had reacted with alarm when it first began, but then he allowed it to happen.

Because his first meditation was identical to my own, I realized that to see in the inner world in a conscious way, it is necessary to have our inner eyes opened. How is this to be done? Through asking, perhaps craving within ourself to be able to understand.

My husband quit meditating after that experience, saying he had found it unsettling. Several years later, after we had each gone our separate ways, he told me of having had the following experience just after waking.

Opening the Closed Door   about 1977

Finding himself standing in a room full of closed doors, my husband stood pondering whether to open one. Finally, he decided to do so. Inside the one he opened, a little old man sat on the floor, bathed in a beam of light. Looking up at my husband, the old man said, "I thought you'd never open that door!"

While my husband did not reopen the meditation door for many more years, he eventually did. It is my view that once opened, the door never stays entirely closed.

Meditations about Meditating

In consulting the *I Ching* I had received lines in various hexagrams that pointed to better ways of meditating. The first line of *The Clinging*, Hexagram 30, had counseled meditating first thing in the morning, when "thoughts run criss-cross." It was important to catch inferior thoughts and impulses just after sleeping, it said, when their energies were at the lowest ebb, and before they became empowered to rule our mind.

My early meditations continued this instruction. Some, such as the following meditation, worked in conjunction with the *I Ching* counsel I had just received. For example, I had drawn the first line of *Coming to Meet*, Hexagram 44, warning me of the danger of meeting inferior thoughts halfway (entertaining them). Once we dally with them, it said, they gain control. They must therefore "be checked with a brake of bronze...if one lets it take its course, one experiences misfortune. Even a lean pig has it in him to rage around." This power was demonstrated in the meditation which followed.

The Lean Pig   early 1972

Almost as soon as I closed my eyes I heard an obstreperous voice shout at me, "If you don't DO something (regarding the problem then bothering me) you will lose everything!" Then I felt a semblance of the fear that normally would accompany such a thought, but, remaining detached, I was able to notice its demanding tone. I realized that this was the lean pig referred to—an emotionally-driven thought which must be resisted at the outset. I had heard it as separate from myself, as if it had shouted in my ear. It was then I realized that just before a thought becomes fully empowered, we hear it as separate from ourselves; once it reaches full power it seems to be ourself thinking the thought. The instant I listened to it as reasonable, it changed from being separate and talking to me, to appearing to be my thought. I also noticed how difficult it had been to discard the thought, since it had sounded reasonable.

Then I heard another thought that was completely ridiculous. I do not remember the exact thought, but it was as absurd as "The moon is made of green cheese." I noticed there was no difficulty in discarding an absurd thought. Only when a thought seemed faintly plausible, I realized, did I entertain it, or "meet it halfway." I realized that the mind sheds absurd thoughts instantly, and greets something that comes through with clarity and insight instantly. The problem comes in the middle region, when a thought generates conflict or hesitation. The fact that such thoughts generate conflict and hesitation should be cause enough to reject them until we have developed a clear insight about them. Being indecisive about unresolved thoughts causes them to slide into the background of consciousness. Simply by not shutting them out of consciousness we endow them with a certain credence, thereby give them a foothold in our thinking. I had previously thought that I had been deliberate about the way I accepted or rejected ideas. I now realized that inferior and incorrect ideas entered my thinking by simple osmosis, through not having rejected them decisively.

This meditation was probably the first in which I became conscious that the screaming, hysterical voice which had plagued me during my waking hours was separate from myself. Sometimes it raged with anger, sometimes it burned with frustration. "Why am I not taking action?" it had asked, presenting to me a picture of myself as stupid and ineffectual.

Having thrown this bad actor out in the first meditation, I heard it in the next in a new guise. This time it tried to return through self-pity. As I began meditating I heard a faint, near-death-like whisper, "Poor me. Alas, How am I to endure?" and similar quaint phrases. It was so faint I nearly missed noticing it. As soon as I listened, however, with just the slightest wondering whether I ought to be feeling just a little bit sorry for myself, the voice instantly changed back to the loud, demanding, tyrannical voice. This, then, was just another tactic by which this other person within me was attempting to regain control.

In subsequent meditations it tried more subtle tactics. The next was flattery. "You deserve better." "Everyone has a right to happiness and justice." Envy, too, showed itself in phrases such as, "How unfair life is. How can they get away with things and I cannot?"

I soon noticed that all the rationales of this other self were based on half-truths which engaged my interest. But these rationales had one purpose only, to return that self to power. Any time I allowed it to guide me, I regretted the consequences and suffered recriminations and conflict, because I had acted in ways that were untrue to my nature.

Through all my dealings with this other self, I noticed that its arguments and rationales centered on my self-image—my injured pride, the way others looked, or might look, at me—and around my comfort or anything that might threaten it. It was totally self-oriented, concerned with its rights, wants, and frustrations, and with whether the world was treating it justly or unjustly.

The more I saw this self in meditation, the more I recognized that it was what the *I Ching* referred to as the "Inferior Man," or, ego. This ego, I realized, was my self-image, or the composite of self-images I had developed over the years.

Keeping free of my ego's efforts to resume control was a long and arduous struggle, but, by persevering, I began to overturn old habits of mind which operated simply because I had never resisted them. Through not resisting them they had become institutionalized patterns, and I had come to think of these patterns as my personality.

By continuing to listen to the first thoughts that entered my mind each morning after waking, I intercepted pacts I had made to "always do this," or "never again" do that; I heard unresolved worries and childhood fears; I discovered that I had accepted many ideas as true simply because they were commonly held, or because someone I admired had believed them. I recalled people and values my family had said were important and not important, and now re-examined the validity of thinking anyone is more important than another. Occasionally, I heard a thought expressed in the exact words and voice in which I had first heard it. I realized from all these things that the subconscious holds things we have long forgotten in vivid memory. Until we intercept them in meditation and re-examine their validity, they exercise power over us.

In the following three meditations I glimpsed the way such stored ideas influenced my thinking.

The Pond Meditation   about 1973

I saw the floor of a pond in cross-section. At the very bottom was clean sand; over this were layers of sediment from which gaseous bubbles occasionally floated up to the surface. I became aware that the clean sandy bottom represented the pristine condition of my mind at birth—pure and open. The gaseous sediment represented layers of accumulated conclusions I had developed or adopted from others about the way things work. The bubbles represented thoughts, loosened by events, which floated up into consciousness to influence my thinking.

I realized that I must remove these layers of conditioning to restore the pure and open mind I originally had.

The File Drawers   early 1973

In another meditation my subconscious appeared as old file drawers stored in a basement. Each file in the drawers represented one of my experiences and my conclusions about it. The files also contained dossiers on people, with records of hurts and unjust actions, along with notations of my anger and hurt pride. Just pulling out the file (remembering) awakened the old anger and pride. Included in the files were perceptions of what the situations meant, and the pacts I had made to react in a certain way should I ever meet like circumstances. Included were justifications for my attitude, such as, "I am this sort of person, therefore...."

The files also contained insights, premonitions, and reflections about life, along with remnants of my childhood hopes, fantasies, and terrors. I saw that these old files, stored beneath my consciousness, constantly influenced the way I identified and related to situations. They were so corrupted that it would be too difficult to sort the good from the bad. The only thing to do was to put the whole mess, along with the file cases which held them, into the fire which suddenly appeared for that purpose.

The Grid   December 1972

In this meditation I saw part of my mind as a giant grid. Each cell of the grid contained an opinion, a pet idea of how life works, a definition, or impression I had placed there. The grid, I realized, symbolized the way we pigeon-hole phenomena and experience to make us feel we "know it." In this meditation I no sooner saw the grid and heard some of the pigeon-holed ideas than an enormous shock crashed the whole structure. While the structure had appeared to be strong, it was really brittle, even more than glass. The shock had caused it to disintegrate. I realized that having such a collection of certainties inhibits us from perceiving things in a new way. Also, because the grid appears neat and orderly, it imparts a feeling of security that our opinions are true. Then I realized that just as programs drive computers, the ideas we place in these grid cells become an internal programming. False ideas or inadequate perceptions act as bugs in our program, causing malfunctions, or conflicts with the life process. This happens, for example, when stored negative memories add up to an embittered attitude. Negative things do happen, but we, as free spirits, have the choice: we will either give them a negative emphasis and make their negativity part of our operating program, or we will view each situation afresh.

Through meditations such as these, in conjunction with the help given by the *I Ching*, we are able to free ourselves from corrupted programs. Chief among my programming defects was my arrogant disbelief—a skepticism derived from believing (1) that we are born into a hostile universe,

(2) that we lack a nature adequate to deal with it, and (3) that no help of a higher nature exists to pull us through. These, in the *I Ching* viewpoint, are slanders on the truth. Incorrect beliefs act as obstructions to attaining harmony with ourselves, and hence with the Cosmos.

A friend of mine had a similar meditation about a grid, except that hers was a honeycomb. Instead of finding honey when she removed the top layer of wax, she found a worm in each cell!

In both these meditations the grids had become sources of trouble and had to be destroyed. In the first, the grid was rigid and brittle. My friend's meditation confirmed that such grids are the source of bad nourishment in the form of stored ideas.

Because our grids give us a feeling of security, we hesitate to throw them out, thereby disarming their capacity for mischief. We are afraid we cannot do without them. Nevertheless, if we realize that our reliance on comfortable, but incorrect, ideas only inhibits our growth, then we can find the courage to throw the ideas out. Many times we think we must put something else—other ideas—in their place, but this is unnecessary. We do not need to have anything in their place. Having nothing in their place is a starting point for learning from the Higher Power.

After my first few meditations I began to approach meditating eagerly. I did not realize that such anticipation would create a barrier to doing it. I had not had a meditation for perhaps two weeks when the following occurred:

The Doctor's Office   October or November, 1972

I found myself conscious of sitting on a hard bench in a doctor's office. I could tell it was a doctor's office because opposite me, hanging on the wall, was the doctor's certificate. No one else seemed to be waiting, just me. I waited and waited, and waited, and waited, all the while a little impatiently, wondering how long it would be before the doctor arrived. Waiting still longer I realized I was being impatient. Then it came to me that this meditation was about waiting, and about accepting waiting. Once this thought occurred, I decided to wait as well as I could, with acceptance. The moment I adjusted my attitude in this way, the doctor came into the room and greeted me. That was the end of the meditation. The message was: waiting in a correct attitude is the essence of the matter. The doctor, in this case, was the Sage.

This experience paved the way for my understanding that "looking ahead, aside, or behind" is the work of our ego. In looking forward the ego seeks to gain something, or to see if what we desire is forthcoming. It will follow the good only if it can foresee getting something tangible (go to heaven, or be saved from the fear of going to hell). It measures our effort as if to say, "if the correct way of making progress is too slow, I will use other means." In looking aside it is ever engaged in envious comparisons, to see if God unfairly allows others to get away with things we are not permitted to do. Looking behind, it paints nostalgic pictures which are out of all proportion to reality. It likewise magnifies griev-ances and feelings of alienation towards others. It is as if, before entering meditation, we inform the Sage, "if you are going to require me to forgive this or that person, I will not do it." It holds tenaciously to petty likes and dislikes, and to anger and alienation as if they were a spiritual birth-right. Because of this activity of our ego, we need to drop, or at least be willing to put aside, memories which condi-tion our way of seeing and relating to others.

In its stance as leader of the personality, the ego looks at all things conditionally, as if to say, "I'll go along with the Sage only to a point." In every way that we hedge in our commitment to following the good, our ego is there, placing conditions on our activities. Such hedging and supervising prevents our entering the place of insight.

The Leaning Tower of Pisa (Receiving the Ruby)
October 20, 1972

In this meditation I saw myself unable to sit up straight. I seemed to be leaning at an angle to the left. I tried propping myself up but this did not work. Then I saw the Leaning Tower of Pisa, and that it was leaning at precisely the same angle. I seemed to be pulled to the left by something I wanted in that direction, and the constant pulling caused by this wanting had undermined my foundation on the left side. The remedy, I realized, was to cease wanting. In trying to straighten up, however, I could not maintain myself in an upright position. My habit of wanting was too strong.

At this point I received help. I perceived that my medulla cortex was being lifted away. With my skull opened above the spine, a large, beautiful ruby was placed in the empty space at the top of my spine in such a way that it faced overhead, straight up. In this position it was aligned with heaven-earth energies, and transmitted these energies as a laser beam. Like a beacon, it kept me upright and balanced within. I was made aware that if I started to drift from my inner balance, remembering the laser beam would help me realign myself. (In a subsequent meditation I repaired my foundation by pouring cement under my left hip.)

This meditation made me realize that in meeting the Sage halfway, through meditating, we attain help in correcting problems. Here the help came in the form of a gift— the laser ruby. This meditation also showed the importance of being balanced within. There is no way we can know, until we see our inner self in meditation, whether or not we are balanced.

The Hearing Aid, or Key of G Meditation
November 14, 1972

I became aware of the Sage's presence, and I perceived that I was in his (doctor's) waiting room. I remembered having heard the day before a faint inner voice that I had not heeded. With regret I later wished it had been louder so that I would have paid better attention to it. It occurred to me, now in the presence of the Sage, to ask for a hearing aid so that I could hear his voice better.

He did not say anything, but I then found myself in a projection room where movies are shown, although it had no seats. Then I heard a faint sound in my ear which resembled radio static. I realized that the fuzzy hum was in the key of G. It came to me that if I listened for this faint sound within, I would afterwards hear the Sage. Then it was explained that my normal thoughts are so many and so fast that there is no room for the Sage's voice to come through, but if I will listen within to that sound, it will obliterate all the other sounds, leaving a space for the Sage's voice to come through loud and clear.

Then I noticed that the front of the chamber in which I stood was the middle section of the brain, lying just behind the frontal, memory section. To hear, we must keep this middle section clear. To see, we must project our point of vision through and beyond the memory section to a point out in space. It helps, when clarity is lacking, to project our inner eyes beyond the front part of our mind. Then the right visions and images can enter to give perspective to our thinking.

I then realized that the Sage could not give me a hearing aid, because this would be interfering with my free will, but if in modesty I would listen within, he would come to my aid.

Many more meditations involved my cranium. In these I appeared to be small, while my cranium was room-sized. In several meditations I saw the middle part of my cranium (behind the frontal lobes) as a projection room in which I could sit or stand. Later on it became an inner theater. Once my cranium was opened up (sawed through in cross-section, as it were), the light (understanding) was capable of coming into it. If I had not meditated for a while it was necessary to reopen it because it had grown over again.

I found it necessary to renew my inner openness repeatedly and consistently for some time, to break my habit of shutting off my inner consciousness. With each new problem or ambiguity I tended to shut off, or barricade, myself by returning to old defenses or by trying to force things to work the way they used to work.

In meditation we do not merely open our inner eyes and cranium. Eventually we open our entire inner self. Only through opening ourself up totally to the Sage can we free ourselves from the fear and doubt which isolate us from the help He can give.

Lenses of Identity   about 1984

In a meditation many years later I learned that the way I see others—the identity I develop of them over the years, forms lenses on my eyes. Through these lenses I see "the way they are" as if they and their habits of mind (or mistakes of perception) are one and the same thing.

I now realized that not only do these *lenses of identity* fix our attitude towards them, but they also prevent them from changing because they feel it useless to fight against our fixed opinions of them.

Also, because it is our ego which "fixes" them, their inner dignity prevents them from conforming to our idea of who they should be. They have no choice but to continue being whatever it is we have decided they are.

Understanding this process, I peeled off the lenses of identity I found on my eyes and placed them on my altar of sacrifice so that I could develop a truly open mind about others and thus free them from these negative effects.

Because of this and similar meditations I make it a habit, during the preparatory part of meditation, to visualize different people to see if in bringing them to mind I can find any traces of emotion or opinion connected with them. If so, I sacrifice these emotions and ideas.

Being Framed   December 7, 1989

I was involved in a situation with a relative in which I became misunderstood, so that everything I said or did aroused suspicion and mistrust.

The *I Ching* counseled me to free myself from hurt pride and attain a moderate view of the situation. This proved difficult, for however I sought to disperse my feelings, they returned.

Having known this person all her life, I shared a view often held by others that she tended to be "difficult."

In meditation I saw her, and then a number of other

relatives, with frames around their heads, as if they were living portraits of themselves. I saw that in her case the frame was my definition of her as difficult. Then I noticed that the frames also reminded me of the others' faults.

Then I realized that these "frames of identity" acted to "frame them," in the criminal sense of setting them up for conviction. Once created, the frames seemed to trap them in their negative behavior. Realizing this, the frames immediately dissolved, along with my negative feelings. I then realized the woman distrusted me because I possessed this frame.

I then saw my six-year-old grand-daughter. Having no frame she was free to be her innocent, loving self.

Throughout my meditative life I have been aware that it is necessary to forgive, but not forget, so as not to fall into presumptions that the relationship is better than it is. How, then, is one to remember without framing the person?

It came to me that the solution lies in holding the greater view that we are all on a path of self-development. We must be neither envious of those ahead, nor critical of those behind. When we frame others we forget that we ourselves are still learning, misunderstanding, making mistakes, and growing.

It also occurred to me how much we "create our reality" by fixing people with frames of identity. When a child behaves rudely, how quickly we give him the identity of "being rude," and so fix him on a self-destructive path.

Shifting into Neutral   about 1978

One day on entering meditation I wanted to know just what was the perfectly correct attitude. If it were incorrect to focus on the future, the side, or the past, where should I focus? I then saw myself in a car shifting gears. As I shifted from gear to gear I noticed a corresponding feeling of being involved, either in moving forwards through desire or ambition, or backwards in dread and flight from anticipated problems. Then I shifted into neutral. Here I noticed no feeling to move in any direction, but also a feeling of great freedom. I realized at once that the correct attitude was to be in neutral—no gear at all. Both forward and backward gears are ego-dominated.

On Becoming a Receiver, Therefore a Transmitter   1978

In a meditation having to do with being neutral, I saw that during times when I am called on to lead, I am not to tell others what to do, or to plan what is to be done. Instead, by being empty within, and by keeping contact with my inner voice, I will act and respond appropriately to each situation. Through being empty I receive thoughts from the higher source. Then my thinking and responses are beneficial to everyone concerned.

The Semaphore in the Night   about 1978

In practicing neutrality I began to notice that during the day thoughts would come which seemed foreign to me. It occurred to me that I might be intercepting other people's thoughts. Upon entering meditation one of these thoughts was voiced. Simultaneously, I saw a distant light flashing rhythmically on and off. Looking at it I noticed that the light pulsations were similar to Morse code signals, such as those which might be sent from a ship at sea. Curiously, they seem to be aimed directly at me. I walked out into a field to find that the light was coming from a semaphore machine which was plugged into an outlet in the ground. I unplugged it, and that was the end of all strange and extraneous thoughts.

How Inferior Thoughts Block Sleep / The Below Ground Room   about 1973

I had been tossing and turning in sleep. Finally, I woke up. To get back to sleep I decided it was necessary to meditate. In the meditation I found myself in a below ground room where a big electrical generator was running. Around the baseboard were dozens of electrical outlets. Each had plugs with wires trailing to the generator. I realized that each wire carried thoughts which had been

31

running through my mind, waking me up. I pulled out all the plugs and dynamited the generator.

As this meditation indicates, meditations often contain harsh or violent acts. We do things in dreams that we would never think of doing in our conscious minds. It is the same in meditation, although curiously, I cannot remember ever doing anything violent in my dreams. Meditation differs from dreams in that the conscious mind is a member of the audience. Violence in meditation simply reflects the great determination and resoluteness needed to rid ourselves of unwanted elements. I am reminded here of Christ's statement, "if thy hand offend thee, cut it off." We cannot assume from this that Christ had a natural tendency towards violence, or that He meant us literally to do such a thing. No doubt He meant it the way the *I Ching* counsels us to be willing to make war against evil within oneself. In meditation, dynamiting the generator is a metaphorical act, similar to cutting off an offending hand, or plucking out an offending eye.

How Being Neutral Makes Us Clairvoyant   about 1973

Soon after learning to be neutral in attitude, I had the experience, while playing tennis, of seeming to hear when my opponents planned to return the ball cross court, down the line, or lob, and so forth. I heard their thoughts an instant before they made their moves, and my body reacted accordingly. My neutrality was making me receptive to other's conscious thoughts.

I also noticed that when I was neutral and empty, my body seemed to play tennis better than "I" could. It was as if I had got out of the way and allowed my body to do what it knew better to do.

Inner Emptiness Invites Unwanted Visitors   about 1978

Inner emptiness seemed to provide space for unwanted songs and ditties, especially those with short, repetitive themes. This happened if I listened to a song, or sang it.

Having turned it on, so to speak, I was unable to turn it off again. In meditation I saw a phonograph playing one of these songs. The needle had got stuck in one of the grooves and was repeating. I took the record off but realized that if I simply put it aside, it might start playing again, so, I destroyed it. This worked well until I once more listened to the same song. In another meditation I destroyed the phonograph as well. So long as I do not listen to or sing one of the same kinds of songs, the problem does nor recur.

How Character Development Stops Unrelated
Inferior Thoughts   about 1973

This meditation began with seeing a butterfly come toward my brain, as if toward an apple on a tree, and bite it. Then it turned into a worm which began to enter my brain as if it were an apple. I realized that the butterfly symbolized the way inferior thoughts "bite," then burrow into the brain, the way a railroad worm tunnels through an apple, enlarging in size as it goes.

Then I saw that as our character strengthens, the effort needed to deal with inferior thoughts lessens because strength of character is like a force field through which the inferior thoughts cannot penetrate. The stronger the character, the stronger and more impenetrable the force field.

How Inner Emptiness Leads to Spontaneous Creativity
about 1978

I was to give a talk on the *I Ching* to a large group of people at a local museum. As I organized my talk, the *I Ching* told me to quit planning what I would say, and to allow the talk to be spontaneous. This aroused considerable doubt and trepidation, but as the *I Ching* continued to press me on the subject, I had to go along. Even while the Curator was introducing me I had no thought how I would proceed, but as I mounted the podium and turned around, it came to me to follow the line of the essential, to explain what the audience really needed to know. The talk unfolded better than any for which I had carefully prepared.

Cleaning Out the Gaseous Matter   April 15, 1976

I saw that our youthful dreams of what life should be are like a haze, or gas, that clouds up our inner space. I saw that up to now I had been measuring my life in terms of old dreams, only to be disappointed.

Then I saw the quick flash that reveals the four leaf clover hidden among the ones with three leaves. Seeing one is such a surprise when you are not looking for it! Focussing on old dreams and hopes makes us oblivious to what is already there, within our reach.

I saw that luck and blessings come to the one whose view is not beclouded with dreams, desires, and wants. Freed of these things, we are open to a wealth that is there all along.

The Empty Meditation   February 25, 1973

I found myself in an inner theater, looking at an empty movie screen. I had gone to bed the preceding night without finishing my *I Ching* reading because I had watched a movie (one I had seen before) and then another TV program, so became too tired to do the reading. Although during the meditation my mind was clear and I might have had an exceptional meditation, I saw only the empty screen. I was told that if I did not put anything into my education I would not get anything out of it. I was reminded of *The Well*, Hexagram 48. We go, as the hexagram says, to the well with a jug. The bigger the jug and the more effort we put in, the more water we can bring up. We receive only according to our effort. Our success depends on our sincerity and consistency.

The Image of the Shining Lake   about 1978

In the *I Ching* hexagram *The Joyous*, Hexagram 58, the image of true joy is given as that of the shining lake. In this meditation I saw the stillness of the shining lake as the perfect state of balance and harmony. I also saw that this perfect stillness is disturbed whenever feelings of wanting, wondering, or worrying begin. They create ripples, and then waves, on the lake's mirrored surface.

After this meditation I needed only to visualize my inner lake to know whether something was disturbing my inner serenity. Sometimes I visualize this inner lake during the early stages of meditation to see whether it is mirror-still and peaceful, or whether it is ruffled by something disturbing it from below, or above.

The Attitude of the Hunter early 1989

After trying to explain to someone how I meditate, I had a meditation in which I was a hunter. On my entering the woods, all the animals hid, so I sat down and became perfectly quiet, waiting the way a hunter would do. In a short time the animals came out again and resumed their normal activities, oblivious of my presence.

This image called to mind the fact that on entering meditation we are hunters, on the lookout for troublemakers in our personalities. The "inferiors" (body self) sense our intentions, and so hide, but being of shallow intelligence and forgetful, they soon return to their normal activities.

I was then presented with an image of Jane Goodall, who lived among the chimpanzees, and of Farley Mowat, who lived among the wolves. Both these people studied their subjects by trying to see things from their subjects' viewpoints. If we adopt a similar attitude towards our inferiors in meditation, we will be better able to understand them, and to acquire their cooperation and interest in helping us (our true selves).

Acid Dropped on the Ground, or, the Power of Purity March 3, 1973

In this meditation I saw the effect of maintaining inner purity symbolized by acid being dropped on the ground. As the acid ate through the earth, its ability to "eat" weakened as it became mixed with other elements. If it could retain its purity, I realized, it could eat a hole straight through the earth. Then I realized that our ability to do great things depends on our capacity to maintain our purity. Because this purity becomes diluted through our involvement in the daily business of life, it must be restored, through daily meditation and inner cleansing.

This was the same principle shown in a meditation about my inner house. I had noticed that although I cleaned my inner house every day in meditation, there was always more dirt to clean up in the next meditation. I kept thinking that at some point it would remain clean. In this meditation I was told that just as a house, by living in it, becomes dirty, our inner self, through contact with the situations of daily life, becomes tainted and must be cleaned up repeatedly.

Looking at the Mundane summer 1989

I had a dream about sitting outside. I thought, afterwards, how mundane! In meditation I found myself wondering why I dreamt about something so silly. Then the message came: Do not pull your attention away, look at what is being said. Then it broke through—One must not refuse to look at the mudane, for the mundane holds the breakthroughs in our understanding.

As the meditations related here indicate, effective meditation requires that our attitude be neutral and detached, but also alert and participatory. We should be open and tolerant, but also firm in seeking what is essential and correct. We must remain detached and unresisting. This means our head is kept empty of thought, our heart empty of emotion, and our self free of attachments and resistances. Keeping detached means we are loyal to our true natures, and to those with whom we have inner connections. We extend this loyalty beyond the way people are at the moment to what is potentially great and good in them. This attitude, which the Sage has towards us, is our model.

4.

Meditations About Attitudinal Defects

Looking back over my meditations, I am amazed at the orderly and systematic way they addressed my problems. My first and most immediate need had been to get sleep. Once my simple beginning meditations solved this problem, my next meditations taught me to meditate better. Interspersed with meditations about meditating were others which freed me from the grip of my runaway emotions. Still others dealt with attitudes which caused emotional distress.

Throughout this process the *I Ching* repeatedly counseled me to quiet the thinking of the heart. We do not normally regard the heart as able to think, but in a number of meditations my heart was seen to be the source of my emotionally-based thoughts.

Heart Infested With Crabs   October, 1972

As the meditation began I heard myself reviewing memories of old wounds and disappointments caused by people I liked or loved. Then my heart became visible and I saw that these old wounds and disappointments were, in my inner life, small crabs which had dug their claws into my heart's outer surface! With the claws embedded in my heart, they were now constraining and hurting it.

The question became how to remove them, for they seemed to have the characteristics of fish hooks, with barbs that would tear away the flesh. After considering various means I decided there was nothing to do but tear them out. Even though I feared this would damage my heart, I tore them out anyway.

Immediately I was presented with a healing oil which I poured over the wounds that had been produced. The wounds were instantly healed.

This was a graphic illustration of the negative effects of

holding onto negative memories. After removing the memories and healing my heart, I felt a tremendous release from their constraining effects.

In a similar meditation a month later I saw that the inside of my heart was infested with bugs of desire. After killing the bugs I became free of a number of frustrations that had been bothering me.

In still another heart meditation I heard small voices issuing from my heart, saying, "It's hopeless," "It's too late now," and "Nothing can be done." The voices were weary, tired to death, oppressing me with feelings of hopelessness. This time I washed my heart inside and outside, and then treated it with the healing oil.

Heart with Seed-Bearing Pockets   November 19, 1972

In this meditation the chambers of my heart were so crowded with seeds of desire that it was difficult for my heart to function. Moreover, the seeds seemed to be generated by seed-bearing pockets which had become attached to the chamber walls. I no sooner removed these pockets than I noticed that my heart became stiff and unpleasant-looking. Then it began to shrink and before I could act to prevent it, it withered away to nothing.

I was disconcerted, thinking it might even be dangerous not to have a heart, even if it were only the one seen in meditation. Thinking I should somehow have intervened I then was made aware that mine had been a troublesome heart, always in need of repair or alteration. Being informed of this, I accepted its loss as for the best.

In a meditation soon after this I saw that my old heart had been replaced by a new, healthy heart.

I had no more meditations about my heart for several years. The following meditation occurred after I had been to a dinner party in which I had been given as dinner partner a man then in the process of becoming a psychiatrist. On being asked (somewhat facetiously) whether he was a Freudian or Jungian, he reacted vehemently, exclaiming that Jung was a barbarian. I felt quite annoyed until I noticed that he had worn two different colored socks. Having found something to ridicule I felt vindicated. My next morning's meditation, however, had another point of view.

The Dragon of Vindictiveness   about 1978

I found myself in a semi-dark room with a vaulted ceiling. I heard a panting sound that reminded me of one of the old coal-fired railroad engines sitting idly on a track, puffing. I also saw smoke rising, as if from such an engine. Each puff of smoke was timed to the panting sound. Then I saw, as the light increased, that I was in the presence of a sleeping dragon. The panting was its breathing.

Finding a spear in my hands and realizing that my chance of killing a dragon must be much better when it is asleep, I thrust my spear into the dragon's eye, killing it. (It seemed that this was the only non-armored entry to the dragon's brain.)

With the dragon dead I felt safe enough to look around at the dragon's vaulted lair, only to recognize that I was standing in a chamber of my own heart! Then I recognized that the dragon's panting was identical in sound to my haughty feelings of vindictiveness, "Harrumph! Harrumph! Harrumph!" This dragon was the dragon of my vindictiveness, and this meditation was a message not to tolerate such monsters within myself.

In later years several meditations illustrated that the heart is not only the source of emotional thinking, it is also the source of emotional seeing.

Heart-Seeing (Dark-Seeing)   January 15, 1981

In a meditation, while I was searching for the cause of vague feelings of dissatisfaction which were causing me to lose my inner balance, I began to be conscious of my recent concern with distressing situations—world poverty, child and animal abuse, and wars.

Then I noticed that I was not looking at these things with eyes placed in my head, but with eyes placed in my heart.

In wanting these situations to be corrected, I was really seeing them as problems that never would be solved. My point of view was hopelessly infected with doubt. Since I had been seeing from my heart, I now realized that all emotional viewpoints are seen from the heart and constitute "heart-seeing."

Heart-seeing, based on wanting, is essentially negative. It is the source of all "dark-seeing." It is as if we have on dark lenses. "I want this because I cannot have it." (We do not want things we feel sure we will get.)

Not only did this dark-seeing jar me off-balance, but its hidden presence also prevented my having a good effect on the problems about which I felt hopeless.

The Creative Power, I realized, can be activated only when we cease doubting its ability to deal with such matters. If we really understand the way of the Creative Powers in the Cosmos, we need not sigh over terrible conditions we see. We need only disengage and turn the injustice and suffering we see over to the Higher Power. *Dispersal of our distrust liberates this power to work towards a beneficial solution of such problems.*

Cleansing the Photo Negative   January 20, 1981

This meditation made me aware that when I took a dim view of people, their prospects, and their paths, I was engaging in dark-seeing. I saw my dim and dark views as photo-negatives.

I now rinsed the photo-negatives with light, which returned the film to clear. This reopened my mind. By opening my mind, I enabled the Creative Power to have a beneficial effect, both on me and on the people I had fixed in my dark view.

I then thought of all the people I could remember, took out all the dim views which came to mind, and washed them with this solution.

The Sturdy Small Boat   December 1979

I saw myself in a very sturdy, though small, boat similar

to the longboats used by whalers in the old days. All around me sharks swam in a circle. In fact, the water seemed to boil with them.

Wondering what would happen if my boat should sink and I should have to swim for it, I put my arm down into the water, only to narrowly miss getting it bitten off.

Then I realized that although there were many sharks around, my boat was sturdy and I need not worry. I could remain in it indefinitely, if need be. Danger would arise only if I got into the water.

Then it became clear that this scene was a metaphor for my looking at problems. Once I allowed myself to look at them, I became involved (put my arm into the water). All I needed to do was cease looking, and stay within the confines of my sturdy boat, in other words, to attend to my own path, to remain safe.

The following meditation was but one of several which concerned the existence within myself of an "intrinsic spot." Although this is the only one I wrote down, I feel they were all vital to understanding the importance of establishing and maintaining my inner balance and self-esteem.

Meditation About the Hole in My Chest (Center of Being)
about 1972

I saw a hole in the center of my chest. I understood that the hole, which was located in the exact center of my being, was my "intrinsic spot," or place where I most felt myself as me. But what did a hole in this spot signify?

Then I noticed that when I desired something, I felt the desire as a hole in this spot. When my feelings were hurt, I felt the hole, and it felt terrible, as if I had been wounded. No doubt when Cupid shot his arrows of love and hate, they went straight to this spot and were felt as a hole. Lack of self-worth, inner emptiness, and self-doubt, all were felt here, as gnawing feelings inside this hole.

Then I realized that because of this hole and its uncomfortable quality, I desired things because they filled the hole and allayed the gnawing feelings inside it. Physical palliatives such as coffee, alcohol, and sweets seemed temporarily to alleviate this gnawing. Occupying myself in a workaholic way kept me from being conscious of the hole and the deficiencies in myself that seemed to be associated with it.

I also noticed that once the hole was filled with the thing desired, or with any of the palliatives, it was soon empty again so that I would once more feel empty and needy.

To solve the problems caused by the hole, it came to me to clean out the hole thoroughly, in the manner of a dentist cleaning a cavity in a tooth, then fill it with cement—a good tough cement, such as a dentist might use.

In a later meditation I saw that my steady work on myself had translated into self-esteem which had healed and filled in the hole, displacing the temporary filling.

In this manner I learned that self-esteem cannot be assumed. Simply saying we are "okay" does not fill in the hole. Neither is self-esteem the consequence of being intelligent, capable, or talented. Self-esteem is unrelated to such matters, or even to self-confidence. Indeed, we can have self-confidence with low self-esteem.

Self-confidence, or lack of it, belongs to the conscious mind. We see ourselves supposedly from a logical viewpoint, either as capable, talented, or intelligent, or as lacking in these qualities. Self-esteem is related to our subconscious knowledge of how we really are. If we have been pursuing a course away from our truthful, kind, mild, tolerant, and forgiving true nature, we fall into self-conflict and begin subconsciously to dislike ourselves. Our subconscious has an absolute knowledge of our inner workings. It knows when we lie, cheat, adopt pretensions, and otherwise betray our true nature. In response, our true self feels ashamed and we feel a loss of self-esteem. We rebuild self-esteem every time we resist denial, decadent attitudes, and unworthy habits of mind. Every time we make the hard choice to follow the good, and to be faithful to our higher nature, our self-esteem grows. Self-esteem, therefore, is the product of healthy work on ourselves. The hole created by lack of self-esteem gradually fills in as we complete our higher natures.

The person with self-esteem also has inner independence. Through growth we shed our dependency on all those personality props which shield us from our fears. It is our fears that make us dependent on others and cause low self-esteem. Inner independence may appear to others to be self-confidence, but unlike self-confidence, it is based not on a feeling of being sufficient unto ourselves, but on our knowledge that we are dependent on something higher than ourselves to guide us.

As we see how following our higher nature works in all situations, we gain confidence in following this path. In every circumstance in which we dare to follow this path, our intellectual perception of its worth is transformed to an inner knowledge which, in *I Ching* terms, is called "inner truth." This truth is no longer mere conjecture; it has been experienced as true and reliable, and it is in harmony with our true natures.

During each of these experiences we also learn that all achievement is the result of our partnership with the Higher Power. Continuing recognition of the partnership and of our dependence on it is essential to inner independence.

Strictly speaking, the inner-independent person is not self-confident. He may know he has talent and ability, but he recognizes the inherent limitations that attach to these as things in themselves. He knows that his talent and ability will only gain scope and meaning through his partnership with the Higher Power. We are really okay only when our self-esteem is based on something more substantial than merely saying we are okay.

The Inertia of Indolence

The next three meditations focus on the inertia of indolence. Although indolence may seem harmless, the inertia that accompanies it is perhaps the major cause of evil in ourselves, and therefore in the world.

In meditation I saw that my indolence was based on dreading the possibilities that lay hidden in change. Dreading is due to a number of hidden fears we entertain about going on with our life. Many times procrastination is based on these hidden fears, which need to be ferreted out of our attitudes.

Berry Picking   about 1981

Recently, walking along a railroad track was the subject of a number of meditations. In all these, although there were others walking along the track nearby, I was always walking alone. Sometimes a train would whiz by on the track, full of people, making me aware that those of us who were walking were certainly taking the slow way.

It was clear that the railroad track symbolized our path, and that those of us who were walking were not meant to ride on the train.

In one of these meditations several of us had stopped in a small field beside the track to pick and eat the ripe berries growing there. As I picked I noticed that bushes growing along a footpath that led away from the railroad track had particularly luscious berries. As I picked these I went a distance down the path. Then I noticed that the path itself was inviting, and I began to feel tempted to walk along it. No sooner had I got some way down it, though, than my meditation called attention to my indolent attitude, noting that while side paths are alluring, I would find myself unhappily lost and disappointed, because I would have left the path I was meant to follow, the path that led to my goals. This made me beware of the inertia and abandonment that attaches to indolence, into which we slip ever so subtly and carelessly.

In following the path of the true we must ever be alert and attentive. Luxury and abandonment are really slippery slides into ravines from which it is difficult to extricate ourself.

Picnicing on the River Bank   about 1981

In this meditation I found myself paddling a canoe down a white water river. In spite of concentrating intensely, I was barely able to keep from ramming into rocks. Finally, however, I got past these threats into smoother water.

Looking ahead, I wondered what might be around the bend in the river. Would it be more white water rapids? Would I have to get off and portage around falls? Would I see and hear rapids or falls in time? I then noticed a pleasant clearing and small beach off on the right, so I decided to stop there to picnic, rest, and restore my nerves.

The message of this meditation was two-fold. First, it is my job to pay attention only to the immediate situation. I should not concern myself with what lies around the bend, out of sight. The entire business of canoeing down a river is to keep our attention on the situation of the moment. If we focus our gaze on what is around the bend, we may not see the rock just ahead that can put a hole in our canoe. The second message is that after dealing with a harrowing situation, it is right to stop and rest. But, as the following meditation, which occurred a month later, made clear, picnicing on the river is not meant to last forever:

I saw myself still resting in the pleasant clearing on the riverbank. I had stayed here picnicing, content not to return to my journey down the river with all its unknown elements. The message of this meditation was that I was not meant to stay here indefinitely, since it was my destiny to go on.

Then I recalled the time I took flying lessons and had to practice stalls, spins, and cross-wind landings. After each landing I had been so relieved to get the plane safely back on the ground that I always dreaded the next lesson. But just as there is no other way to learn to fly but to expose ourself to the risks involved, there is no other way to find that our perceptions can be trusted than by putting them to the test of experience. Indolence is based on the hidden doubt and fear that we cannot trust our inner knowledge, and that we might not get the help we need during the difficult moments. We need to deal with these doubts and fears; they are the source of all easy, luxurious indolence, for they keep us from growing, and from going on. Indeed, this is the nature of all procrastination.

Still another type of inertia, or indolence, was the subject of an early meditation.

Taking One's Feet Off the Bottom to Swim   about 1973

During my first year of consulting the *I Ching* it had helped me bring my runaway emotions under control, made me aware of my ego, and strengthened my essential self. In spite of having experienced dozens of small miracles and improvements in my external situation, I clung to my original "doubting Thomas" attitude about the *I Ching*, "We'll see what it can do for me."

During the two weeks prior to this meditation my *I Ching* readings were inexplicable and unrelated, for the first time ever. The Sage, who had spoken so reliably to me through it, seemed to have closed his door and gone elsewhere. Moreover, I felt a gradual decrease in the supportive love I had begun to experience. Finally, meditating, my "let's see" attitude was presented to me as if someone had written it on the blackboard as the subject of a lecture.

Then I saw myself teaching swimming—something I did as a life-guard during my last year in high school. My seven-year-old students had already learned to hold their breath, kick their feet, and paddle correctly. On this day they were to take their feet off the bottom and swim only a foot or so, to the safety of the end of the pool. I remembered explaining that they were to push off towards the shallow water, taking their feet off the bottom for only a moment.

Then I remembered the first time I had done this, and the courage it had required. I then was reminded that all year the Sage had proved himself to me over and over again as trustworthy and reliable. Although I no longer actively distrusted, I had not divested myself of passive distrust. It remained present in my attitude simply through inertia. Like a crutch I no longer needed, I had not given it up. It was time now, I was told, to take my feet off the bottom and swim. I was made to understand that up to now the Sage had tolerated my indolent distrust, but to go on I must give it up. At this point giving up my distrust was not even a big thing. It required only that I decide to give it up.

The following meditations called attention to subtle attitudes I might not ordinarily notice. The first of these contrasted the impotence of striving with the power of acceptance.

Dealing with the Obstructing Wall   September 24, 1979

In this meditation I was walking along a mountain path. Suddenly erected before me and straddling my path was a great wall. There was no way to get over it or around it. For an instant I wondered if I might have taken the wrong path, but a moment's reflection made me realize this was not the case. Then it came to me that this wall was put there by Fate as a purposeful obstruction. It was my job to find out the correct way to deal with it.

I tried to climb around the wall, only to realize that was impossible. Furthermore, if I persisted I might fall off the mountain. Then, next to the wall I noticed a ghost-like light force which I understood to be the Creative. It simply walked through the wall. I decided the only thing to do was to accept the fact that I was blocked. Immediately, the wall disappeared, permitting me to continue on my path. The message was clear: acceptance of obstructions leads to a resolution of the problems they present.

See No Evil, Hear No Evil, Do No Evil   December 9, 1979

The old saying, "see no evil, hear no evil, do no evil" was the subject of the following meditation.

I heard someone say negative things about one of my sons, and I replied, "Get down, you're obstructing my view." Then I saw walls on all sides of me on which were displayed pictures of my family and friends. The people in these pictures seemed to be observing my behavior and measuring me in some way, and it was they who were saying the negative things.

Then I saw the walls on which these pictures were hanging being pushed back farther and farther until they dropped off what turned out to be a mountainside. Suddenly and unexpectedly I was free and able to see that I was on a mountain-top with a grand view of an entire range of mountains. Off to the East, the sun rose up over the mountains, beautiful and serene.

In saying "get down, you're obstructing my view," I had freed myself from the anxiety I had had about being criticized and measured by others. My new freedom enabled me to see far and wide, while before I was only able to see them, and hear their possible criticisms. By being resolute with them, they (or my preoccupation with them) obligingly dropped away. Then I realized they had monopolized my view because I had not been resolute with them in the first place.

It then became clear that evil arises from fear and doubt. This is the essence of the dark power. Once we allow fear or doubt to enter, by worrying that we are being watched and measured, all those parts of ourself which are struggling to do the right thing begin to feel discouraged and hopeless. If we do nothing to bolster these parts of ourselves, they give up. If, on the other hand we resist doubt by being resolute, these hard-working aspects of self fight back tooth and nail and thus defeat the dark power.

Then I saw merit in the saying, "see no evil, hear no evil, do no evil." Evil—the thing we look at that makes us fear or doubt—is always there and will draw our attention. Instead of continuing to look at it and becoming involved in it, we resolutely disengage from it and turn it over to the Cosmos to solve. This is what it means to see no evil. No longer watching evil in our minds, we disperse the arguments and justifications that keep us involved with it. Through refusing to continue hearing these arguments, we avoid doing evil by struggling with it.

The following meditation helped me see to the source of the Dark Power, and thereby to become insulated from it.

The Sooty Black Cave / Power of the Dark   about 1988

A door appeared to open into a cave, or dark place which I somehow knew contained the most awful thing I had ever feared. As it opened, the door creaked as if it were on rusty hinges. Once it was fully open, I felt it was too stiff ever to close again. I knew this meant that once I had opened myself up to my inner fears and faced them, they would never again dominate me.

Then I walked into the uninviting opening. It was the blackest of places, as if it were a cave lined with soot. The air was close and stifling as if it were inhabited by a horrible creature. As I waited for something to happen, the most terrible yowlings began. Although they moaned on and on, nothing happened. They simply moaned and yowled, as frighteningly as possible.

Afterlistening for some time to the moaning, I realized that that was all there was to it. Nothing happened, nothing was inside, there was only noise. The power of the dark, I realized, lies in the noise it makes, and the awe it inspires. We only fear it when we forget the power of the Sage, and the power of light and truth. We think we are alone, without help. Once we are exposed to the emptiness of fear, it never again is able to wield the same power over us.

The following meditation concerned pride as an attitudinal problem. On numerous occasions I had been made aware by my *I Ching* readings that pride was isolating me from the help of the Creative, and preventing progress. After getting rid of big, obvious elements of pride, I still had smaller, subtle elements of pride that were just as destructive as the larger elements.

Getting Rid of the Last Little Bit of Pride   about 1988

On this occasion my *I Ching* counsel called for getting rid of that "last little bit of pride." On receiving such counsel it is my usual practice to examine my attitude to see if I harbor any residual alienation or resistance. This time, however, I could not identify anything. Before going to sleep I asked the Sage for help to identify the problem.

The next morning I got up with that sense of grogginess that holds us suspended for a few moments between sleeping and waking. As I dressed I remembered my dream of the night before.

I had been in Russia, where I was required by the authorities to clean up a radioactive mess, even though I was not properly protected, and had on only short sleeves and shorts. I had concentrated so hard on the job that by the time I had finished, I had forgotten the danger. Only afterwards did I remember the contaminated dust particles that must have gotten into the pores of my skin. Although I washed carefully and vigorously, I could not wash the dust off. As the dream ended I thought I would surely die of radiation poisoning.

In meditating I was presented with images of various family members. Most were tainted with something that had pigmented their skins greenish-yellow. I noticed that the taint on them was related to how they had hurt my pride in some past time. The more deeply my pride was hurt, the more deeply pigmented their skins.

Then I remembered my dream and the feeling of distress I had had on realizing that I had been permanently tainted (and damaged) by the radioactivity on my skin. Realizing that the two situations were related I knew that I must somehow take away the taint of pride that stood between me and all those close to me.

The question then arose, How was this to be accomplished? Obviously, simple forgiveness was not enough, for in my heart I had already forgiven them. The taint existed only as a memory of their mistakes. As I reviewed each person, I realized that each person had become identified with his mistakes, even though he had left them behind long ago.

Just then I was presented with a large, bath-sized container of magic liquid. I realized that were I to bathe each of their images in the liquid, they would be cleansed of all taint, so I washed all of them by dipping them in the magic liquid, much as a Baptist minister baptizes converts. As soon as I had completed this task I washed myself and found that I had become free of the radioactive contamination I had incurred in the dream. By freeing them I had also freed myself.

After the meditation I also realized that the wounding of my pride was sometimes unavoidable as I kept making the effort to believe in people. It was important to know how to give pride up, so that I could keep free of its damaging effects.

The work of self-development, as these meditations show, is to rid ourself of faults that prevent us from engaging the Creative. Perfection is not required, only sincerity of purpose. We are always going to make mistakes. The highest good, the *I Ching* says, is not to *be* good, but to "know how to become free of blame"—which is to return to working towards the good.

The next two meditations informed me of the dangers of idle curiosity.

The Black Snake   about April, 1973

This meditation followed a day in which I indulged my idle curiosity to inquire where my husband, from whom I was then estranged, was going, and what he would be doing. I had had faint warnings while doing this that I was exceeding my limits, but I did not listen because my curiosity was too compelling. The result was negative, for in addition to exposing myself foolishly, I received insults.

In the meditation I saw a black snake curled up in the grass. As I tried to grab it by the back of the head I got bitten. Obviously, the snake was much quicker than I was.

Then I perceived that trying to pick up the snake symbolized my curiosity. The problem lay in the fact that I was in the snake's territory, bothering it; it was not bothering me. Being on the defensive, it was faster than I was. This warned me of the dangers of overstepping my limits because of idle curiosity.

The Gordian Knot / The Old Logging Road that Went Nowhere   July 4, 1974

In this meditation I saw the famous Gordian Knot which no one could untie. I examined it, looked at the way it was entangled, and found no ends to grasp or unwind. I perceived that someone had knotted it with all sorts of unusual knots, and after tucking the ends inside, had then rolled the massive knot upside down. I perceived that knots are generally composed of an end which is tucked inside a loop then pulled tight. Knots cannot be untied unless one can find the ends, for they are the only places the tension can be released from the knot. I saw how one could examine and pick at the Gordian Knot forever without discovering how to untie it.

I then saw a road I used to see many times in childhood at my aunt's farm. I always wanted to follow this road to see where it went, for it appeared to go to the top of the mountain where I was sure there would be a good view. Every time I asked my cousins about it, however, they had no interest in going and said that the trees at the top made it impossible to see the view. It was just an old logging road used to take timber off the mountain. Their explanations never satisfied me and I remained forever curious about this road.

As I contemplated these images I suddenly understood that picking at knots and following roads that went nowhere were a kind of idle gaiety—a concern with the 10,000 things of the world. Alexander the Great had no time to waste on idle musings; he saw that the best answer to the riddle of the Gordian Knot was to cut it in two with one stroke of his sword. Too much gaiety, idle curiosity, or fantasizing, leads to loss of the inner continuity and strength that is necessary for worthwhile achievements.

Furthermore, seeking comprehensive answers is like trying to untie the Gordian Knot. Making grand and great explanations of things is folly—creating roads that lead nowhere. The best way to live life is to live it one day at a time. The solutions we need are to be found at the time we need them.

Leaning On Things   November 21, 1979

One time as I entered meditation I had the sensation of falling over abruptly. Indeed, when I looked around to see what had happened I realized the stool on which I was leaning had been yanked out from under me. Then my attention was drawn to a pixie who stood aside, observing with an amused expression on his face. He was a small man in lederhosen and shiny black shoes, and he had on a green felt hat with a feather in it. Obviously, he had been the one to pull the stool out from under me.

I immediately demanded, "Why did you do that!"

He replied, "Because you weren't supposed to be leaning on it."

I recognized him as Fate, and that it is Fate's business to teach us not to lean on anything, whether it be a person, a belief system, or a line of thought which arouses great enthusiasm. It is important to follow the mean, and remain balanced.

The Empty Packing Boxes
(The Danger of Waiting with Expectation)   July 9, 1984

I saw a room full of empty packing boxes, all broken down and stacked to the ceiling, waiting for something to be put into them.

Then I realized I had stored the empty cartons in anticipation of things I expected to be given, for things I expected to come in the mail, for people who had yet to put themselves together, for the chance to go somewhere special, or to do something I've always wanted to do.

Then I thought of the hexagram *Waiting*, Hexagram 5, and of the fact that we spend a good portion of our lives waiting. The person who has not yet found the right mate must wait. Resolving differences and enlarging understanding requires waiting. Often we must wait for payment for our work, or for the right time to say or do something we think must be said or done. This hexagram, however, says that we need to develop an attitude that is free of expectation.

How, I wondered, is it possible to wait without having all these "boxes of expectation" in the back of our minds.

I then saw that it is essential to give them to the Sage to be filled when he sees fit, and to let go of all expectation.

Then I saw that people sense when we wait with "empty boxes of expectation" piled around us. If they are resistant for any reason they will disappoint us simply because of our lack of inner independence. As soon as we give up waiting with expectation, people stop resisting and begin to do the right thing.

This meditation came just before I visited the buyer at a large bookstore chain. I realized that it was important that I not go with an empty order box (or begging cup) in my mind. Having presented the best reasons I could think for their stocking my books I was to let it go at that.

The Influence of the Bum   January 14, 1981

Prior to meditating I had talked with two different people who had spoken of situations that appeared "nearly hopeless" to them.. The first was a young man who had moved into the city from the suburbs. He had remarked that people in certain areas of the cities live, "almost like rats, breeding, being indifferent, trashing, and drinking." His house, he told me, was separated from a bar by a vacant lot. Every morning he cleaned up the trash thrown into the lot by the bar's night customers; he had also rescued an abandoned, starved, and nearly frozen kitten. Then he had intervened on behalf of a four-year-old boy who was locked out of his house in the zero cold, too afraid of his mother, the man had discovered, to ask to be let in. He just stood there, crying. My friend banged on the door until the mother let the boy in. All these experiences had provoked the man's shocked attitude and negative observations.

When the second person I met began telling me similar things, I found myself repeating the first person's words, "it almost seems hopeless." That evening my *I Ching* reading was *Splitting Apart*, Hexagram 23, and another hexagram which counselled me to "avoid hardness and alienation," and to try to arrive at a "just and moderate view of mankind."

As my morning meditation began I saw a dwarf-sized, grizzled derelict in tattered clothing sitting on my shoulder, making hopeless observations. Then it got off and walked around me, gesticulating and ranting about the hopelessness of situations. I realized that this tiny bum had hopped from the first man's shoulder onto mine, (because I had not resisted the hopelessness in what he had to say), and I had then passed the bum onto the next person I met. Then I realized that when society as a whole starts to feel that people as classes and groups are hopeless, those classes and groups become trapped and give up on themselves as well.

I was reminded of the movie *Oh God!* and the message God (in the movie) had brought to the world: We *can* do it; all of us have it in ourselves to make things work, to get along, to get on. Then I saw that it is up to each of us to reject the derelict attitude which operates to say that people are hopeless. If even a few of us develop our full personalities, and keep our minds open to the thought that people, left to themselves, can make things work, then things *will* get better. The way will be found, step by step, to solve our problems and make progress.

If there is anything that characterizes our modern American society, it is our tendency to give up on people. That is the reason for the nearly 50% divorce rate. We give up on our mates, we give up on our children, we give up on ourselves.

People become emotionally disturbed and schizophrenic when we do not believe in their potential to come to the correct viewpoint, or to make something of themselves. Otherwise normal people feel defeated because of society's derelict attitude: it is hopeless to try, working leads only to disappointment, and you can't get ahead no matter what you do; you might as well get what you can by whatever means, or otherwise be content to "bum it," settle down and wallow in envy and discontent. The derelict in us is our defeated person. Accepting the bum in others leads to lassitude, indifference, and defeat.

Perhaps it will have dawned on the reader, as it gradually dawned on me, that evil in the world exists only in defective attitudes. Added up in the populace, these attitudes amount to an evil force.

Good, likewise, exists in the world only as it exists in each of us. As each of us rejects indifference, hopelessness,

alienation, the luxury of anger, egotism, self-righteous-
ness, and vindictiveness, we purify our natures and place
ourselves in harmony with the Cosmos. Doing this, we
arouse the power of the Creative and the power of truth and
good to become manifest in external life. Thus we are able,
through working on bringing forth our higher natures, to
unleash the power of good in the world.

5.

The Inner Life—a Journey of Destiny

For a long time my meditations seemed unrelated to each other. Gradually, however, I began to sense that I was tapping an ongoing inner life. This inner life seemed related to my external life in some ways and unrelated to it in others.

My true self was first seen and felt in meditation as weak and dominated by my ego-self-image. As I became more disciplined in my responses to problems, my true self became stronger and my ego-self-image shrank. Eventually, I rarely saw it in my inner space. As my true self began to exercise more command, my body self became less fearful and frenetic, whereas before, this self had been exceedingly vocal if not catered to continually.

Gradually, the body self changed in meditation. At first it appeared as numerous dwarf-sized, pasty-faced children. Later, these children appeared as adults.

At first I thought that my inner house, and the other objects I had seen in meditation, were simply metaphors by which the Sage taught me the lessons intended. When I later had meditations that presented views of my whole life, I came to feel that an inner world exists, even though, while we are alive, we may experience it only metaphorically.

I also began to have the impression that the inner world I saw in meditation was there before I was born, and that I would return to it at death. The people in Dr. Raymond Moody's book, *Life after Life*, described experiences quite similar to those I had in meditation.

Changes in my inner life occurred only when I related correctly to my external situations. My inner world condition remained static until I grew, through my outer-world experiences. This fact made me conclude that if we neglect to develop the higher nature that is potential in us, we remain undeveloped, perhaps even nonexistent, in the inner world.

The inner life seemed to parallel my external life in other ways, as if it were a shadow existence. For example, my early meditations were seen in black and white. The views were somewhat bleak. I did not then know that this corresponded to the fact that my outer life was also bleak and dark, from a spiritual point of view. My thoughts at the time had been full of doubt and despair. I later saw that in the inner world I had been crossing a "plain of pitfalls" in the night. As I dealt with my doubts and fears, this inner night passed.

In other matters parallelism between the two worlds ends. For example, inner world values seem to be almost the reverse of outer world values. Society tends to view leadership as the ability to take charge and wield power. In the inner world, leadership is exercised by the one whose attitude is most in harmony with the Cosmos. He influences invisibly, simply through possessing the power of "inner truth." Such a person is also free of any need to be recognized. Similarly, things that preoccupy us in the outer world—how we look or what we wear—are unimportant in the inner world, where the only thing that counts is the quality of our inner thoughts.

In saying this I do not mean to say that beauty of form is unimportant, or that society has no need for visible leadership. I mean, rather, that inner world values have a greater priority and validity. Form is important, but it is not the main thing.

The following meditations demonstrate some of these characteristics of the inner life.

The House Meditations (1972-1980)

In the first chapter I described seeing myself in a dark, dirty, floorless and windowless log hut. The hut appeared in many more meditations. As I began keeping it clean, it improved, soon having a floor and windows. As I began to adhere to Cosmic values, the hut became lighter inside. After a year or two it became a neat Swiss chalet, and its original dark location changed to a pleasant meadow, up on side of a mountain where there was a view. These changes corresponded to improvements in my inner condition.

A few years later, during a period of isolation, the house became a cabin located on top a mountain peak.

On Top the Mountain   October 31, 1975

I saw myself in my inner world cabin and noticed that now it was located on the top of a 15,000-foot peak. Here I had a gorgeous view of the surrounding world, and despite being above the tree line, the house was surrounded by beautiful plants and shrubs. Strangely, the peak possessed sheltering winds; while elsewhere the winds blew as usual, here they did not. Sun and calm prevailed.

Then I understood that although I was here alone, in a strange place to carry out my life, everything was fine because I had not resisted where I was.

This scene made me realize how important it is not to resist where we are, and what is happening at any given time, such as being isolated. By having a non-resisting attitude, we find that the time is spent comfortably and peacefully, and the Sage keeps us company. I also realized that the time of isolation passes; we are not meant to live on the mountaintop forever. A period of isolation, it seems, is necessary to one's self-development. It is as if, for a time, we must go into a monastery.

Four years later, in 1979, I saw myself leaving the mountaintop to go down into a valley where I would mingle with people and be useful.

Six months later my isolation ended. Fellowship with others began again. My immediate family who had been doubtful about my intense interest in the *I Ching,* now became respectful of my point of view.

I never again saw the cabin, either in meditation or dreams. My next inner house was a Victorian style house.

The Victorian House   1979

I saw myself living in a rather large Victorian house with many rooms. The main rooms and hallways had dark wood panelling; it was what one might describe as a dark house. There was, however, a remodelled room upstairs that had a skylight. Although the house was obviously mine, and represented what I had achieved for an inner world habitation, I realized that with the exception of that one remodelled room, it did not have the light, airy quality of a house I would choose.

Then a voice explained that I could have this well-made, comfortable, and roomy house "forever" if I wished to go no further in my self-development. I could stay or go on. Then the voice explained that to go on meant that I would have to face my worst fears. Although the thought of facing my worst fears brought trepidation, I realized almost immediately that I had no choice. This dark house, though nice, was not "my house."

It was perhaps as much as five years before I saw my next inner house. This time it was the house I had seen in an early meditation which had presented me with a panoramic vision of my life.

In the meantime, as the next meditation describes, I came to live in "temporary quarters."

Slipping into the Other World   March, 1980

Up to this point, except in a few meditations, my visits to the inner world had an outer-space-like quality in which the surrounding atmosphere was black rather than blue.

I saw myself at the top of a black dome of empty space. Above me was an unusually small man-hole, but I was just able to wriggle through it. Then I found myself looking down from a similar dome of space, except that now the surrounding atmosphere was blue, and the world below was bright, colorful, and beautiful. I seemed to be only a few thousand feet up, looking down on a pleasant town located beside a beautiful lake. It was like a 19th Century Dutch town, well-tended and well-built, with cobblestone streets and attractive buildings adjoining each other. I then found myself on the ground, walking into the town, where I was given a room in one of the buildings which had a view of the streets and lake. The room, although somewhat bare of furniture, was pleasant. I was aware that it was to be temporary quarters while my house was being built outside town on the slope overlooking the lake.

Now the meditation backed up to show me that the black area of empty space contains wandering debris such as guilt, unresolved anger, and negative thoughts which must be dealt with before one can reach the entrance to the colorful world. I also noted that one must shrink in size to get through the manhole entrance. Everything but one's essential self must be shed to get through.

The house meditations, more than any others, made me aware that it is our destiny to develop our higher nature—to complete, as it were, a Cosmic image, or potential of ourselves that is kept in the mind of God.

The Well Meditations   about 1972 and 1973

Another group of early meditations showed me my inner world location, and explained how I had gotten there. Taking place during the first two years of meditating, they illustrate and explain the dark period.

In the first of these meditations I experienced myself falling endlessly through black space. This image came without any explanation and had passed from my mind when I had another meditation in which I again experienced myself falling, as before. This time, however, I came to an abrupt halt. As soon as my eyes had adjusted to the dark, I could see I was down about 30 feet in the bottom of a dry well, in the company of a lizard. Light was dimly visible above, and for about a minute each day, as the sun passed overhead, sunlight came down into the well.

I immediately realized that my long fall into what had seemed an abyss, had ended. Moreover, my situation was not as desperate as I had first thought. Instead of falling endlessly, I had fallen only into a well. I wondered, though, how I would get out. The rocks on the sides were slippery and allowed only small toeholds. Trying to climb up, I slipped back. I did not feel discouraged, though, I was only relieved that I had not fallen into an abyss.

In a meditation two or three months later I had climbed halfway up the well. My feet were braced securely on the sides. Applying some of my *I Ching* lessons to external world situations had translated into progress in climbing up this far. Several months later I found myself within four feet of the top, and not long after this I saw myself climbing out of the well. This time it was barely dawn, and I could see in the dim light that prior to falling into the well I had been crossing a plain full of well-holes, or pitfalls. Beside the well was a lantern I had been carrying, but it was obvious I had not lit or used it. Through self-confidently crossing in the dark, I had fallen in.

The well meditations made me aware that there exists, in everyone's inner life, a plain of pitfalls. Occasionally, I realize, while talking to someone, that he has fallen into one of these pits. Anyone who is surrounded by a set of inexorable limits is in such a pit.

Generally speaking, the pit is the *pit of despair*. We have not seen or understood our purpose in life, and have allowed our ego to decide that there is no purpose in life. We have thus allowed ourselves to close our minds to the possibility that things will work out.

Very often we encounter the pit when our ego has decided that we have been thrust into the external world without possessing the capabilities to achieve what must be achieved. We accept the ego's contention that help from the Higher Power is not forthcoming, or that there is no Higher Power there to help. We may have decided, as novelist Warren Dieping put it in *Sorrel and Son*, that there is only the "Great Indifference."

The Jail Cell Meditations   about 1972

At the same time that I had the Well Meditations (which I sometimes called the meditations of the black pit), I also had meditations which made me understand other meanings of "being in the pit."

In the first of these I found myself in total darkness. I

struck a match to see where I was, only to recognize the bars of a jail cell. I was in the Cosmic Jail.

Later on, near the time I was climbing out of the well, I saw myself again in the jail cell, but this time the light of dawn was coming through a high window. It was enough light to see, on looking around, that the cell door was open, and that I was free to leave.

The Straitjacket and the Corral   about 1972

In addition to seeing myself in a jail cell, I often saw myself in a straitjacket. This was a metaphor for the extreme sense of limitation I felt at the time. It seemed that if I even thought anything incorrect, a penalty was attached. I could move only an inch in any one direction without hurting myself. If I struggled I only suffered.

The reason I felt so limited, of course, was that every time I reverted to ego-directed ways of doing things, my external situation would immediately deteriorate, or even fall apart.

This sense of being in a straitjacket did not last too long. It gave way to seeing myself as a horse in a corral. I, like a horse, checked the fence and tested it, only to find it had been electrified. As long as I did not seek to force my way out, or fight the fence, I did not get hurt. As I adjusted to my limits, the corral enlarged to a comfortable pasture, though still with a fence around it.

The Burned Out House   December 9, 1972

The reader might well ask how I got into such a bind. I had permitted within myself a variety of luxurious and arrogant attitudes which broke Cosmic Laws. Among them, I participated in what I now call the *trampoline effect*, an image I once saw in meditation. One or both marriage partners test their relationship to see how much stress it can take.

In meditation I saw the burned-out ruins of the inner-world house my husband and I had built together. Through carelessness we had allowed it to burn down.

I saw that when we are young and first go out into the world, we test for boundaries. Not finding them immediately, we develop luxurious attitudes. In a childish way we assume that life is a grab bag of goodies made especially for us, and that there are no moral laws or obligations. We fail to accept our responsibility to be loyal to those with whom we have inner ties. If our partners, children, and friends do not behave as we wish, we give up on them forthwith. We even guess that Fate has granted us a special licence to demand that life work out our way. However, the day of reckoning eventually comes. The result, in the case of our marriage, was the destruction of our inner world house.

These and other meditations made me realize that a hidden body of Cosmic Laws governs life. Excessive pride led to my stint in the Cosmic Jail; vindictiveness led to my being bound up in the Cosmic Straitjacket. Once I made even small changes in my point of view, I was released from the straightjacket into the less confining Cosmic Fence.

These meditations also made me aware that there are Cosmic Duties beyond those implied by society and what we are taught to do. These duties apply to our attitudes towards each other, towards animals, and towards the earth and the use of our resources. Wherever we are luxurious and careless in our conduct or thinking, wherever we are indifferent and lax, wherever we assume rights, we exceed Cosmic limits and expose ourselves to Cosmic Punishment.

I was to understand more about the nature of Cosmic Punishment in the following meditation.

Fate as a Canal   about 1974

Sitting still in meditation I suddenly felt I had been rudely bumped by something. Then a scene materialized in which I was in a small boat which had rammed into the side of a canal, jarring me. The canal was as one might imagine the Panama Canal to be—massive walls of concrete. Surveying the scene I realized that instead of something bumping me, I had run into it.

I wondered why this had happened; it was then explained to me that as long as my boat went in the direction of the canal, all went well. When I had decided there were no Cosmic Limits and that I was free to do whatever I wished, I had disregarded my intuitive knowledge of moral limits and had taken a wrong direction.

Since I was the only one in my boat, and my hand was on the tiller, my boat had rammed into the side by my own doing. I realized that by self-confidently feeling I was free to do whatever I wanted, I was doing what was not justifiable. In the face of the Unknown we must be modest and careful, and not thrust aside carelessly our intuitive knowledge of right and wrong.

I also realized, through this meditation, that what I often felt as Cosmic Punishment in the form of unpleasant events, were only externalized consequences of my inner carelessness.

Through accepting my limits I was let out little by little from tight constraints. When I relapsed into carelessness or arrogance I was reined in again. I once saw myself in the horse's place, with the Sage as the rider. When I insisted on going "my" way, I was prevented. The more I became sensitive to where the master wanted to go, and the more willing I was to reverse direction when asked to do so, the better things went for me. I was reminded of Kate in *The Taming of the Shrew;* she was required to agree with her husband's absurd statement that the moon is made of green cheese. It is necessary to attain just that sort of acceptance.

Once I gave up my rebellion, I began to experience wider freedom. The day did come, seven years after the meditation of the burned-out house, when I was finally free.

The Return of the Lost Credit Card   October 22, 1979

I saw a credit card that looked as if it had been hidden in the leaves on the ground for quite a while. I instantly saw it was one which had been lost, and knew it was mine (although I had never seen one quite like it before). I was surprised and pleased to realize that I now had it back.

Then I realized that before beginning work on my self-development I had charged up so many errors without getting the bill that I had come to think I would never have to pay. I had presumed on my good fortune. That was when my credit card got lost (or revoked) and Fate closed in to straighten me out. It did so by making me pay on the spot for my mistakes, with the price sometimes tripled over what it once was.

The return of my credit card did not mean I could start getting by with things again, but that my credit had been restored. It was an acknowledgement of my "good faith," and that I had redeemed my integrity. Small mistakes would be overlooked so long as I remained conscientious enough to see them as mistakes, and if I did not pretend it was all right to exceed my limits, or otherwise excuse myself for mistakes. Above all I had to make sure that having a credit card did not become justification for my being less conscientious.

Up to the time I lost my Cosmic Credit Card I had felt a sense of being loved and protected. I did not know the source of this love, though I suspected it came from a power higher than myself. I had always marvelled that it was there for me no matter what I did. Finally, when I decided it would always be there for me, I lost it. Possibly falling into the well was a metaphor for the loss of this sustaining love. Of all my losses at that time, this was the greatest, for without it I knew for the first time true loneliness.

No doubt this loneliness became the driving force for developing myself. The instant I began consulting the *I Ching,* increments of this love returned. With every increase in my humility and acceptance, and in my willingness to sacrifice anger and frustration, the love increased. When I regressed to an indifferent, lax, or arrogant attitude, the love waned and was soon gone. Return of the love made me know I was on the right track. Little by little the love stayed. Little by little, as I became more stable in my way of life, it grew in intensity. Then one day I suddenly recognized that the source of this love was the Sage, my flawless, invisible Teacher.

These and other meditations also made me aware that the lantern—help—is always there and available, if we will but ask for it, look within ourselves, and rely on it. I had arrogantly disdained my inner life. I had become careless in my personal relationships. I had refused to listen to my inner sense of things to the point that I lost my ability to hear within. Through self-development and the help of the Sage, I regained my inner hearing.

My meditation experiences showed me how I had come to have my adversities, and how, by working on spoiled aspects of my character, I was able to make my way out of them. With the help of the *I Ching* the perilous night of misunderstanding and folly came to an end. The dawning of understanding had begun. In the last Well Meditation I could see a path leading up over a hill, out of the Plain of Pitfalls. Although many challenges lay ahead, the worst was behind me.

The nature of the inner life has continued to be revealed throughout my meditative life. Other meditations throughout this book contain insights into the way the inner life works. These have made me realize how ignorant we are of the inner life at the beginning of our self-development. We are, as the *I Ching* puts it in *The Wanderer*, Hexagram 57, "strangers in a strange land."

I relate the next meditation to demonstrate that we communicate with each other constantly on the inner level, and thus never really deceive each other.

The Greek Amphitheater   February 2, 1974

I saw a highly polished, mirror-like, circular floor which resembled black onyx, and which was illuminated by a torch burning opposite where I stood. This circular floor was surrounded by an ancient stone curbing. Before I had a chance to realize where I was, or what I was doing, I whispered one of my inmost thoughts out over the floor. Though I had barely whispered it, it seemed peculiarly audible, like a stage whisper that reaches the far side of an auditorium. Then I saw to my left, tiers of ancient stone and 20,000 pairs of eyes. Shockingly, I realized I was in an ancient Greek amphitheater which was acoustically perfect. Everyone had heard everything I had said.

Then I understood that, on the inner level, each of us knows what each other's innermost thoughts are. Even though our knowledge is "only subconscious," people are influenced more by it than by anything we say. This was why my *I Ching* counsel had been so concerned that my innermost thoughts be pure and good. These innermost thoughts create the trajectories of action in our lives that determine our fate.

Our inner life journey is concerned with conquering the fears and doubts which rule our lives, for they comprise the dark power. The dark power, we learn, is not a passive force; it is an extremely active force.

Everyone's subconscious is tuned to the other's on the inner plane. When a person's attitude is in harmony with Universal Truth, he possesses what the *I Ching* calls the "power of inner truth." His actions are automatically correct and he automatically conveys to others truth and light. When he is not in harmony with Universal Truth, he conveys only weakness and inner conflict.

The purpose of making this inner world journey is to bring our true natures into being, and give body to our character. The journey is also a process by which we are repeatedly tested and challenged, so that our experience of inner truth slowly becomes freed of all doubt.

These tests expose us to many dangers, the greatest being that we might give up, get stuck in convention, or misunderstand the way things really work in the Cosmos. If we will remain aware of these dangers and resolute to carry the process of growth through to the very end, we will complete our journey and fulfill our destiny.

In working on self-correction we do more than rescue ourselves. Those around us subconsciously watch to see whether our path is safe to follow; our perseverance lights the path for them, and gives them courage to follow their higher natures.

Through manifesting our highest natures, we act to stop the cycles of misery that pass from one generation to another through decadent traditions. This is why the Chinese have long held that we can only correct the world through correcting ourselves. Correcting ourselves is the most creative job of all.

6.

The Inferior Man, or False Self

For quite a long time I did not understand what the *I Ching*, in its ancient language, meant by the Inferior Man, or, for that matter, by the Superior Man, and the Inferiors. Although it soon became evident that these designations referred to parts of myself, I could not distinguish between the different parts other than to realize that once my mind was consumed with fears and worries, the Inferior Man must be in control. Learning about my interior makeup took a number of years of meditating in conjunction with the *I Ching*.

Although the *I Ching* refers to the Inferior Man, the Superior Man, and the Inferiors in the masculine gender, gender is superfluous. The following meditation explained something of these divisions of self. The meditation made use of my having recently seen the BBC's Masterpiece Theater television series, *Elizabeth Rex*.

The Elizabethan Court Scene   November 29, 1972

I found myself listening to the strident demanding voice of a man who stood before me, explaining why I should do this and why that. He was very pompous and authoritative, and from his fancy dress and the way he stood out from those around him, I saw that he was the Prime Minister, and those around him, members of the court. For my part I saw that I was sitting on a throne. Looking at my fancy clothing I realized I was, indeed, a queen. This seemed flattering until I noticed that I was being bossed about. Worse, I was quite docile about it, as if I had no thoughts of my own. I assented to ideas the minister presented without any question on my part, as if it were unthinkable I should know anything. I also realized that he alone defined "our" goals. I was a rubber stamp, nodding yes. The more he talked the more I realized he was presenting reasons which echoed the very thoughts I had recently been thinking which seemed to have been expressed in terms of "we," as in, "We ought to be doing this." If I were truly reigning, it should have been "I," not "we," operating in my thoughts.

Acknowledging my impotence, I thought of Queen Elizabeth I, who certainly knew her mind. I needed that kind of courage and perseverance. My first act as ruler of myself was to throw out this Prime Minister I had allowed to rule. This had a great effect for some days. But after a while, being unused to ruling, I reverted to listening to doubts he continued to insinuate into my ear and so allowed him to resume power.

In many more meditations about my inner court, I ejected the usurper again and again, until I gradually gained strength in commanding myself. It was a two steps forward, one backward process. Although I was bothered less and less by these incursions of the ego-self, to this day I remain watchful lest, by not paying attention, it surely will regain command.

Hearing and seeing the ego in meditation enabled me to realize that all its complaints, statements, and threats were expressions of fears about what will happen if I do not do things "the right way," and what others will think. It constantly projected the fear that I would lose out in some way, or that I would not succeed in attaining my goals, or maintain my life style, or similar fears that were connected with my image of myself.

In time I learned that the ego (Inferior Man) initiates itself through the moods. It gains my attention (my docile, undeveloped self) by introducing things it has taught me to want, or worry about, or wonder about. There is always a certain whining quality, like that of a spoiled child, in these moods, which changes once the ego attains full command. Then its tone becomes goading and demanding. When it was displaced through my growing ability to resist it, or through losing face by its bad judgment, it changed to grovelling, flattering, or complaining in self-pitying tones, to intimidate or trick my real self into allowing it to return to power. The instant I entertained its complaints, self-pity, or flattery, it resumed full power and began demanding.

Once I caught on to these tricks, it would direct my attention forward in anticipation of things happening, or to the side at how things weren't going right, or backward, at how much better (or worse) things were in some past time. In looking forward its scenarios were either of gloom or doom, or of some scheme which promised wonderful results: a more comfortable circumstance, or more recognition of my abilities, wit, grace, charm, etc. In looking sideways it engaged me in envious comparisons—making me discontent with people who seemed to get away with things, not do their share, and so on; in looking backward it projected memories in which "poor me" had played the role of the tragic heroine, or martyr, or the reverse, "See how I sang, see what a success I was, how I have achieved this or that, and how I have figured out everything."

I was not to recognize for many years the many stances the ego-self-image could invent, or the tricks it could play. The worst of these tricks was getting me to think it was me thinking its thoughts. In meditation I had seen it was not me, but it had a way of getting me to forget that. Through many of these experiences I learned how insidious an intruder it was. It would try almost anything to slip back into control, and I have never permitted it to do so without suffering bad consequences.

Several more meditations confirmed that the Inferior Man was my ego-self-image. The most important of these came in response to my need to understand a problem then occurring between me and my husband. In following the *I Ching* I had begun to shed my self-images. Since my husband was proceeding in a different direction, the chasm of misunderstanding between us widened.

The Elizabethan Stage   May 17, 1973

I saw my husband and myself opposite each other on a well-lit stage. I was clad only in a simple dress that might have been made from a feed sack. Beside me were the full trappings of an Elizabethan gown I had just removed. I somehow noticed that I looked a good deal younger than I had looked before, when I still had the dress on. My

72

husband was dressed in full Elizabethan costume, with doublet, cape, broad-brimmed hat with a feather in it, and lace at the neck and cuffs. All over the front of his clothing were labels which announced him as "writer," "artist," "photographer," "teacher," "father." There were so many I did not read them all, but I noticed that the ones I saw corresponded to self-images he held at the time. Towards me he was guarded and defensive, but I noticed that something seemed to be struggling behind his cape. Then my perspective changed so that I was permitted to view the scene as a member of the audience. From my new position in the orchestra I could see that his real self was struggling behind his cape. Also dressed in simple clothing and youthful in appearance, this self was gagged and bound, hand and foot. Only his eyes were free, and they looked imploringly to me (in the audience) for help. Curiously, his gaudy self was still facing the young version of me still on the stage, carefully guarding to insure that she could not see what it was he was hiding. He was unconcerned with the fact the audience could see everything. Then I was informed by the unseen teacher showing me the scene that if I gave up on his real self by believing that his real self no longer existed, that self would die. Indeed, this meditation made me realize it was my mandate to strengthen and rescue this real self by never giving up on him. I have also interpreted this as a general message never to give up on anyone's real self, regardless of what is showing.

Another message implicit in this meditation was the ironic fact that everyone but the person involved can see through the pretensions of the ego. That person may think he has succeeded in projecting an image that fools others, but he is mistaken.

The Ego as a Snake, and as Alberich, King of Dwarfs
December 25, 1972

In other meditations I saw the Inferior Man as a snake which whispered scenarios in my ear, and as Alberich of Wagner's *Ring Cycle*, who stole the Rhinemaidens' gold. Characteristic of the ego's search for power and glory, Alberich's intention was to have a ring forged of the stolen gold, the possession of which would enable him to rule the world.

The Ego as Defensive Crutches   about 1973

This meditation focused on the ideas which provide a basis for the ego. I saw the ego-self-image as a crutch which provides defenses against the Unknown. I saw myself as one-legged, so that my progress in self-awareness was slow. The Sage gave me a temporary leg so that I would not have to depend on defensive images, pacts to do or not do things, and policies of how to respond in this or that instance. Such defensive maneuvers had become institutionalized in my mind so that I reacted and thought defensively nearly all the time. This defensiveness occurred because I saw my natural reactions as flawed (one-legged) and not good enough to protect me. Now, I was informed, it was necessary to give up the crutch if I were to make progress. This meant that I must trust the Unknown, and allow myself to be led.

I saw that such crutches keep us victimized simply because we are afraid we cannot do without them. I was to use the temporary leg until I could grow my own, through learning to trust, in small ways.

The following meditation was perhaps the most interesting one I had about the nature of the ego. It occurred the morning after a friend had been trying to convince me to join him in trying out for an operetta. I had been a little tempted, but noticed that the temptation brought self-conflict. I had left performing behind only a few years before as inconsistent with what I really wanted to be doing with my life. Nevertheless, the lure of the limelight returned from time to time.

The Three File Boxes   December 13, 1976

I saw three dead-file storage boxes roll out on a conveyer of rollers and stop in front of me. I opened the one on the far right, only to find soot and ashes on the bottom. In the center of the ashes I caught sight of a high school ring, and remembered the person who gave it to me. Although at one time I might have experienced some emotion on seeing this ring, now I had none. A few other mementos from that period of my life seemed to be there as well, but they meant nothing to me now. Obviously, this box contained items from a dead past.

The second box was full to the top. The first thing I found was a suit of clothes I had liked. As I shook it out I realized how musty, even mildewed it was. Then I realized that something stored beneath it was semi-decayed, and the suit had absorbed its unpleasant odor. Hastily, and without any regret, I put the suit back and closed the box.

Looking in the third box, the first thing I saw was a beautiful black dress, crisp and clean. Although I had never owned such a dress, it obviously was one I might use in performing music. I quickly and without second thought put it on, only to become alarmed when it immediately began dancing off, out of control. I hastily unzipped it and scrambled out before it was too late. With difficulty I stuffed it back in the box and clamped the lid down tight. Then the scene disappeared.

Shortly, the explanation came. The first box and its contents symbolized attachments I had in my youth, now totally forgotten. The second symbolized another part of my life, now dead, but to which I could still relate with a certain nostalgia. The third represented my recent performing past. It was clear I could not become involved in singing again without getting caught up in the destructive vanity of that part of my life. The meditation was also a statement of the nature of my ego, and of the limits I must observe. Just as the alcoholic must not indulge in alcohol, I was not yet free enough of my vanity that I could indulge in singing.

Six Characters in Search of an Author (Pirandello)
about 1973

Not only did meditations draw on my daily and past

experiences, they drew on the TV programs and plays I watched, and all the literature I had ever read. Once, on reading the preface to Pirandello's play, *Six Characters in Search of an Author*, I was struck by something I had noticed in my own earlier attempts to write plays—that once you define a character, that character no longer enters and exits on cue, conveniently, to suit your purposes. It wants to do its own thing and have its own say. This causes considerable trouble for the playwright. Now I realized that as we grow and become acculturated, we develop images of ourselves to compensate for imagined deficiencies or defects. Once created, these images are no longer content to be mere figments of our imagination. They demand their own reality. They are unwilling, moreover, to serve us. Quite the opposite, they dance their own dance, and like the black dress, they take over, with us in them. There is no friendly meeting ground where they compromise with us, or we compromise with them. They swiftly develop their own defenses and devices to keep power. Often this is achieved through flattery of the self; often through intimidation; often it is through making the self feel it is too weak to resist its insistent hammering. It maintains power by seeming harmless, deluding us into thinking we can manage it.

These are only some of its many tricks. There is no possible compromise with it.

Goals of the Ego, or Inferior Man (An Essay)
November 4, 1973

The ego-self-image, or dark force in a person, seeks to complete itself in the capitulation of others. It does so to obtain a "high," a fulfillment of self, an existential awareness of being.

This fulfillment of the ego is found in feeling it exists, although it never can, because it is only an image we have created. Even though it is only an image it seeks the existence of the real self.

In contrast, the real self finds confirmation and fulfillment in attaining an inner harmony that is free of all competition and striving. We experience only humble gratitude. It is like the selfless appreciation of sunlight falling on wet leaves, or the quiet wonderment at serene beauty found anywhere. The fulfillment of the ego creates a swelling enthusiasm that *temporarily* fills the hole in the center of our being caused by feeling insufficient. This hole can be filled permanently by serving the true and the good, not by aggrandizement.

The inferior, or false self, in its quest for existence, strives to achieve the joys of the real self, but it mistakes the source of joy. It thinks it can create joy, and to obtain its desires it plunges ahead ambitiously, sacrificing dignity and self-esteem.

When we are under attack by another's ego, we tend to build defenses, in order to gain relief from the tensions exerted on us. These defenses come in the form of tempting inner attitudes such as, "I can't stand this person anymore," or "I'm fed up." Such defense mechanisms, coming from the inferior element in ourself, are a form of capitulation to the situation—the very effect desired by the other person's ego, for this effect feeds his ego's feeling of existence. Not only does our capitulation affirm his ego, our ego is aroused in the form of injured pride.

The only real defense against evil in another is to develop and maintain a correct attitude. We adopt no defenses or resentments; we build no barriers. As Lao Tzu put it, we become opaque; we disengage, retreat within, and persevere, though grieved. This attitude deprives the other's ego of energy, its needed affirmation, and saves our personality from damage.

When the other's ego fails to achieve its aim to unbalance us, it must then turn back on itself. As a line in the *I Ching* puts it, "When the dark force has wounded all it can, it must then destroy itself as well."

In striving to engage our egos, another's ego may also employ flattery. By adopting the mask of caring, sincerity and sensitivity are simulated, to engage us. If these ploys are unsuccessful, more clever devices may be used; these failing, the person may resort to intimidation, one-upmanship, or even force. Depending upon the person's resolve and the extent of our relationship with him, an inner war may begin which is manifested by intimidation, then mean assaults. If at any point we waver, the inferior nature of the other person, sensing possible success, will become more aggressive. It is essential, therefore, to be firmly resolved to keep on our path.

To adopt no defenses is to achieve the strongest position. We also avoid feelings of alienation. We simply forbear in modesty, and wait. Modesty is both a shield and sword, for without doing anything we overcome everything. We allow ourself to be defended. We should not think why the situation is happening, for this would embroil us in conflict. We need to recognize only that it is happening, that it is incorrect, and then turn it over to the Cosmos for rectification. Remaining in contact with our inner voice, and remaining firmly disengaged, we see that the seemingly irresistible wave of negative energy passes by. A second wave that comes is only half its strength. The third and final wave is merely a ripple which exhausts the energy of the dark force.

To maintain inner forbearance is to exert the quiet power of inner truth which in the *I Ching* is called the *Power of the Great*.

Crescendo of Awfulness   about 1985

This meditation occurred after an *I Ching* study group I ran had been challenged by a newcomer's worst ego nature. This person challenged and verbally assaulted the group for four consecutive meetings. Nearly everyone, through great effort, remained disengaged, so that the person retreated. The entire situation demonstrated the power of perseverance.

It came to me that we were being put through a Crescendo of Awfulness. Such moments of challenge are also moments of opportunity. If we can retain our integrity throughout the situation, we act as a mirror, discrediting the other person's ego before his higher self. In this moment of truth, the wrongdoer is turned towards the good, even if only momentarily.

The following shows the tendency of the ego to pursue a straight line course to proving how wonderful or right it is.

The Path of the Billiard Ball   August 13, 1977

On the previous night, while driving with someone, our car began to be followed closely by another car. To get free of this annoyance I turned down a side road, but the other car followed. My passenger suggested I drive extra slowly, or even jerk to a sudden stop, to teach the person a lesson.

I explained that it was not my philosophy to engage someone else's ego. Pulling over, I forced the other car to pass, causing my passenger to comment that I was "too nice." Seeing that my passenger's ego had been aroused, I felt it was no use trying to explain my philosophy.

In meditation the next morning I saw a pool table with scattered billiard balls. One of these was shot across the table. It bumped first into one, than another ball, each time changing its course. I thought how it must take a master to plot the course of a billiard ball that hits more than one ball.

Then I thought that people who are rigid in their point of view are like billiard balls. Each time they hit something in their way, their course is altered. They would have to be exceedingly clever to end up where they want to be.

A more flexible person would have the ability to go around obstacles in the way and resume his original course. Even if he did not end up exactly where he wanted to go, he would certainly increase his chances of doing so.

7.

The Superior Man, or True Self

Alas, the loud voice of my ego—the Prime Minister of my court meditations—and those unidentified others who plagued me with interruptions, seemed to be the only voices I heard in my thoughts, other than the calm, authoritative voice I had identified as the Sage. I was certain that voice was not my own. I rarely heard it, for it mostly spoke during emergencies to warn against dangers. Where, then, was the real me? As yet I could not identify any voice that seemed to come from me.

A Pair of Eyes and Ears   about 1972

As if in response to such wondering, in meditation I saw myself simply as a pair of eyes and a pair of ears. I saw that I could direct my attention outward at the external world, or inward at the inner world. A pair of eyes and a pair of ears—that was all there was to me! I felt astonished and puzzled—it seemed too little.

Actually, it *was* all, then. At the time I had not gained command of my inner domain. I was still ruled much of the time by my ego-self-image, and although my newly developing self was getting stronger in terms of commanding my internal self, I was still without an image. However, I was conscious of my enlarging reservoir of "inner truth" derived from the meditations. I was learning to hear, and rely on, my inner voice.

Elizabeth Rex, or, Learning to Rely on My Inner Voice
November 29, 1972

After a period of seeing nothing but a blurred scene, a strong, clear image came of Queen Elizabeth I, when, as a prisoner in the Tower of London, she had learned to listen to her inner voice. Doing so had saved her life on several occasions. When she was older she continued to rely on it.

Then I knew that listening to my inner voice was to be my *modus operandi*. I was told that I would be entirely on my own, and that I would have to rely on my inner resources and listen to my inner voice. Then I saw myself as blind, dependent on listening to my inner voice.

Other thoughts then "ran by" before I could hear them. Asking the Sage why I was unable to hear my inner voice, He replied, "A river grows cold before it turns to ice." This astonished me until I realized that when the truth is no longer audible within, it is a warning that I have lost my receptivity.

While this meditation made it was clear that I was to be the ruler of my inner domain, it did not mean that I should develop an image of myself as a queen. Instead, I was to free myself of all self-images.

Recently my granddaughter was watching a TV cartoon in which Daffy Duck was being pursued by its enemy, the cat. At one point Daffy Duck dropped an anvil onto the cat, then picked up the anvil and peeled off the flattened cat. It occurred to me that the ego's flattening of the real self was a similar phenomenon. Once freed from the domination of the ego, the flattened and squashed real self develops and assumes its natural form. Unlike the ego-dominated self, which is only an inflated nothing, the real self is not an image, but what we manifest through developing our highest nature. It is something that simply "is," and that is enough.

The Tree Meditations   1973-1974

As I began to grow in inner stature I no longer saw myself as "only a pair of eyes and ears." I saw myself as a seedling just sprouting. Later, I had wriggled up through the soil, twisting around rocks, and stretching upwards. Then I saw myself as a young plant, exposed to the beating sun, the driving wind, and the rain. Later I was a young tree whose bark, though still thin, now protected me from the elements. Still later I was an older tree, better established, with an adequate root system. These transformations, like those of the house meditations, took place over a long period of time. Seeing myself in these symbolic forms confirmed that while nothing had changed in my external life, I had achieved much within myself. These meditations helped me stay on my path.

The Engine Meditations   1973-1976

Another series of reassuring and explanatory meditations showed me an automobile engine. In the first of these, the engine was in parts, lying about, as if someone had been assembling it but had gotten distracted and forgotten to return. This was obvious because some of the parts, through neglect, had developed a thin layer of rust. It was necessary, therefore, to clean and polish them. Cleaning and polishing was the work of this meditation, which was to say, before we can even begin to put the engine together, we must get rid of this old matter.

In a later meditation I saw the engine half put together. All the parts had been cleaned and oiled, and the work was proceeding well. Still later the engine was fully assembled. As if to demonstrate the value of my work on myself, the engine was started up. I recall its being around 350 horsepower, capable of pulling a very heavy load.

Ironically, growing is a process of subtraction. Every time we subtract or sacrifice what is false, our real self gains that much more strength. The following two meditations demonstrate this principle:

Crutches   May 7, 1982

I have had many meditations in which I have come into the presence of the Sage sitting in a small garden. The garden is a semi-circular area in front of a rock facing. Everything in the garden is natural except a hedge which outlines the boundary of the garden, and a small walkway of brick that wanders through it. It is simple, but attractive.

The Sage, unlike the setting, is not distinct. He is rather a presence sitting there in human form, but blank-faced. Once in His presence I seem not to notice the form, as if it is not important. I only notice, when I first sit down there, that being in the company of this presence is invigorating and pleasant.

Often the meditation begins with my being outside the garden, unable to pass through the gate. The meditation revolves around discovering what prevents me from entering the garden, hence coming into the presence of the Sage, who could then help me with my problem of the moment. Since the thing which prevents my entering the garden usually involves a habit of mind, or image of myself that stands in the way, I search myself for the obstructing element.

This time I discovered that I did not feel free. Looking at myself I noticed I was enclosed in a sort of iron maiden which I must take off, or break through. After some difficulty I removed it and saw that it was a hardened image I had put on to protect myself from others. Obviously, in an effort to "be firm" I had adopted an image of "being firm," in hopes the image would protect me. All I really needed to do, however, was to be clear-minded and firm in my values, and trust them to guide me through the challenges.

On shedding the iron maiden, I also shed my clothing, which seemed surprising, but then I realized my clothing reflected what I thought of myself, and was also part of my self-image. I kept subtracting images, one layer after another, until I got down to my real self—a formless lump! At first I resisted this idea, but then accepted it. Accepting it, I found myself within the garden walls, no longer an outsider. Then love seemed to be showered on me in response to having shed my self-images.

Then my attention was drawn to a shallow pit which looked like an empty goldfish pool. As at the shrine at Lourdes, France, it was nearly full of crutches, braces, and the paraphernalia of sickness. My iron maiden was on top the pile. Obviously the pit was a place for giving up things on which we lean—things we think are indispensable—defense mechanisms, self-images, ideas of how we "need to be" or "have to be" to get along, and our attachment to our personality as some sort of prerogative. I realized that if we can be no personality at all, we find the perfect way of relating to everyone. Then everything we say or do comes from our essential self instead of the self-image, and is spontaneously correct.

On Being a Nub   May 9, 1982

Continuing my lessons of the past few weeks I had been shedding every last vestige of being that is not part of my essential self. In this meditation I saw myself reduced from a lump to a mere nub. The lesson revolved around the feeling that I needed to possess answers. I realized quite suddenly that I do not have to know, or have an answer for something, even though all my training has made me feel ashamed not to know, and not to have answers. Indeed, feeling I had to know often made me think up answers that trapped me in uncomfortable positions. Then people were able to manipulate me because they perceived I was fixed in the gear of "having to know," and that having come to a position, I would have to defend that position.

Then it also occurred to me that I did not "have to worry." Somehow I had the idea that if I did not worry about money, or other matters, nothing would happen, and I would not get money, or solve those matters. I saw that it was enough to be careful and conscientious. I also saw that my doubt was often expressed as a need to "keep my eye" on a situation, "otherwise it would get out of control." However, keeping my eye on the situation only indicated the presence of the doubt which kept things from happening. Doubt is the element that activates the dark force and keeps us isolated from the power of the Creative. I saw that what I needed was to detach my gaze from the situation in a willing suspension of disbelief.

Then I saw that in meeting certain sorts of situations, I had perceived that I had to "be tough," "be angry," "be alienated," "be hostile," "be easy going," or, "be nice." I saw that all these additions to being were superimposed attitudes, defenses I had adopted because I did not know how to relate to the situations. I feared that not taking a position would leave a dangerous vacuum. When these devices failed to protect me, I then attempted to force matters, again out of fear that doing nothing was cowardly, useless, or danger- ous. I saw that all such tactics and devices, because they were related to inner weakness, were ineffective. Also, my weakness was intuitively perceived by others, who were then put in a position of strength. I realized that sometimes I took a defensive or offensive position because I doubted the other person would do the right thing. Feeling my doubts about them, they remained resistant, and I was unable to invoke their potential for good. I saw that doubt also shut me off from those elements in the Cosmos which aid all that is good.

Through such meditations as this I became aware that as our true self becomes more established as leader of the personality, traits and qualities we formerly distinguished as ourself are seen as superfluous. With insight we relin- quish them and they disappear. With growth we are more consistently empty, neutral, and attuned to the Cosmos. Through carefully adhering to our values we are better protected from being impressed by flattery, or being drawn in by the seductions of vanity. We more actively disperse anger and recognize the fears and doubts of our inferiors. We are more tolerant and persevering. While we do not shut the world out, we are more resistant to being pulled off balance by it. Our state of mind is somewhat like that of a tight-rope walker.

Although I have never been a tight-rope walker, I grew up in railroad town. My cousin and I used to compete to see which of us could walk the farthest on the rails without falling off. I well remember the concentrated, alert state of mind needed to maintain balance.

The Meditation of Total Decrease   about 1978

In a lecture I once talked about the "real self" as being devoid of self-images. One of the audience said they thought that was terrible. "Who would even want to work towards such a goal?" she asked.

Certainly, up to now I had been doubtful that being empty within could lead to much of anything. However, thinking that a total submission of self was what the Higher Power required, I became determined to shed every last bit of "myself." Having decided that I was the enemy, tears in great streams began running down my face. Although at first I felt awful, in a short time I became detached from this feeling and sat, as it were, watching my body cry. My body was detaching its allegiance from the ego-self-image.

After crying for a while, I became devoid of feelings. Then suddenly everything began to change. Where before all had been black, all now became light. Through voluntarily giving up "myself" I was blessed. I had been showered with love from a hidden source. What was the lowest point for my ego became the beginning point for my spiritual existence.

To find our true self, we must let go of all the defensive postures of the ego. This means we cease relying on structured defenses which shut us off from perceiving better, more effective ways of dealing with situations. We are not, as we might think, left unprotected. With our mind open, we are better able to respond effectively to the challenge of the moment.

To elaborate, the best tennis players have the best technique and training in strategy, but they also are the least "grooved." They know the rules of strategy, but are still free to respond to the ever-changing situations. Similarly, the concert violinist may practice a phrase for an hour, but as Isaac Stern put it, "I never know how I am actually going to play it until I play it." He relies on something that comes out of the moment, and although he may play the phrase almost the same as he did before, there will be something unique and fresh about it. Similarly, a singer may sing a Puccini aria in the style set by Madame Melba, who first sang it, but she must find the essence, or heart of that aria if she is to give it life. The ego, relying on the cleverness of a carefully contrived approach which allows no suprises, is an enemy to this, the Creative process.

By leaving ourselves open and unstructured, we are able to invoke the creative powers of the universe to aid and defend us. Being open and unstructured, we have an antenna out, so to speak, and are able to receive insights. When an insight occurs, we follow it. Something happens and Aha! we know what to do. Sometimes the insight is so mundane and commonplace it is astonishing. The solution seems just too simple, but it is the correct one. Perhaps our ego would like to jump in, once we have succeeded, to say it did it, but that simply is not so.

8.

The Inferiors, or Body Self

In the meditation of the inner court I had found that I was a beleaguered Queen, dominated by a Prime Minister, and harassed by undisciplined others who, surrounding me, pointed out what I ought to be doing. They constantly asked, "What about *my* needs?" as they intruded noisily in my inner space. They presented their needs as if they were the only important needs of the self.

I soon noticed that their concerns were physical—when and what to eat, complaints about being uncomfortable, or tired, feelings of being over-used and abused, unappreciated and tread upon, neglected, and never recognized for their part in the scheme of things. As spokesmen for various aspects of my body self, I realized that they were what the *I Ching* calls the "inferiors." Though they interrupted and made meditation difficult, I eventually had to acknowledge that their presence in my inner space was legitimate. The problem with them lay in the fact that they were untrained and undisciplined.

Disciplining the inferiors meant that they must learn to wait and to allow themselves to be guided by my higher self. The type of waiting was specific—perseverance. Once the inferiors began to accept this guidance, their true purpose and worth emerged. They reminded me of appointments and kept me abreast of what needed to be done in my normal areas of existence. I learned to keep a notepad beside me during meditation, to write down their suggestions. But I also learned to say, after giving them a certain amount of attention, "enough is enough." While it was a mistake to pay no attention to them, it was equally wrong to pay too much attention to them.

The inferiors, then, are our body cells. Highly vocal, they represent the interests of the body self. In meditation they appear as people. When I first saw them they were pasty-faced children who reminded me of the Walt Disney version

88

of Snow White's dwarfs. Their housekeeping was bad and they were given to being grumpy, dopey, sleepy, and happy. As I grew, they became less pasty-faced and more disciplined, and I found I could put them to use in interesting ways. I could go to sleep, posting them to alert me if anything important arose, and to wake me up at whatever hour I wished. They faithfully executed these requests. I even tried putting them on guard to alert me to the entrance of the ego. While that was unsuccessful then, lately I have had some cooperation in this area.

Although their intelligence is childlike and their interests mundane, it surprised me that they could be so verbal until I had given the matter more thought and realized that it was they who, through infinitely small steps, learned to talk and walk. It was their particular talent to learn small repetitive tasks. Through identifying and relating sounds to activities, they learn to speak. The same ability enables us to learn to hit a nail with a hammer without hitting our thumbs. Through repetitive practice fingers learn to play passages on the piano and can continue to play these passages even when we are thinking of something else. With this sort of ability, no wonder our inferiors can dominate our inner space with idle chatter. Chatter, however, is what it is. There is no depth to the thinking of the inferiors.

It would seem that the body has a variety of ways to communicate, both with itself, and with us. In addition to being able to communicate verbally, our cells communicate through feelings of pleasure and pain. If we have turned ourselves off to how our body feels, and ignore its needs as insignificant, our body may begin to communicate with us through pain, discomfort, and illness.

On first seeing the inferiors, I shooed them out of my inner space, which appeared to be a room, and locked the doors. Even then, they seemed to crowd around the windows to stare in at me until I found a way of blocking them from view. This method of handling them worked only for a while. Then I got the *I Ching* line from *Keeping Still*, Hexagram 52, Line 3, "In exercises in meditation and concentration one ought not to try to force results. Rather, calmness must develop naturally out of a state of inner composure. If one tries to induce calmness by means of artificial rigidity, meditation will lead to very unwholesome results." Gradually, I began to listen to their concerns, and to acquire their willingness to leave me alone in meditation.

The following meditation was one of the earliest in which I saw the function of the inferiors in my personality. At the time they were in a dangerous state of disorder, so much so that it was necessary to deal harshly with them.

The Columbus Meditation   1973

I found myself on a ship halfway across the ocean. The ship was square-rigged and I swiftly became aware that, as on the voyage of Columbus, the ship's crew was in a state of mutiny. They were assembled on the main deck, and were angrily haranguing me for "not knowing where I was going," and for allowing myself to be led blindly by "this *I Ching* thing." They were certain we would fall off the edge of the world. Listening to them from the quarterdeck, I looked at the ship. Because of my crew's neglect, boards were loose and sticking out, and the sails were in tatters. Surely the next storm would sink us. Their rebellion was dangerous, and it occurred to me that I had to get rid of them.

No sooner did I realize this than I found myself armed with a bow and arrows. I shot all who did not jump overboard at once. When none were left the thought came, How would I manage, here in the middle of the ocean, without a crew? But it would be better to have no crew, I realized, than to be stuck with this one. Then I thought, How will I navigate? How will I know the way? The words came, "Follow what is constant." I remembered Columbus's journey. Certainly my ship was just like his, and so were my circumstances. It came to me that the North Star always stays in its place. Keeping its location in mind, I realized, was like laying a path out across the water. Then I saw this marvellous path, burnished by the evening sun, that led straight west.

Wondering at the symbolism of the North Star, it came to me that it symbolized Universal Truth, for the Truth is constant. I could rely on it utterly to point the way. Even if I did not know what the truth was, it would show itself at the right time, when I needed it.

This meditation reassured me to go on.

I saw my ship soon again in another meditation. This time I had an entirely new crew and the ship was completely repaired.

Although it may seem strange that I killed the unruly inferiors, since the idea came to me, together with the weapons to do it, it was right for me to do it. Similarly, on seeing diseased body cells in meditation, I might cut the diseased area out, cleanse the wound, and pour a healing oil over it. That usually solves the problem.

Although the action parts of meditation happen fast, we seem to have all the time in the world to notice things. For example, I immediately noticed that the inferiors were obsessed with what I was doing (leading them on that risky voyage); meanwhile they paid no attention whatever to their job of keeping the ship in good repair.

Once I had killed off this unruly crew, my inferiors were easily led. I only needed to tell why I needed them to do a thing for them to do it. Once disciplined they were both loyal and brave.

The Hospital Ward   1984

After having an appendectomy I noticed that the areas on each side of my incision were unusually tense. Whenever I feel bodily tension I tend to meditate in an effort to free myself of it. This time, however, removing the tension required an unusual amount of effort. At length I succeeded, then forgot the whole incident.

Three weeks later, having recovered from my operation, I had an accident which caused injury and pain. Deciding to meditate to deal with the pain, I quickly slipped into meditation and found myself in a hospital ward. I noticed that the ward was full of children—patients from six to ten years old, in all stages of injury. A few were in a coma, some badly bruised, some only slightly injured.

I realized that these were my body cells in various stages of injury. It came to me to embrace, comfort, and reassure them that the worst was over, and that they would soon heal and be well. As I did this, I noticed that their worried faces relaxed and they became content. When I arose from meditation my pain was entirely gone. Even though the injury was considerable, the pain never returned.

As is often the case in meditation, realizations continue for days afterwards. I realized that the tension I had felt around the incision after my appendectomy was the result of fear. The bodily inferiors had not been told something was going to happen. Then, after being operated upon, they did not know whether they might be subjected to some other unpleasant experience. It was up to me to tell them what had happened, and that nothing else would be happening. In the future I must prepare them in advance by explaining to them what is to happen, how long they must endure the unpleasantness, and why it for their good, and necessary. Pain, I realized, is mostly bodily fear. To ease this fear doctors prepare their patients by saying, "now this is going to hurt a little," or "only for a moment." Advance preparation eases their fear, minimizes their anticipation, and helps them be brave.

Not long after these experiences two friends came to visit who did not know each other. One had a kink in her neck, the other had completed training to be a chiropractor, but had never practiced. The chiropractor fixed the other's back with a stroke of the hand. This caused me to tell her about my recent experiences. She then explained that when a back muscle is strained, all the muscles surrounding it seem to freeze in a protective stance. Then she remarked of my experience, "it's as if pain is cellular freakout." I thought this a very good description.

Another experience reinforced the importance of preparing my inferiors in advance.

When my youngest daughter left home, her horse, then four years old, remained. It had been trained to a dressage method of riding, while my training had been a cavalry style of riding. After having problems riding this horse, I decided to take lessons from a dressage teacher. This teacher pointed out that I was giving the horse "mixed signals"—one set of commands by voice and pulling on the reins, and a contrary set through my body weight. It was necessary to synchronize my body weight with my intentions. Thus, if I wished to stop, I must shift my weight by sitting back, and not continue sitting as if I were going at a trot, or canter. I soon found that I hardly needed give any voice or rein signals at all to stop. I merely needed to sit back. My teacher also recommended I give the horse just a moment's advance preparation for whatever I intended to do. If, for example, I wished to trot, I should change the tension on the reins just a fraction to signal the horse to expect that something new was about to happen. Through these small changes all the horse's nervousness and confusion ended. He no longer showed the resistance he had been showing.

Later I noticed an identical pattern between a mother and her child. The child happened to be playing with another child when her mother decided it was time to leave. She went to the child, took her hand and said that now it was time to leave. The child, lacking time to adjust her mind, broke into tears. I have since made a point, even with adults, to give them just a bit of advance preparation to expect an upcoming change on my part. All our inferiors need just a little advance preparation.

I have concluded from these and similar experiences that the inferiors, or body cells, have a child-like and limited intelligence. Unable to perceive things as a whole, they react to stimulus the way the proverbial blind men reacted to the elephant. For this reason, when we are injured, or taking treatment that is painful, it is important to tell the inferiors what has happened, or is about to happen, and how long their patience will be required. It is also important to give them moments of rest. Leading them requires that we help them understand how, if they do their best, the whole will be served. If we are honest and sincere in this effort, they will bravely do what is required of them.

This is what the *I Ching* means in *Enthusiasm*, Hexagram 16 in the phrase, "setting armies moving in our behalf." Through rallying the enthusiastic support of the foot soldier (inferiors) great things can be achieved.

The Fire Tower Meditation   about 1986

In this meditation I saw myself atop a high fire tower. Looking down at the ground I saw a crowd of my "people" standing about looking up at me. They were no longer children, but adults of various ages. From where I stood, high above them, they seemed so remote. It occurred to me that it was wrong to be separated from them in this way so I climbed down and walked among them, only to find that I was like a Gandhi to them. While I was appreciating them, they appreciated me. They brought out two or three of their own who were ill and on stretchers. I expressed my sorrow at seeing them in such bad condition and did what I could to comfort them. I decided that I must visit my people more often, and be more aware of their needs.

This meditation made me realize how indifferent to my body I had been when I sat too long at writing, or when I worked too hard and long, or ate carelessly. I realized the importance of balancing my activities.

Now, when I begin meditation, I devote a few moments to becoming aware of my body, its aches, pains, and complaints, and to expressing thanks for its help. This attitude has been full of rewards.

Often in my early experiences with meditation I was in the "out of body state." This was good for me then, because being out of my body kept me from being overpowered by my body-mind. Now, however, it is better to be "in my body," because my light energy vivifies my body and makes me healthier.

At first I was heavy-handed with my inferiors. Now I soothe them when they need it, and apologize to them when I have required them to endure undue stress. They, in turn, are loyal and patient. They seem to derive energy from serving the higher self.

Training your inferiors is like training a horse. The job is one of gaining the animal's confidence. I will never forget a friend who took a three-year-old thoroughbred rejected from the racetrack, and trained it to be a first-class hunter. She was also one of the best ballet teachers in our area. The first year she only walked the horse. If we rode together she told me, "I want nothing to upset my horse." Things did happen, though. Once, at the beginning of the hunting season, an unseen hunter who was not far away shot his gun in our direction. Her horse remained very controlled for a three-year-old. Her willingness to go slow and to be endlessly patient had already won her horse's confidence. The next year she spent three months teaching the horse to trot at slow, medium, and fast speeds. Then she did the same thing until he had developed three speeds at the canter. She had him practice every new thing until he was bored of it. By the end of the next year her horse would go over every manner of jump and frightening obstacle in utter calm. On hunts, he behaved perfectly. All the horse's fears and herd instincts for flight had become disciplined and controlled. Through teaching him in small steps to take ever bigger risks, and by making sure he would be successful in completing each step, she trained him to trust his abilities, and to trust that she would not ask more of him than he was capable of doing.

Our relationship with our body is no different. When our inferiors are disciplined, and when we deserve and gain their confidence, we fulfill the *I Ching* definition of a fully developed personality—"though the thunder terrify for a hundred miles around, he does not lose a drop from the sacrificial spoon."

On Dying—Being Pulled Across   about 1985

One of the chief fears of the body self is death. To a great extent this fear is due to the influence of the ego-self-image, to which death really is oblivion, for the ego, unlike the true self, must die.

Fear of death is not necessarily natural to the body self, whatever we may think. Individual body cells die all the time without our notice. It is only when we lose large numbers of them at once so that we also lose functions or limbs, or when our appearance changes drastically so that it becomes noticeable to the ego, that the death or sickness of our body cells becomes of concern. A great part of the ego-self-image is tied to our physical appearance, therefore the ego's fear for the body self is exaggerated.

Growing required that I understand and deal with my fear of death. My fear had not been of dying, but of how I might die. During the time that I was puzzling over this question I had a meditation in which one of the experiences mentioned in the book, *Life After Life*, flashed through my mind. In nearly all the experiences mentioned in that book, those undergoing the near-death experiences had hovered nearby, watching those who were trying to revive them.

In my meditation I saw myself dying in a situation which I thought would be extremely painful. Then I saw the outstretched arm of the Sage reaching for me from a cloud of light. On grasping it I was pulled out of the bad situation, relieved of pain and misery. Dr. Elizabeth Kubler Ross's experiences with the dying verify that once people "accept" their deaths, they feel no more pain.

In time I was to see that we, our bodies and our true selves, are co-participants in life. Curiously, to operate as a whole we first need to see these two selves as interdependent co-inhabitants of the same space. If we see ourselves only as a single entity, we fail to understand their interdependence, and cooperation between the two selves cannot be initiated. The body self, likewise, is unable to accept its true purpose to serve the higher self. Worse, if the body self remains dominated by the flattering ego, which asserts the body's survival as the pre-eminent concern, the true self remains undeveloped. If we are preoccupied with how our body appears to others, our ego may be causing us to sacrifice our health and well-being to appearances. For example, although steroids are known to be harmful to the body, athletes take them to achieve physical prowess. This shows the ego's domination of the body. Conversely, if a person holds the intellect to be all-important, he may allow the interests of his body to languish while he sacrifices his eyes to incessant reading, his muscles to excessive sitting.

Even though the ego gives the body self the message that it is devoted to its interests, the ego only uses the body for its purposes. When things go well the ego takes all the credit. When its plans fail the ego may tell the body that life is not worth living. When people say they would rather die than lose their present good looks through an accident, their egos are speaking. People going through a "to live or to die" depression are only responding to their ego's death-wish. When the higher self is in control, there is never a flirtation with death. There is only acceptance to "carry on" throughout our lives in the same way to a natural end.

Our well-being, ultimately, is based on balancing our activities; we neither neglect the outer world nor the inner world; we neither neglect the development of the higher self, nor the needs of the body self.

At first the inferiors' attachment to the ego is hard to dislodge. Then, when shock collapses the ego, the inferiors become hysterical with fear and anxiety. The real self must become strong enough to rein them in, and learn enough about them to understand and re-educate them. To the repressed real self this seems impossible. *Everything is accomplished through perseverance.*

Perseverance is made easier by the pressure of necessity, for there is really no other direction to take. Because for a long time there seems to be a lack of improvement, we seem to be going backwards. Nevertheless, while we are shedding the old, we are also developing the new. Danger occurs only when things go well, for then we think we have exaggerated the problems. When we relax our perseverance, the ego slips back into control. Mistakes like these are part of the self-development process. To become masters of ourselves it is necessary to gain our inferiors' confidence and help, and to remain vigilant throughout our lives against the ego's return to power.

9.

Healing, and Dealing with, the Body Self

It is tempting, having witnessed the healing effects of bringing myself into harmony with the Cosmos, and having discovered how emotions and subconscious attitudes produce illness, to say, "Here is the way to cure yourself." However, while I firmly believe that I can and have influenced my own health through meditation, I cannot say that someone else will be able to do the same by following a few simple steps. I must leave this matter entirely in the reader's hands. He must find the way to heal himself.

It is my view that to a large extent, health is related both to our physical and emotional nourishment. Bad nourishment disturbs the inner balance that is essential to good health. We cannot feed the body endless messages of ill will, anger, alienation, and hopelessness without a negative effect on our health. Similarly, fear and doubt, and the inevitable self-conflict that accompany them, may become manifested as illness. Getting well may require that we ferret these elements out and rid ourselves of them.

Through meditation, in conjunction with consulting the *I Ching* on a daily basis, I have frequently become free of pain. By this I mean that through following the *I Ching*'s counsel, I attained help from the Higher Power. It is my experience that no benefit can be achieved until we engage the help of the Higher Power. Moreover, the Higher Power remains aloof until we attain the proper degree of humility.

To achieve our goal of returning to health, perseverance is needed. Discovering harmful attitudes and uncovering hidden fears takes time. Progress never occurs in a straight line. The way of the Tao is zig-zag—two steps forward, one backward.

Nature works slowly, in small steps, which amount to trajectories. Reversing a trajectory that has become manifested as illness requires that we perceive and halt the destructive attitudes fueling the negative trajectory. Simply by halting the negatives we create a new trajectory towards health.

Often the process requires peeling away layers, lifting off weights, and freeing ourselves of inner obstructions. This process must be slow and thorough, because it requires that we change many attitudes and habits of mind. The *I Ching* is indispensable to this process.

Once we begin working with the *I Ching* and meditating, regardless of what has gone before, we are at a *point of beginning*. We need to acknowledge the impasse at which we have arrived, and put up no further resistance. If this impasse is ill health, the state of our health is the point of beginning. We make our way up from here. Every time we suffer a reverse we need to look at our new position as a new point of beginning, without dwelling on things getting worse. When things improve we need to be equally vigilant not to lose our inner discipline. We need to view each new situation as the starting point for making progress. The sooner we accept reverses as inevitable and greet them with equinimity, and the sooner we view progress as a temporary respite in our work, the sooner we will make enduring progress.

Each stage of our work presents us with a new problem, or puzzle; to find the correct way to respond. Solving the problem requires that we learn something about ourself. Once we understand the problem, it ceases to exist. In going through this process it helps if we view each new problem as a test of will. The important thing is to keep our will steady. Keeping our will steady often requires that we correct our inner attitude in some way. Once we grasp the lesson intended and make the correction, we proceed to a new phase in our development.

We need to pursue each new problem with sincerity. By this I mean we avoid being too focussed or goal-oriented. Indeed, the first key to the problem is to limit ourself to "one day at a time." When we are goal-oriented our ego leads. In a hurry to "get there," it measures every advance, puts conditions on everything we do, and demands immediate, measurable progress. Its activities contradict the process of healing from within, and of working with time as the vehicle of progress. Acceptance is the perfect healing balm. However, even acceptance cannot be forced. We can achieve acceptance only by dealing with our resistances and their causes. By acceptance I do not mean that in being thrown overboard we accept drowning; we begin to swim.

The following meditations provide imaging techniques which may help the reader deal with his body self.

I have already mentioned how in meditation I saw my body cells as children who needed reassurance and love, and how reassuring and loving them freed me from pain caused by injury. Loving our inferiors, forgiving ourself for errors, and reassuring ourself; these are important techniques that help one become well.

Mental Surgery   1972

In this meditation I saw an area in my kidney that was "black." I carefully excised it, cleaned out the damaged tissue with my Cosmic Vacuum Cleaner, and treated the area with healing oil. After that the pain I had been experiencing in my kidney area stopped.

Whenever I have a physical problem I mentally visualize the area causing trouble and do whatever seems appropriate to do. Sometimes I use mental surgery, sometimes I use cleansing techniques. The benefit of such mental images is remarkable.

Occasionally I have seen pain as moving red lines. I usually shine a light on these red lines. If that does not work, I treat the pain with an imaginary healing oil. I do these things in addition to all the medical things one would normally do.

Not long after I first saw my vertebrae in meditation I began to regard as a problem anything I saw in my meditations as black. Black seemed to symbolize fear that had taken up residence in my body. The following meditation showed me how, on seeing these fears, we can nullify their power over us.

Fear Which Casts a Giant Shadow   about 1975

I saw a huge black unidentifiable form which immediately inspired fear. Upon closer inspection I could see it was simply an image that had been flashed upon a large screen. In looking for the source, I saw a very small snail that was placed in front of a light so that its shadow was enlarged many times, and projected onto the screen. Then I found myself looking at the snail to see if there was anything unusual about it. When I tried to inspect it, it quickly withdrew into its shell, but not before I noticed that it was black. I realized that being black, it symbolized fear, and that it had hidden itself to keep me from realizing that it was really harmless. It struck me as remarkable that the fears we store from childhood, small and insignificant as they are, can throw frightening shadows.

The next meditation showed me how our inferiors are controlled by fear. Once I understood this, my ego's control over my inferiors was lost.

Controlling Inferior Nourishment   August 26, 1978

I found myself in a dark room carved out of rock inside a mountain. I knew the room to be one of the dark rooms of my inner self. A small light was coming from a fire in the middle of the room. Huddled around the fire were little people, extremely agitated, urging me to look at a huge, spectre-like face glowing on the opposite wall. Obviously, they were being terrorized by it.

I saw at once that although they thought the image was real, it was being projected by a movie projector. The inferiors were being fooled by the one running the projector. Then an explosion blew out the walls of the room. I could see that while I thought I had been deep inside a mountain, the edge of the room had been only a couple of feet from the mountainside, which was now exposed, so that daylight streamed in. The spectre-like face was obliterated by the light. Moreover, the one running the projector had been killed in the explosion. The little people, relieved of the terrorizing sight, were surprised to find that they had been fooled.

Then I saw that the mountain was honey-combed with similar rooms in which inferiors were being terrorized by fear-inspiring images. I seemed to realize that this scene symbolized the way people in general and society as a whole are dominated by fears suggested by others, and then projected by their own egos.

Curing a Bad Back Through Meditation   1972

A short time after learning to meditate my husband had a meditation in which he rid himself of a troublesome back problem.

Often while getting out of a chair or bed he suddenly would be gripped with pain that would last up to six weeks. One day in meditation he saw his vertebrae in front of him. At the lower end of the spine he noticed a crook. Reaching forward, he straightened out the crook with his fingers.

To my knowledge he never again had a back problem.

It seemed that he had retained an image of his back as "permanently" injured, with a crook in it. This image, in combination with the fact that his cells were constantly on guard in anticipation of being strained, made his back easy to strain. By changing his stored mental image, he effectively healed his back.

While working on this book I had an accident in which I broke my collar bone and injured my shoulder and chest. While meditation helped, pain in my shoulder persisted until I remembered to change my newly developed image of torn ligaments and broken collar bone back to a normal shoulder and unbroken collar bone. Once I did this I had no more pain.

Curing Cancer by Burying an Old Conflict   1981

In Chapter 11, I relate the Gravestone Meditation which tells of a friend who was having her second bout with thyroid cancer. In that meditation I saw her in a graveyard, standing before a man who was handing out gravestones.

Pondering whether to accept one from him, she decided not to do so, and walked out of the graveyard. Her inner rejection of death preceded by some months her recovery.

During that time, two of my friend's sons were working on a Navajo Indian reservation in Arizona. One evening they attended a medicine meeting. At these meetings the Medicine Woman stares into a fire and describes any images that present themselves. On this occasion she described the illness of "the mother of some of those present," in such detail that they were certain the Medicine Woman was referring to their mother. The sons arranged for their mother to fly out to meet with the Medicine Woman, who then repeated the ritual. This time, the Medicine Woman saw the cause of my friend's illness as her failure to bury her dead father. After the ritual the Medicine Woman helped my friend perform a symbolic burial of her father. Immediately, my friend's blood cancer level fell from 20,000 units to 1,000 units. The planned operation was called off and my friend has not had a recurrence of the problem.

What the Medicine Woman did not know was that, during the preceding ten years, my friend had worked on a project memorializing her famous father.

My friend's experience, combined with my own, as follows, convinced me that we can easily become victims of our past by holding onto old issues and problems through self-conflict.

Releasing My Father   June 14, 1979

When my father died in 1976 I was surprised that I had few feelings about it. All our lives my father and I had had difficulty understanding each other, and my lack of feelings now caused me inner conflict. I felt that I must be deficient in some way. The question persisted of what it was that caused this distance between us. I would picture him, then my feelings, trying to find some relationship.

On this day, in meditation, I saw my father lying on a mortuary table. Although his body already showed considerable decay, he sat up and looked at me a bit sternly, and with some despair said, "You must let me go."

I was astonished, but it made me realize that, by allowing my inner conflict to carry on, I was holding him back from going wherever it was he was supposed to go. For my part, resolving the conflict required only that I let go of it, along with the question, "What should my relationship with him have been?"

A month or so later, a friend told me she had dreamed that she and her sister-in-law had been walking along the beach when they came upon a mound in the sand. Just as they were about to pass by it, the mound, or person in it, sat up, as if he had been covered over by children playing at the beach. The person was her grandfather, who had recently died. He just sat there looking at her in a haunting way. Thus her dream ended.

In telling this friend my meditation about releasing my father she seemed to understand her dream.

In addition to freeing her from wondering about her grandfather, her dream may also have answered questions about death. It made her realize that her grandfather was not gone permanently, as she feared.

These meditations strongly imply that we are not meant to torture ourselves with past relationships and mistakes; holding onto them is potentially damaging. The perfect attitude towards life is total acceptance. It is also forgiveness. We forgive everything and everyone: fate, life, people, events, ourselves. We rid ourselves of all resistance. This selfless attitude, which is in harmony with life, is also healthy.

For a long time now I have had no doubt that many diseases are caused by mental attitudes and continuing inner conflicts. Two of my very good friends died of cancer not long after they expressed deep frustration at not being able to deal with their problematical marriages. I felt they caved in to feelings of hopelessness. During the period of my life that I felt the most depressed I was also the most susceptible to illness. My experiences with the *I Ching* and meditation have made me convinced that there is a strong relationship between illness and hopelessness.

Balance the Secret of Good Health   November, 1973

In this meditation I saw someone swimming the crawl, becoming tired, then turning to the back stroke for a bit of rest. Although the crawl enables a swimmer to make fast progress, he quickly becomes exhausted. Changing to the back and side strokes enables him to avoid exhaustion while continuing to swim.

Later that day I meditated while my husband and I took a sauna after playing tennis. In the middle of meditating I suddenly noticed the difference in our breathing. My breath had nearly stopped and my heartbeat seemed almost non-existent, but my husband's breathing was noticeably faster and heavier. I realized that his heart was not resting as mine was. I also realized that meditation rests the heart the way a quieter stroke rests the swimmer. When we are balanced and serene within, the heart is spared. Being able to detach and become quiet in meditation must lead to better general health.

Finding the Secret Room   January 1, 1981

Once, near the end of a bout with the flu, I had a meditation about the cause of my illness. As I sat down to meditate I noticed that I yawned twice. I immediately associated this with harboring a depressing idea that had also made me ill. (From the *I Ching* point of view misunderstandings and outright falsehoods cause inner conflict.)

In meditation I caught a glimpse of a figure ducking into a small hallway. During this fleeting moment I shot and killed it with a golden arrow. Looking at it more closely I saw that it was a thin, bespectacled woman whose hair was drawn back severely. I was reminded of an extremely inhibited and self-conscious history teacher I had had in college. The figure, despite her impoverished appearance, also seemed to be a teenager with clothes styled in my college days in the late 1940s. Exploring the hallway into which I had seen it darting, I was led to a small room with a desk. Above the desk were racks of pigeon-holes like those in post offices. Each pigeon-hole contained a long rolled-up plan. I realized that the young woman worked here developing plans of all sorts. Although the room was a part of myself, I had never seen it before. On reflection, however, I remembered a time when I knew this part of myself better, a time when I had busied myself with all sorts of plans to achieve a variety of goals. Though this part of myself had not been active in recent years, a part of me had remained here, still busy at planning.

I now became aware that when no apparent progress had been made towards my goals, this element had held up images of myself as a failure because I had not followed its plans. Having killed this inner operator, which had been the source of inner conflict and blame, I realized that I had also thrown out the cause of my illness.

Guilt must be Released   February, 1989

This meditation followed a situation involving one of my children, then over 30 years old. I saw that our elbows were tied together like Siamese twins by a thick steel joint like that from a large tractor. There was no weakness in the metal whatever, nor was there any way to separate the joint. The joint itself had a small leather patch over it, which I took off, to see whether I could get the joint apart. All I found, however, were maggots and dirt under the leather. I cleaned these away even though they did not affect the joint. Then I decided that the only thing to do was to carefully cut our skin away where the steel was attached to our elbows. This operation was successful.

Contemplating these images I realized that this child and I had been tied together by an extremely strong bond created by old feelings of guilt on my part. I felt I had paid less attention to this particular child than to the others. My guilt, which was as damaging to my child as it was to me, had formed into the steel bond I now saw in meditation. Cutting through our skins, I could see, entailed a certain loss of self, but doing it released both of us.

I also realized that when I release my feelings of guilt about another, I free the other from the impression he is defective in some way.

An Observation on the Power of Our Thoughts   1984

For a long time I did not know that my feelings could create strong reactions. This was demonstrated to me in an unusual way.

I had two horses—a gelding and an old mare. The gelding, now ten years old, had been with the old mare since he was six months old. When one was taken away the other became agitated until they were back together again.

One night the old mare died in her stall, which was next to his. When I found them the next morning, the younger horse was calm and composed. He seemed to know she was dead. He never looked in her direction, whinnied, or seemed disturbed. About a week later, I thought, as I patted him, how he must miss her. Suddenly, he looked towards the place where she had been buried, stiffened up, and whinnied almost violently, the way he used to when she was away from him. I immediately realized he was responding to my thoughts so I decided not to think of it again. From that day on he was content. This was a great lesson to me about the power of my thoughts.

How Mental Habits End as Diseases

Both meditation and actual experiences have convinced me that bad mental habits end as diseases. The *I Ching* pays particular attention to nourishment—both to what we feed ourselves in terms of ideas, and to how we nourish our bodies with food and drink. Many illnesses, both physical and mental, result from being careless about what we take in as nourishment. What we entertain in terms of ideas, how we amuse ourselves, and how we cater to our physical senses, has much to do with our health and well-being.

Conversing with a friend who had had a massive heart attack, I listened as he told me that prior to his attack he had been angry for quite a long time. Anger, with all its poisons coursing through the blood stream, could certainly affect the tissues of the heart.

As I related earlier, a great many of my early meditations were about healing my heart. Desire had been one of my worst problems. To cure it, I had had to cease desiring, then deal with the sores the desires had created on and inside my heart.

Vindictiveness and failure to forgive no doubt constrict the arteries and valves. Other organs must similarly suffer from other bad habits of mind.

Bad attitudes, repressed guilt, incorrect perceptions, faulty habits of mind all cause inner conflict, diminish our self worth, and create feelings of inner emptiness. Self-conflict and feelings of inner emptiness are not sustainable.

The following are two meditations of friends which give an interesting perspective on smoking marijuana.

Our Symbiotic Relationship with Plants   about 1980

A friend, a young man, had recently taken up the *I Ching* and had begun to meditate. That summer he stayed with people who were smoking marijuana. In a meditation he saw a field of marijuana. The marijuana plants were talking among themselves about how they had managed to assure their survival by getting human beings, who otherwise were generally destructive to nature, to become addicted to them. This meditation caused the young man to give up smoking both marijuana and tobacco.

On a Man Under the Influence of Marijuana (From a Friend's Meditation)   about 1974

I once asked a meditating friend of mine what she thought about a young man who attended our *I Ching* group. It was obvious he was always under the influence of marijuana. I wondered whether she thought he got anything out of our group, because he seemed always to be "somewhere else."

Some weeks later my friend told me that in meditation she had seen him as a burn victim, bandaged all over, but there was a small hole where his mouth was, and in it was a straw from which he was able to sip tiny amounts of nourishment.

The meditation verified to her that although he was able to take in only a little nourishment at a time, he was getting some nourishment. About ten years later this man visited me. In the intervening years he had put his life together, and was living very creatively. He had long since quit smoking marijuana. There was almost no resemblance between this new man and the one who used to sit there in our group.

Each Person Must Discover the Cause of His Illness 1989

In regard to illnesses, life-threatening or otherwise, I believe that in a great many cases their causes and cures lie in discovering images and attitudes stored in our subconscious.

Recently, an old friend told me she had a kidney problem. I asked her how she generally felt about her body. She replied that she felt it was never up to all she wanted it to do, that she was generally impatient with it. I thought that perhaps there was a connection between her illness and her feelings of impatience and dissatisfaction with her body.

A week later another friend had a violent allergic reaction to something she ate. Never before had she had any allergies. I asked her the same question—how do you regard your body? She replied that she had been rushing around with the thought that once she got to her vacation spot she "would collapse." Again, it seemed there was a connection between her attitude and the allergy. The allergy may have surfaced only because she allowed herself to become overstressed.

I recall two other people who told me they welcomed getting sick, because it was the only way they would really take the time to rest properly. One of these people became quite ill and suffered extensive paralysis on one side of his face. I related this story to the second person so that he could see we sometimes get more than we bargain for.

Since to a certain extent we create our own reality through the attitudes and ideas we permit within ourselves, we would do well to reflect on how we feel about our bodies and ourselves in general. My experiences make me think that good health may be related to a caring and conscientious attitude towards our bodies, and that sickness comes because we are careless and luxurious in attitude.

Even though we may not be able to cure birth defects, injuries caused in accidents, or hereditary ailments, who can say correctly that these problems cannot be helped through meditation and attitude corrections?

On Trying to Heal Others Through Meditation

During my first year of meditating I became enthusiastic that I might be able to treat others by meditating about them. Then I had the following meditation.

The Giant Ear   November 30, 1972

I saw myself looking into a giant ear, as if I were a Lilliputian. It was difficult to see whose ear it was, but as I returned to normal size I perceived it belonged to someone close to me, about whom I had been concerned. I looked at his eyes and realized he could only see in the inner world if his memory grid was cleaned out, which I then tried to do. Then I tried to repair his hearing, which was also out of order. After attempting this, I saw that there still seemed to be something else wrong. Apparently his heart was connected in some way to his hearing. It had to be healed and opened up before he could hear.

Then I saw his heart. Although it was in the process of healing, it still had a lot of sores and scars. I tried pouring healing liquid on it, with no effect. Then I asked the Sage if he would do something to repair the situation. He touched his heart and instantly it was made whole and healthy. Then the Sage said, "If you will only leave things to me they will go so much more easily."

Three other meditations of this period (late 1972) concerned this principle. The first was a meditative effort in which my friend had focused on another's problem, in hopes of helping him. She did a number of the things one does in meditation, such as pouring healing oil on his heart.

About a week later she had a meditation in which she saw herself pushing him up a ramp in a wheelchair, only to lose control and have him go careening off it. The ramp represented her efforts to lift him to a higher plane of consciousness, but instead of helping him by attempting to rush his development, she had harmed him.

The third meditation was mine. It followed similar efforts on my part to help others by meditating on their behalf. I had also received *I Ching* lines which warned me not to skip steps in development, nor to try forging ahead to achieve things by force. In the meditation I saw that my attempts to make things happen in meditation were what the *I Ching* calls "forced meditation." We must be guided in our work in the inner world as well as in the outer world. If in meditation we see someone with swollen eyes or a diseased heart, it is correct for us to respond as it comes to us to do. If it does not come to us in meditation to do something, we must ask the Sage's help and detach from trying to do anything. We must also detach from watching for any improvements.

On Retiring, and the Principle of Carrying On
September 2, 1979

The idea of retiring, so popular in our culture, could very possibly be a morbid trap. Flattering to our vanity (especially the idea of being able, financially, to retire), retiring is presented as a national goal. Consequently, nearly everyone has some pet idea of being released from the cares of work and responsibility, and from the risks of being in exposed positions. We envision, as our aches and pains increase with age, and our limitations begin to set in, being saved by someone taking over for us, or by something happening which will release us from our duties.

In all this fantasizing we seek to let down our will to go on, to collapse into indifference, to pursue our whims and "do what we want for a change."

It is not that retiring itself is bad or harmful to our health. The idea of indulgence, of letting down our will, is against our fundamental nature, and causes harmful self-conflict. I have found that if we are willing to accept what comes, we are gradually "let off the hook," protected from undue stress, and given a measure of freedom from galling responsibilities and risks, but only if we are willing to accept what life brings. When we seek to protect ourselves from all risks and to shut life out, life breaks through all our barricades.

The person who looks at his inevitable decline as a challenge to keep his will and inner light shining brightly, is the person who keeps the meaning of his life. He does not allow himself the fantasy of indulging in complete comfort. He values his inner light more than all else. This carries him through all adversity and he has no regrets. His life is a success.

Mental Illness (Bats in the Belfry)
about 1973

Because of a situation my daughter once described, I had a meditation on the cause of at least one case of mental illness.

My daughter attended a school which was like Summerhill. She told me of a student there who bordered on being psychotic. The girl never spoke, and she stayed by herself. My daughter spent some of her time at school sewing, and little by little this girl became interested in what she was doing. For a while the girl only watched from a distance but gradually she began to feel at ease and allowed my daughter to help her. After a while she also sought help from the sewing teacher, and soon her problems with the other students and adults began to disappear. By the end of the school year she seemed nearly normal.

I had been thinking about this girl prior to meditating. In meditation I saw the belfry tower of an enormous Gothic cathedral. The entire ceiling of the belfry was covered with bats hanging upside down; as soon as I noticed them, they all flew down toward and past me in a disconcerting manner. A voice told me to hold my ground as they swarmed around. On my standing firm, they gradually began to fly back to their roosts.

I was then made aware that the belfry tower is like the head; fearful thoughts are like bats that roost and swarm about in it. If we fail to stand our ground they will stupefy us with terror, even though in and of themselves they are harmless. It is our perception and fear of them, rather than their actuality, that creates the harm. Then I realized that some insanity is exactly described by that ridiculous saying, "He has bats in his belfry." The terrible mass of fears stupefy a person's mind with terror and force him to escape to a place of safety which he creates by drawing a curtain between his consciousness and the threat. This "place" resembles a state of shock from which the victim is unwilling to return, for fear of another encounter with the masses of fears.

It occurred to me that the school's lack of pressure on the girl to achieve, combined with my daughter's friendly and kind attitude, allowed the threats to subside, and helped the girl regain her natural strength to deal with her feelings of weakness.

Looking to the Sage about 1985

The following thoughts came during meditation, in response to my looking to sources other than the Sage to resolve my problems.

If you look to the doctors (solely) for your health, the doctors may, or may not, be able to make you well.

If you look to others for money, you may endure hardship, because sometimes they will help, and sometimes they won't.

If you look to the law, or to the police, for retribution and security, you may or may not win protection.

If you look to the Sage (Higher Power) for your needs, you will be given all you need.

This is called leaving it up to the Playwright to write the script.

Natural Abortion   about 1973

While most of this chapter has been devoted to healing ourselves, one other health-related issue—abortion—was the subject of a meditation which I include here. It occurred in answer to a dilemma that arose when I got pregnant in my early forties. At the time the youngest of my four children was fifteen, and all the circumstances of my life made the prospect of having a baby a very difficult one to face.

I had been consulting the *I Ching* for two years, and had learned to trust it. My first question was, "Is a woman obligated to have a baby once she gets pregnant?" My second question was, "If not, is there something I can do that is correct to prevent myself from having one?" Abortion was something I had ruled out as an option.

The *I Ching* counselled me to withdraw from the question entirely, to compose myself, and to allow myself to be guided, which I did.

In my next meditation these questions of pregnancy arose again. The answer came that while *I* may not want to have a baby, my body, by instinct, does. If I am not to have a baby, I must become free, not only of my desire to have one, but of all my body's desires to have one. I must be completely free, even of the slightest longing to have a baby. This would not be wrong.

I had always loved having babies and children, but I realized now that I must say no to all parts of myself. In seeking through my feelings I discovered an image of myself cuddling a baby, and felt the warm pleasantness that accompanied this image. I realized that this was my baby self wanting to cuddle a baby, the way a child wants to cuddle a doll. I was lured by this feeling only for an instant, then firmly said "No" to that part of myself. Once I did so, all feelings of longing departed.

Within five days, I miscarried.

This experience made me realize that I was in no way obligated to give birth simply because I had become pregnant. There was a natural and correct way to end the

114

pregnancy. This, of course, happened within a month of being pregnant. It has since occurred to me that if during pregnancy we have mixed or negative feelings about having a baby, we fail to provide a proper inner setting for the emerging child, and we may even harm that child. We need to be decisive in such matters.

My experiences in meditation lead me to conclude that many of our physical problems are the consequence of incorrect ideas we have absorbed from our culture, the product of thinking only in this world's terms. We fail to take into account the other world and the possibilities which come when we engage the Creative Power. Certainly, if we think it is up to us to do everything, everything is left to us to do. When we learn to engage the Higher Power, we receive the help we need to deal with whatever problem or challenge is put before us.

Every thought has some inner effect. We need to be circumspect about what thoughts we lightly accept as true. Many thoughts are based on half-truths, and therefore "slander the truth," as the *I Ching* puts it. The *I Ching* regards the ideas we take in, as nourishment. This nourishment affects our bodies as well as our spiritual nature, for our physical well-being is very much dependent on our self-esteem and inner balance. We need to ask ourselves, "How does this idea nourish me?" Any idea which causes conflict, anger, frustration, or despair, if allowed to continue for a period of time, will damage our health.

I also have found that the imaging techniques I learned in meditation are helpful to others. We may try them, but if they are not effective, we must be open to others that may help. If one set of mental images is not effective in dealing with a physical problem, another comes to mind.

We also need to be aware that the cure for one problem is not always the cure for another. For example, once when a sickness hung on tenaciously, it came to me to give in completely to the sickness, and to relinquish all efforts at trying to cure myself through the imaging techniques I had learned. I turned the matter over to the Sage and let go of it. This worked and I improved almost immediately.

In all my efforts to heal myself I did not rule out taking aspirin, keeping wounds sterile, following hygienic practices, or using normal first-aid remedies. I have not made pacts to forego medical help, nor do I rule out seeing the doctor, or going to the dentist. I try to be open-minded and responsive to my inner voice. I find that it generally leads me along the route of common sense. It is important to recognize when we are dominated by fear, and to learn to disperse distrust. We should beware of rigidly following pacts never to do something, or to always do things in a prescribed way. If we can remain open to our inner voice, we will know when it is appropriate to visit the hospital, and when we are merely being barraged by fear and doubt.

Finally, it is my conclusion that each person must follow his own path. Ups and downs, good times and adversity are characteristic of the life process. If we persevere in greeting difficulties as opportunities to grow and learn, the chances of finding our way past them will be very good.

10.

Problems in Close Personal Relationships and Marriage

As the reader will have realized by now, many of my meditations concerned my relationship with those around me: the Sage, my husband, children, friends, business associates, and clients. Personal relationships were probably the most frequent subjects of my *I Ching* consultations and meditations.

The *I Ching* counselled withdrawal from many old attitudes and opinions which created problems in these relationships. These were attitudes and opinions carried over from what the *I Ching* calls the time of standstill—the time before acquiring it as a teacher of inner world affairs. Chief among my problem habits of mind was giving up on people, and intervening powerfully to effect changes.

Instead of dealing with problems in the old way, I was to withdraw from all perceptions and attitudes which fueled the inner lawsuits and wars that had developed in my relationships. Eventually I recognized that this guidance aimed at de-energizing my ego, to allow all the accumulated hostile energies to dissipate. Then, by allowing higher truths to penetrate through to me, I, unconsciously, would transmit these higher truths to others. Gradually, my developing inner sense of truth would create a new basis for relating.

Years passed before I understood how and where the *I Ching* was guiding me. I only knew it felt right. For the most part I had to progress blindly while it revealed its way to me in tiny, nearly imperceptible steps.

I was also to learn that time was to be the vehicle of progress. Having started from a behind position—behind because of the need to unlearn so many things—I had no idea how long the road would be. Nor did I understand that the real purpose of my trials and tribulations was to make

117

me develop myself. Certainly, I would never have bothered to make changes had there been no pressing need to do so. However, once I began to see the good sense of this path there was no turning back, regardless of the periodic outbursts of my inferiors who clamored to know "how much longer" it would take before there would be some measurable progress.

At first I did not realize to what extent my attitudes had been a factor in my personal relationships. I did not understand that our inner thoughts are so potently dynamic. I had no understanding of my own inner workings, or of those of others.

I was to learn that people's actions, especially when inner lawsuits and wars exist, often are misleading. When our egos are strong, others carefully hide behind masks to protect themselves from us. It is difficult, therefore, for us to perceive their real feelings, and the fears, doubts, and wounds that cause them to act the way they do. Sometimes their actions are the result of an inner conflict going on within themselves, therefore we mistakenly judge their actions to be against us personally. During such times we need to try to be objective, patient, and tolerant. Making an effort to remain open-minded and unstructured gives us the strength needed to hold to our path.

The *I Ching* had put it to me that having attained help for myself, I must not then look down on and dismiss those around me as hopeless. They, like myself, were capable of starting from the barest nub to develop themselves. Through remembering their potential for greatness, I would help rescue them.

Curiously, the business of rescuing others involved persevering through many difficult situations without doing anything at all. It involved developing the inner independence to follow my own path without watching them. It meant that I had to stop lifeguarding them, and intervening in their lives. I was to detach and focus only on keeping my inner thoughts correct. I was to relate to them when they were receptive and withdraw when they were not. I was to let them go entirely, without giving up on them. I was not to forget or abandon my perception of their true selves, but to hold true and steady to them inwardly. I was to learn to wait in the correct waiting attitude, which meant to trust them to find the way for themselves.

Seen purely externally and logically, I had done nothing to create any of my problems; it was the others who had acted selfishly and arbitrarily. Gradually, however, I began to see that all my adult life I had followed a path of comfort and desire which had led to compromising my principles. Through what I regarded as love, but which was really weakness, due to my fear of alienating those I loved, I failed to hold to the standards of equality and fairness that would have maintained their loyalty and respect.

I had not yet understood that it is an individual's responsibility both to be just and correct in his own way of life, and to settle for nothing less than what is just and correct in others. If we take the trouble to see that there is nothing arbitrary and selfish in our principles, and that they are so correct and just that anyone could agree with them, then we make them the basis of our relationships with our mate, children, parents, friends, and all those with whom we associate.

In love, when the two become intimate before these fundamentals are clearly established, each holds unresolved doubts about the other. These doubts become a source of continuing problems. An individual must care enough for himself that he is willing to wait however long it takes to win the loyalty and respect of the person he loves. He can achieve this degree of perseverance only if he has first "married" his principles.

By this I mean we withdraw when others around us depart from correct conduct. We do not try to convince them of our point of view, or tell them what to do; we only say what we are willing to do, or not do. We leave it up to others to perceive our inner standards. If for the moment they do not, we leave it to them to see things as they will, and let them go their way. We do not give up on them or on the situation simply because it has a negative appearance. Instead, we hold that the truth of the matter is momentarily eclipsed. We hold that like the sun, the power of truth will emerge from the clouds to correct the situation. If a time of misunderstanding or separation develops, we accept the misunderstanding, and the time of separation as essential to correcting the situation. If we are led towards agreement or unity, we accept that, too. We trust the power of truth, and our firm resolve to follow it, to resolve the problem. Meanwhile, we may need to recognize that the more important the relationship, the more time and perseverance may be required to correct it.

Often, during the first meeting, a person seeking a relationship with us will tell us his main fault, as if to warn us that he expects to have his way in certain matters, or that it is his custom to get away with something. This telling may occur in a somewhat offhand way, in the middle of a charming or entertaining circumstance, so that we tend to overlook it, or regard it as an insignificant comment. Wrong situations invariably begin in charming circumstances which seduce us into temporarily forgetting our responsibility to ourselves, and the seriousness and importance of our decisions; but, this happens only because we have failed to pay attention to insuring that things are correct at the very beginning. Afterwards, the person who has made such offhand remarks is sure to respond to our disappointment with the comment, "I warned you, back at the beginning."

Whenever we ignore the small warnings that invariably present themselves, we lose the power of our position because we agree to something incorrect. By involving ourselves before the basis for a true commitment is established, we set the stage for continuous frustration and conflict. As the *I Ching* puts it in *Holding Together*, Hexagram 8, Line 6, "If the beginning is not right, there is no hope of a right ending." This statement is not meant to imply there is no hope of correcting things. Correction is possible, but only if we work on all the attitudes that have spoiled the relationship. Even though a couple may divorce and remarry, if they have not corrected their faults, the same problems are likely to surface again.

Giving up on those closest to us is endemic in our society. The problem put before me by the *I Ching* was to rescue all my troubled relationships. What did it mean? That by holding to the slightest glimmer of others' essential selves, we help them to throw off the domination of their egos. I once saw the completion of this process symbolized in meditation as a man who held in his hand an enormous pearl. The pearl symbolized his collected creative energies crystallized around a moral nucleus.

We do not work to rescue others to achieve a benefit for ourselves. We do it because it is our higher nature to do so.

Everyone who rescues himself acts automatically to rescue those with whom he has inner ties. The rescue happens on the subconscious level. The person rescued is not aware of who is nourishing and strengthening him. Gradually, we extend the principle of rescuing those to whom we have inner ties, to those further away in a general and nonspecific sense. This is the message of the *I Ching* —that by rescuing ourself and correcting our life, we act to rescue the world.

If our children are to grow up whole, they need the example of at least one parent who is committed to solving his problems with those around him. Then our children will not flinch from the difficult job of solving the problems of their families and of their time. If, however, they see that we give up on our most important relationships, and if they see that self-gratification is our main concern, how will they have the courage to see their lives through, and to fulfill their true natures?

On Coming to Meet Halfway, the I Ching Principle of Unity

The way we are meant to relate to others is defined in the *I Ching*, particularly in the hexagrams *Fellowship With Men*, Hexagram 13, and *Coming to Meet*, Hexagram 44.

Fellowship with Men focuses mainly on the principle that we can enter relationships with others if and when, and only so long as both parties are open, honest, and just with each other. The warnings in this hexagram have to do with "secret reservations of attitude." A secret reservation of attitude occurs when one of the parties secretly hedges on committing himself to fair and correct conditions, or when he holds some reservation by which he seeks to ambush the other to gain an unfair advantage.

True fellowship can exist only so long as both parties adhere to what is universally just and correct. Everyone, in his heart of hearts, can agree that the conditions are fair. The hexagram also states that we must reserve our commitment until these fundamentals are firmly established.

Coming to Meet puts forth the principle that we can safely come to meet others only when and if they are willing to meet us halfway. That is to say, if they, as well as we, are just and fair. Sensitivity and mutual respect must exist. The moment sensitivity and respect are inadequate, we should withdraw and wait to be guided further. Our firmness in this conduct will create the sensitivity and respect that establishes trust, but we must be prepared to wait until it has done so.

Consistent with the *I Ching* point of view is the fact that we cannot know someone overnight. As it is put in *The Marrying Maiden*, Hexagram 54, Line 4, a relationship based solely on desire is fraught with difficulties. If we are willing to wait until the relationship has become established on correct terms, happiness will be achieved, "though belatedly." We must be willing to allow the relationship to grow to the point where mutual trust and respect are securely established.

The hexagram also discusses ways of relating to an unjust situation in which we are already involved, or have become involved through circumstances beyond our control. This requires "working on what has been spoiled." Sometimes it is necessary to stay in the relationship until we have become emotionally detached enough to leave it without giving up on those involved.

The meditations that follow were in response to difficulties I experienced in my close relationships.

Cannot Rescue Him Whom He Follows   about 1972
(*Keeping Still*, Hexagram 52, Line 2)

I saw myself and my husband walking in opposite directions. I was surprised since I expected that my having followed the *I Ching* path would cause him to move towards rather than away from me. Then I saw that he seemed to be aware that I was following my path for this purpose, so he walked away from me with even greater determination.

Then I saw that I must disengage from any thought of whether he would follow in my direction. Doing this required putting blinders on my eyes (so that I no longer watched for his reaction), and proceeding without regard to what he was doing. I was to follow my path for no reason other than that it was the correct path.

As soon as I corrected my attitude in this way, I was permitted to see the effect this change had on him. When he saw that I was proceeding on my way with inner independence, and that I no longer looked in his direction, he halted in going away from me, and began to consider the value of what I was doing.

Why We Settle for Less, or, The Clean White Bridge and the Cheap Shoes   November 17, 1972

In this meditation I saw a newly-built bridge of clean white lumber. It was strongly-made and bridged a deep ravine.

The bridge was strong enough to hold up a tractor. I danced over it lightly, back and forth a few times. Then I saw my husband standing on the opposite side of the ravine looking as if he would like to cross over to my side, however he seemed unable to do so. Thinking he was afraid the bridge might not be strong enough, I did some work on it to make it even stronger so that he would feel reassured that it was safe enough to come across. Then I noticed his feet were stuck in mud. My side of the ravine was sunny and light; his was dark, rainy, and muddy, and he was unable to move his feet. I told him to step out of his shoes, but he only stood there complaining.

Another scene appeared in which he had gone into a discount store and come back with a pair of shoes like those on display in the store's window. I noticed they were marked $12.95. Looking closely, I saw they were cheaply made. I recognized these as the same shoes he had had on when he was stuck in the mud.

It came to me that the ravine symbolized the depth of the misunderstanding that had developed between us, and that the shoes symbolized bargain relationships he now preferred, which required no investment on his part. I realized that he was presently afraid, or unable, to invest himself in a high quality relationship.

One reason for his inability to invest himself was revealed in a meditation which occurred several years later.

Pact Made on an Old Grave   about 1976

I saw my husband at a much earlier time in his life, before he met me. He was placing flowers on the grave of the woman he had planned to marry, but who had been killed in an accident. I heard him make a pact to be faithful to her for the rest of his life. I then saw that not long after we were married, he remembered this pact and began to take back his feelings of commitment to our relationship.

I now saw that the pact provided justification for his withdrawal.

Although this meditation helped me understand inner conditions in his mind at the time, I did not realize for a long time that he remembered the pact only because I had failed to hold to my standards. This failure disappointed him, and remembering the pact made him feel less guilty for withdrawing his commitment to me.

The following meditations had to do with resisting fear and intimidation.

The Gaudy Dragon; the Cat and the Mouse; the Snake and the Birds   about 1973

In this meditation I saw a dragon, gaudy and flood-lit. It stared at me with fierce eyes, and I noticed that fire and smoke were coming from its nostrils. My impulse was to flee, but a voice said, "Stay, look at it," giving me the courage to do so.

Seeing that I had not been frightened, the dragon snorted and roared again, and again looked to see if I was frightened. When it saw that I was not, it lost all its power. Once I realized that its bravado was only a charade, it withered away to nothing. I then became aware that everyone's ego is a paper dragon. If we can resist giving way to fear, the ego's power is defeated.

Then I saw a cat hitting a mouse until it became unconscious. When the mouse regained consciousness, the cat hit it again until it ceased to move. I noted that the cat was interested in the mouse only when the mouse was active.

Next I saw a snake coiled around a nest in a tree which had two birds in it. One of the two birds was terrorized by the snake while the other was indifferent to it. The snake was interested only in the terrorized bird and ignored the disinterested one.

All the above images—dragon, cat, and snake—symbolized aspects of the ego which are predatory and bullying, and which are dependent on the reactions it can create in others. The snake, for example, represented the aspect of the ego which feeds on the fear it creates in others. When, through all its threats and tests, we are able to maintain our inner independence, the ego's power is defeated.

The Bullfight Meditation—Dealing with Unreasoning Anger   about 1973

Prior to this meditation I had been harassed for an entire week by someone's anger. Moreover, his anger seemed unrelated to me and without reason, as if I just happened to be present at the wrong time. I was being goaded to defend myself and fight back. After reacting badly at first and making the situation worse, I became determined to find out how to handle the situation the *I Ching* way.

All my *I Ching* lines called for disengaging. I thought this meant to withdraw and say nothing. Saying nothing, however, only made the other person angrier.

In meditation I found myself facing a bull, which was racing straight for me. Feeling panic I realized that there

was a red cape in my hands, which I held out, the way a bullfighter would do. To my relief the bull's horns touched the
cape and passed by. The bull charged two or three more
times, and I diverted it successfully with the cape. Finally
it became fatigued, gave up, and walked away.

Contemplating this scene I realized the bull symbolized
unreasoning anger, and that doing the bullfighter routine
was the way I was supposed to relate to anyone who was
"charging" me angrily. I did not know how I was to carry
this out, but I did understand that I was to keep disengaged, and to relate to the person in such a way that he
would only think he was engaging me.

Later that day I was again verbally attacked by the same
person. Having nothing but the memory of the meditation
in mind, and being disengaged, I found myself replying
nonsensically with any verbiage that came to mind. The
effect was astonishing. The other person suddenly stopped
haranguing and said, "You never did make any sense!" and
stormed out.

This experience made me realize that when a person is
filled with unreasoning anger, a reasonable response
makes no more sense to him than a nonsensical one. The
nonsensical reply satisfied his need for a response and at
the same time defused the energy of his anger.

Restoring the Ruined Garden   February 17, 1973

This meditation included a number of images. The first
was of a garden I ruined through putting wrong materials
on it in the hope of making it grow things better. The next
was of an island that had been devastated by a volcano
some years before, but which was beginning to show signs
of life. I next saw cities bombed-out in World War II, and
how people had labored to restore them. I also saw land
eroded through careless methods of cultivation so that the
growing capacity of the soil was diminished. In all these
things I saw that it takes hard work, carried out over a
period of time, to recover the use of something that has been
ruined.

Then I saw that each of us is born with an adequate

quantity of good soil within us upon which our spirits may be nourished, but our parents and society are careless with this soil. They are too severe in some cases, putting wrong materials on the soil; in other cases they are too lax and do not conserve the soil.

Then I saw that even when the soil is right and the seed grows, we sometimes damage the plant; we crop it too much, crowd it, or allow weeds to grow up and choke it.

Then I realized that nurturing others in the right way is the role of the developing person. By this nurturing we rescue their potential, thus restore the ruined garden. Too often we do not recognize the importance of our task, or we feel hopeless about it. We content ourselves in idle and useless diversions, thereby miss our opportunity to do something worthwhile.

By nurturing the essential self in others, we are able to help them realize that self. In doing this we take part in the reconstruction of society, and so fulfill a higher purpose.

Big Dumb Carol   April 29, 1973

This meditation illuminated a longstanding problem in my relationship with my husband.

I saw a stage with actors on it, but the stage and actors were so small I had to bend over to see them. Then I saw a big actor who had to cock her head to one side to keep from hitting the top of the stage. Nothing happened, so I waited, realizing how that large player would be handicapped in playing any role on that small stage.

Then the scene shifted. I now saw a farmhouse in a pleasant setting, and a large, peasant girl going towards the house. She was big-boned and plain, wearing a simple dress and apron. Then I realized I was watching a distinct part of myself. The name came to me, "big, dumb Carol." As she went into the house I realized the house was much too small for her. She was so cramped she could not accomplish anything without tremendous effort.

It came to me that big Carol was all that part of myself that was devotion and the urge to be kind and friendly with people and animals. It was also my wish to be pleasing, and my natural affection and trust in people. There was no question, though, that she was too simple—dumb, in fact. She was also easily wounded.

Memories began to enter of big Carol's dumbly inviting indifference and mistreatment from others. I saw how my big dumb Carol had given herself so totally to my husband that he had to see it as dumb. I saw times when she had trusted people blindly and got into difficult situations. No wonder he had allocated to her only a tiny space (house) in his heart, a space in which she was cramped and ineffective.

Now big dumb Carol had mentally outgrown the cramped specifications designated by her old attitudes. She must no longer live in a space that was too small.

I also realized that I could no longer allow big dumb Carol to lead my personality. I had to take back all of myself that big dumb Carol had given away. What right did I have to give myself away, anyway? I saw that we are given to ourselves by the Creator, and we do not have the right to transfer our sovereignty to anyone else. All unity, I realized, is tripartite—ourselves, the other person, and the Higher Power. All unity, therefore, requires we do nothing in our relationship that would exclude the Higher Power, or what is good. If our mate requires more of us than what is correct, we cannot correctly follow.

Taking Back Our Heart about 1981

In this meditation I saw that I had given my heart to my husband. I had held it out to him as if it were a crown on a velvet cushion. In giving it I relinquished sovereignty over myself. This was the way I thought it should be, having heard the words of the traditional marriage ceremony. It now became clear that I must take back my heart, that I had no right to give it to anyone.

Punishment by Withdrawing Eye-To-Eye Contact
November 28, 1973

This meditation concerned punishing subtle types of aggression by disengaging and withdrawing. Punishment, the *I Ching* notes, is not to be accomplished by overt means. Instead, we deprive the person's ego of the emotional response that gives it energy.

I saw the ego as a person who was trying to gain my attention by waving his arms, dancing, and making faces. When I looked at him, he reveled and said "Aha! She sees me, she believes in me!" as if he had achieved a great victory. Then I turned my eyes away, in embarrassment. Though I looked away, I was able to observe that in response to my disengaging, he suddenly turned ashen and evaporated! My looking at him had given him the energy to exist, and my decision not to look at him had made him disappear.

I realized that to exist, the ego must see its reflection in someone's eyes. Because it requires continual verification, it flatters; if it is unable to gain a favorable response by flattery, it resorts to pinching or hurting, if only to hear us say "ouch, you're hurting me."

When people behave aggressively we are meant to withdraw. This punishes the person's ego by denying its existence. I saw that this was to be accomplished by denying the person eye-to-eye contact until the ego has given up, and the person has returned to relating to us sincerely. In *Biting Through*, Hexagram 21, a line says that in punishing someone we are to be like "yellow gold"; though we "naturally incline towards leniency," we must do our duty and remain reserved.

In *The Wanderer*, Hexagram 56, we are warned against punishing another arbitrarily, just to punish. The purpose of punishment, it says, is to bring about a correction. Once this correction is achieved we must punish no more, otherwise we transgress.

Biting Through also warns that we must be sure our ego is not the punisher, for then, in addition to defeating our purpose, we bring Cosmic punishment on ourselves.

Duty requires that we punish those who arrogantly wrong us, but it is not the *I Ching* way to follow pat routines in handling situations. Instead, we are meant to grasp what is happening, to really understand its nature. Then we do what comes as appropriate and correct to do.

Lifeguarding People   about 1974

This meditation had to do with my concern about mistakes one of my teenage children was making.

I saw myself sitting on an embankment as lifeguard, but I noticed that the child I was lifeguarding was far out in the water, swimming with the sharks. For my part I was standing and shouting to him to swim back to shore. Even though he heard me, he went on as before, unconcerned and determined to do his own thing. Then I realized that he felt invincible because I was watching. My watching made him feel safe, as if no matter what he did someone would be there to save him. I realized that so long as I stayed there as lifeguard, watching him with my inner eye, he would feel protected and invincible.

On being told that the only remedy was to leave and turn the matter of his safety entirely over to him, I thought this very risky. How could I justify myself if something went wrong? As it was, however, I realized that I was giving the swimmer the message that no matter what he did, he was safe.

Then I realized that lifeguarding people means that I do not trust them to do the right things for themselves. By keeping them in my inner gaze I am doubting them. My doubt also disturbs their belief in themselves. Realizing this I got up and moved away. When the swimmer saw that I was gone, he quickly got out of the water.

Within about six months I began to see a big change in the behavior of that child.

Lawsuits   about 1985

Observing other couples and divorces, and reflecting on my own, I have come to feel that at the heart of the love relationship is the glimpse of the essential self that each person sees in the other. This glimpse, combined with a sudden awareness that each is linked to the other by some inner tie, releases the wellspring of love.

For reasons of their own, or because of prior conditions, one or both partners may revert to old masks and defenses. Covering up and hiding their real selves, they may cause the other to doubt what he originally saw. This doubt initiates the disintegration of their relationship.

At first, the one held in doubt may try to re-establish his credibility with the other. If he fails, he may suffer a loss of self-esteem and wounded pride. This may cause him to seek retribution, bringing about an inner lawsuit.

An inner lawsuit does not end simply because people divorce. It continues with every feeling of retribution, and every hostile and negative thought one has of the other.

The remedy is for at least one of the two to cease participating in the lawsuit. This one must cease thinking negatively about the other and remain disengaged through all the jibes and tests the other can devise. He will also need to remember and reconfirm to himself the original glimpse he had of the other's essential self. Gradually, if he remains constant in these things, the lawsuit will die down, the wounds will heal, distrust will give way, and confidence will be restored. Then growth will resume so that the problems which originally disrupted the relationship can be resolved.

In no way can the relationship be resumed until all the problems which have disrupted it have been worked through. Rushing back into a comfortable, careless, and self-indulgent relationship only revives the ego and creates setbacks. Any temptation to rush back together prematurely must be firmly resisted by the one trying to correct the relationship.

We can identify the presence of an inner lawsuit when a person's behavior becomes a problem to those surrounding him (i.e., the alcoholic, the drug addict, the philanderer, the spendthrift, etc.). His behavior is retribution for the others' having played God by condemning him as hopeless, or worthless, or by the others' thinking that they are better, smarter, or more important. We also play God when we write the script of a person's life by saying, "He will never change," "That will never happen."

The Atom Bomb   about 1983

In this meditation, which occurred some years after my divorce, I saw myself walking through a city which had been bombed years before. Although an atom bomb had been dropped there and the city was still uninhabitable, grass had begun to grow in crevices. As I reached the outskirts of the city I came to a one-room cottage which was intact and inhabited. Entering it I saw nobody, but I was impressed that it was in good condition and conscious of its being carefully tended by somebody. Standing in front of the opposite wall, a pedestal held a large book. This book, I realized, symbolized truth, and I was impressed that the book occupied such a central position in the room. I was reminded of a church setting, since candles were burning on either side of it. Obviously, someone here revered the truth.

Wondering what the scene represented, I heard it explained that the city represented my marriage. Although it had been destroyed, one place still survived in which the truth had a home.

Some days after this meditation I was enlightened about the meaning of the atom bomb when I exploded angrily at one of my children. My lack of discipline caused so much poisonous fallout that we could not relate to each other for months afterwards. I could only deal with the fallout.

King-of-the-Heap Game   about 1986

I once saw in meditation a king-of-the-heap game like that which boys played when I was a child. In this game one boy would stand on top of a small knoll and push the others off until someone managed to push him off. One boy was very good at this game. Hardly anyone could push him off.

This meditation occurred after I had been reminded that some people are good at projecting intimidating self-images. We are never quite certain what they will do or say, so we always feel a little anxious and out-of-balance around them. I now realized that people who project intimidating images are playing a version of the king-of-the-heap game. Every time they make someone feel out of balance, they win the game. But as in all games, someone can win only if another plays the game with him.

People who compete for salary advances and better positions often play some form of the king-of-the-heap game. We need only ask ourselves why a particular person makes us feel out of balance, to realize that we have been participating in this game. When we no longer participate, the game ends.

Another version of this game unfolded when an old friend, who I had not seen in years, visited and asked, "What do you think about such and such?" At first I did not realize the question was merely rhetorical, so I answered sincerely, only to hear in reply, "You couldn't possibly think that!" I recognized how I could be drawn into an exchange in which I would have to justify my views, so I simply said, "Well, I happen to think that, but it's not worth justifying." I saw how her statement was the first move in a polite form of the king-of-the-heap game. I saw how this game could take many subtle forms, and that its only object is to disturb the other's inner balance and independence.

On Sex, Desire, and True Love

From time to time I quite naturally had questions about "sex." I put quotes around this word simply because I found that when I put any issues labelled sex to the *I Ching*, it would not reply to me in those terms. Instead I would receive *Fellowship with Men*, Hexagram 13, or *Grace*, Hexagram 22, or *The Family*, Hexagram 37, and lines from other hexagrams which made me realize that it would not address my inquiry in those terms. Sex, as a thing in itself, it seemed to say, does not exist. There is only the issue of fellowship, how individuals relate to each other, and whether this relationship is just and correct.

Fellowship with Men stressed that an intimate relationship be free of secret reservations of attitude. I learned that this was a warning against being intimate purely to obtain something personal and selfish.

Paying attention to sex as a thing in itself was, as the hexagram *Grace* put it, paying attention to the beard as more important than the chin on which it grows, and to focussing on form as a thing in itself, instead of the content which provides the essential basis for form.

The Corners of The Mouth (Nourishment), Hexagram 27, reiterated the principle that we must not nourish the lower, body self at the expense of the higher self. Each of these references confirmed that sex is not a thing in itself, and that to discuss it without regard to the underlying relationship of which it is but a manifestation, is to deceive oneself about a number of important issues. Rather than speak of sex, we might speak of a situation in which a man and a woman come to meet each other. We are better served by viewing it as a "coming to meet" situation.

The way two people come to meet each other is the essence of the matter. When correct, their coming to meet fulfills the requirements of a true fellowship—a bonding that is the result of careful preparation, self-discipline, and selflessness. It is one which, when it occurs, is free of hesitation, doubt, selfish considerations, and harmful reservations of attitude. Then, true joy comes as a gift.

This gift cannot be produced or reproduced by effort or device, by flattery or by wooing. It comes on its own when its requirements have been fulfilled, as a blessing from the Higher Power. We may be momentarily deceived into thinking that through giving freedom to our desire we have produced joy. But, this is a self-deceit; the ego has overridden and temporarily suppressed the real self. The real self always re-emerges, sooner or later, giving messages of conflict and regret.

Finally, the *I Ching* makes it clear that this gift comes in its own time. As another line of the *I Ching* puts it, "The king gives his daughter when he sees fit." One party may be ready but the other may still hold secret reservations and distrust, or as the third line of *Fellowship with Men* puts it, may "hide weapons in the thicket." This means a person intends to use the other for selfish gratification, or to make a point, or to fulfill some secret lust or fantasy. In cosmic terms this is no different from stealing.

The gift of true joy is granted freely in the first innocence of love. Later, if we have spoilt our relationship it is necessary to achieve duration of character before this gift is given again. Both must be trustworthy in the cosmic sense. On his part he is mentally chaste; on her part she is loyal.

People first experiencing love are granted the gift of true and unabated joy because they see only what is good and great in each other. If or when they luxuriate selfishly in each other's love, joy evaporates and they lose this special feeling for each other. Efforts to reproduce the gift do not restore it. The gift of joy is similar to stumbling onto the inner place of meditation. One may stumble time and again onto this inner place within oneself without becoming aware of how and why it happens. It happens always when each sees in the other the manifestation of his higher self. This alone draws and holds them together in mutual happiness. Keeping themselves correct within is the only thing that makes their happiness endure.

I was made aware in the following dream and subsequent meditation that to indulge in sex as a thing in itself is a throwaway of self which harms the personality.

Dream of the Torso   August 6, 1974

I saw, lined up like a row of headless and footless ancient Greek statues, different nude, alive torsos which were sexually stimulating. I also noticed, however, that as I viewed them I had feelings of humiliation at feeling sexually stimulated. Once I awoke I meditated. In the meditation I saw the images again, only this time I remembered those aspects of the images which had stimulated me. Next I saw these contrasted with images that did not stimulate me, but which I was made aware might stimulate someone else. That is to say, some had hair on their chests and some did not; some were lean and trim, others were massive, others fat.

Then my attention was drawn to the fact that all the images were torsos. I was struck by the fact that torsos, which have no relationship to specific persons, are capable of arousing sexual feelings. I realized that when a person makes love on the basis of sex alone (note that here the language puts it correctly, he "makes" love), he is involved only with the torso image which stimulates him. In his mind he does not see their heads or feet. Any recognition of their personality is purposely suppressed. Thus, in sex strictly for sex's sake, words such as "I love you," mean only, "thanks for making your torso available."

To the extent that we use another, or allow ourselves to be used in this manner, our higher self is humiliated and diminished. We suffer an accompanying loss of self-esteem. Undoubtedly, for this reason, the *I Ching* asserts the principle that the pursuit of pleasure invariably leads to suffering.

Providing it is meant to be and sanctioned by the Higher Power, attainment of the unity and harmony of love is predicated on each person's cleansing himself of seductive images which intrude, humiliate, and denigrate the other person. Unity is something that occurs naturally, spontaneously, and beautifully when the obstructions created by vanity and selfishness have been swept away. Ironically, mutual attraction occurs when both have a chaste mind.

Who is the One Meant for Us

One of the *I Ching* lines says, "The King gives his daughter when he sees fit." (See *The Marrying Maiden*, Hexagram 54, Line 5.) We receive this line upon thinking, "When is my life going to work out?" It would appear from this that not only are our mates chosen for us by the Higher Power, but also the times when things are meant to work out.

We only complicate our lives when we become impatient, disregard Fate, and decide to do things our way. Then we enter what the *I Ching* calls "an embarrassing obligation," from which it takes time to extricate ourselves. Fate often requires that we work through these obligations. We are not let off the hook easily.

It is best to accept our situation patiently, disengage, and go on our way. Above all we need to cease looking with our inner eye for the thing we want, to happen. Fate, it might be said, always comes one day late—the day after we have decided to give up looking and go about our business.

It comes when our virtue has become reliable and is not just a thing adopted to get what we want. We must become trustworthy in our goodness. Fate comes when our ego is truly out of the way. If we can be patient, as indicated in the *Marrying Maiden*, Hexagram 54, Line 4, even though the time appears to have gone by for thing to work out, we will find the mate meant for us, and receive true happiness.

On the Correct Basis of Unity Between a Man and a Woman
August 6, 1974

During the past few days I have had several meditations about the correct basis for unity between husband and wife.

The first of these concerned the simple realization that the foundation of unity is the spiritual purification of both people: a return to an innocent, chaste, and pure state of mind.

The second concerned the same thing, except that it had to do with desire as an improper basis for relating (the torso image).

Now it came to me that before an enduring unity could be attained, each person must become free of the dominance of his ego.

I also realized that we cannot work for unity as a goal, any more than we can work for joy as a goal. Both unity and joy are products of something else, and are not attainable as things in themselves. Rain comes from a cloud only when other conditions make it possible. In the same way, unity results when two people profoundly respect and appreciate each other. This respect and appreciation can be generated only by qualities of character. When either of them seeks to selfishly luxuriate, seeds of disunity are sown. Unity can endure only so long as both of them seek to follow their higher natures.

11.

Meditations Which Foretell the Future, or Prepare Us for Changes

In a number of instances I had the good fortune to have meditations which foretold events, as if the Sage thought I ought to know what was going to happen.

In the following instance I was concerned about a friend's illness. She was about to have her second operation for the same serious type of cancer. I wondered whether she might die, however, my meditation reassured me that she would recover.

The Graveyard Meditation   about 1984

To my left I saw a golden wheat field, the heads of wheat fully ripe and hanging over. Then, to my surprise, I saw the rounded tops of old-fashioned New England gravestones sticking up above the wheat. My attention was drawn to two gravestones, upon which were written the names of two people, an older couple who were, at that time, alive. Then the words came to me, "But no new graves have been opened yet," meaning that their deaths were scheduled, but not immediately.

Then I noticed a wagon path that crossed the middle of the field and passed through an opening in the stone wall. To my right my friend with the cancer was standing before several piles of flat slate gravestones. A man stood behind the stones, offering her one. It was clear that she was considering whether or not to accept it. As I watched, she made up her mind not to take one and walked along the wagon path, up out of the graveyard.

I felt confident from seeing this scene that my friend was not going to die, and indeed she did not. In the following months she had the remarkable healing experience I have already related in Chapter 9, involving the Navajo Indian

Medicine Woman.

Two or three years later I asked my friend what her state of mind had been at the time of her illness. She told me she had felt purposeless, wondering what use her life had been. She mentioned that it was like being in a black pit.

The older couple? A party was given that summer honoring the wife's 90th birthday. The next spring she died, and in the late fall her husband died also.

Even though this meditation foretold my older friends' deaths and the outcome of my younger friend's cancer, I do not believe we can receive such answers in meditation if we are only idly curious. I believe the answer came because I was genuinely concerned.

In working with the *I Ching* I had had the goal of saving my marriage. In devoting myself to self-development, I thought that somehow divorce would be averted. I was therefore unprepared, at least on the conscious level, for my husband's leaving. Only in looking back on my meditations preceding his leaving at the end of August, 1974, did I become aware of how well I had been prepared for this event on the subconscious level. The following meditations were that essential preparation.

On Disengagement, Freedom, and Will   May 26, 1974

In this meditation I saw the replay of a tennis match I had watched on television between women's teams from Chicago and Boston. A member of the Chicago team, which had been losing, had become increasingly gloomy, while another had grimaced, and another had even kicked the floor. The women of the Boston team, by contrast, had been remarkably cool and disciplined. No setbacks had fazed them; neither had winning points. They had remained disengaged, from first to last.

Seeing this scene again made the point that to win it is necessary to keep disengaged, and to maintain a persevering attitude. When our will remains firm, no setback or defeat can have more than a momentary effect.

Then I remembered my husband's saying, in a disconcerting way, that he needed his freedom. I remembered how his saying this had wounded me.

Then the idea of freedom suddenly seemed illusory. I remembered reading of a Russian nobleman, imprisoned by the Czar, who sang every day in his cell. The prison inmates and guards had been amazed. "This is no place for singing," they had said. The prisoner, however, never allowed his will to be dominated by his circumstance, thus retained his inner freedom.

Then I recalled the first line in *Darkening of the Light*, Hexagram 36, which describes being wounded by the Prince of Darkness. I realized that what is wounded is our will to carry on. Our will can be wounded only if we see no prospect of success.

I saw that keeping our will going is like playing a tennis match. Every shot, every volley, every serve must be played and then disengaged from. If we fail to disengage, each bad shot damages our will. Losing our inner freedom in this way, everything we do is hampered.

Then I realized that we are only truly free when we are free of the dominance of hopelessness and despair, with its thousand tentacles of negation. This is the freedom for which people search outside themselves, but which can be found only within themselves. This freedom enables the imprisoned man to sing in his cell. It enables the strong person to lose the fight but not the battle.

The next meditation told of our breakup, but also of a good outcome in the end.

The Plane Crash, or Disaster Site   June 16, 1974

I saw flashing before me a plane crash. My next view was at the site where the plane had hit the ground and burned, leaving its imprint in ashes and ruin.

As I pondered what to make of the scene, an enormous jewel became visible in the center of the crash site, where the fuselage had been.

As I waited for the significance to be revealed, the words came, "Though the path lead through a thousand disasters,

the only important thing is that one remain true to oneself."
The jewel meant that in the final analysis, only good can
come of following the path of the true and the good.

I remembered a line I had recently got in the *I Ching*
from *The Abysmal, Danger*, Hexagram 29. "Water does not
hesitate from any plunge but flows on, remaining true to its
essential nature." We must not shrink from danger, but
follow our lodestar through all life's situations. "Above all
to thine own self be true," as Shakespeare said. We need
consult no other guide.

In all situations we find ourselves consulting tradition,
what others have told us in youth, what psychiatrists say,
and so on, but as Joan of Arc, or Shakespeare, or the *I Ching*
would say, "I must follow my inner voice. I must be true to
myself, and to the path I follow."

The following meditation reassured me that even
though I could not see where my path led, it did indeed lead
to the appropriate solutions to my problems. Meanwhile,
there was no way I could rush matters. I would simply have
to accept time as the vehicle of progress.

The Conveyor Belt   June 19, 1974

In meditation I found my mind occupied with wanting to
know what the lines meant in *Before Completion*, Hexagram 64, which said to "develop the strength to complete
the transition," and to find the correct "vehicle for the crossing."

Looking for problem elements in my attitude I recognized a certain impatience within myself, which I cleaned
out.

Then I saw myself on a conveyor belt at an airport. Although I could not see where it was taking me, I felt sure it
led to the appropriate destination. Noting its slow, steady
pace I wondered if walking might be faster, but I realized
that would just be energy wasted.

Then I saw that if I were to walk around those standing
on the conveyor, I could get to my destination twice as fast,
but then I had to acknowledge that carrying my baggage

would require too great an effort. I decided it was best to content myself with being carried forward.

Then I realized that the conveyor belt represented time, and that time has a direction and motion that takes us with certainty to the correct destination. We need only trust it to do so. If we can simply wait patiently, preparing ourself for the eventuality of getting there, we will have found the vehicle for crossing, and our strength will have been put to the proper use. The vehicle for crossing is acceptance and patience.

(Now, in 1989, I will add that when we allow impatience to take over, we skip steps, only to compromise ourselves. If we seek comprehensive answers, or solutions promising quick progress, we find ourselves entangled in new problems. Or, we abandon the struggle (get off the conveyor belt), thinking we will change our Fate, but we only arrive at the wrong place.)

The next meditation prepared me to keep my inner balance during the difficult time to come.

The Rain Falls, There Is Rest   July 8, 1974

The *I Ching* counsel of the night before concerned finding a safe place when surrounded by danger (*Development*, Hexagram 53, Line 4).

During the usual self-cleansing stage of meditation I found a "soft spot" within myself (soft in the sense of containing a wish or want). I did not define what the wish might be, but recognized that its presence had a potential for self-conflict and weakness. The soft spot had the appearance of being a cavity in the area of my heart. After filling the cavity with a gold filling I put my repaired heart onto my altar of sacrifice.

Immediately after placing my corrected "soft spot" on the altar, I saw rain falling. I understood and felt this to be a blessing, as if I had received nourishment from heaven. Then the message came that the gift of nourishment always comes from Heaven, metaphorically speaking, from the power of the Sage. Though we must wait for this nourishment, it *will* come. To cling to this knowledge is to find safety in the midst of danger. (This clinging is the principle of Hexagram 30.)

Then I saw that in a thousand small ways every day we can reinforce our awareness of Heaven's nourishment. This requires only that we cultivate within ourselves the humility to see the small things that nourish us—the beauty of the flowers, the warmth of the sunshine, the food we eat, the affection of our children. Even the short line at the bank, or the parking place that opportunely opens, is a hidden blessing. Shall we overlook such things by consuming ourselves in sadness over what is missing? Are we too self-important to notice the small things? A dog may be simple-minded, but its heart is big and devoted. Surely we may say it thinks only of its food and so dismiss the little it has to give, but why look at it that way? The gardener is grateful for his tomatoes, his potatoes, and corn. If we can look at the gift of sunshine, the bee busy at its work, or hear the bird sing, if we can find in the midst of squalor that free gift from heaven, in the midst of imprisonment, the sound of music, we can reinforce our awareness of Heaven's nourishment and build our understanding of the way Heaven works. If we can reduce our self-importance enough to experience the divine within, all misery, squalor, and imprisonment will become unimportant. This is what it is to be renewed, and to find a safe place in the midst of danger.

The next meditation prepared me to retain some sense of balance when the shock came.

Justice: Due Measure   August 20, 1974

I saw a man in a courtroom who had committed a crime. He appeared to be a normal person who may have suffered regret. Although I did not as yet know what the crime was, I felt a certain sympathy for him as he stood there facing the court of justice.

Then I saw an image of a generic man committing a generic crime. The aggression and the suffering of the innocent struck me with an awful sense of anger. Without regard for the person who committed it, the situation plainly called for retribution.

Then I saw myself looking at both situations. I realized that when I looked only at the man, my attitude was too lenient, and when I looked only at the crime, my attitude was too harsh. "Although one inclines towards leniency," as it is put in *Biting Through*, Hexagram 21, Line 4, we must be just and impartial in administering justice. The proper path is between these two extremes of attitude.

Then I saw that when the person who commits a crime has a hardened attitude, we must be even more firm, yet still not extreme. We must retain a just and moderate view of all mankind (see *Dispersion*, Hexagram 59, Line 1).

Although the subject of the following dream and meditation was my daughter, its message was about the dangerous consequences of giving up our path.

The Demonic Delusion   August 28, 1974

In the dream my daughter seemed ill, so we decided to visit a doctor. The doctor was very concerned and told us the situation was hopeless. With sympathy and hand-holding he sent us away to a place where she was to dress herself to die; then the people at that place would obligingly finish her off.

On our way there my daughter and I were despondent. Although accepting the situation, we wished there were a different solution. Arriving at the place where she was to be dispensed with, we just stood outside, sighing.

Then it came to me to resist the diagnosis. "Why should you lie down and die," I asked her, "unless you absolutely have to? You are walking. Nothing is *that* wrong." In fear and trepidation we decided to risk going against the doctor.

Once we made this decision we began talking about the doctor and his hand-holding sweetness and sympathy. I remembered seeing him before, some time ago, when something had impressed me that he was a charlatan. As my memory and focus sharpened, I realized he was not a doctor. Immediately we went back to his office and exposed him as a charlatan. What shocked us most was the fact that he had almost succeeded in talking us into giving up her life.

After waking I meditated. In the meditation it came to me that demonic voices "reason" with us to get us to give up on all sorts of things, and that these impostors very craftily disguise themselves as the Sage, appearing as doctors, judges, engineers, or other authorities. I also realized that my daughter was influenced by whether I believed in these "authorities." If because of them I gave up following my path, my example might damage her. I saw that many people are dependent on me in this way, and that to give up could demoralize and defeat all of them.

At the same sitting, I also had the following meditation. These meditations occurred only two or three days before coming home from visiting my parents, to find that my husband had moved out while I was gone.

Climbing Mt. Everest   August 30, 1974

A group of us were on our way up the last part of the ascent of Mt. Everest, with only 1000 yards to go along a narrow edge of ice. I saw that this last part of the climb, with the top in sight, was certainly the hardest, because our desire to get to the top might obstruct the sense of caution we needed. To rush now, when we were stressed the most in the high altitude, when blackouts could occur, where the ice was hardest and most slippery, where sudden gusts of wind could blow us off the mountain, could endanger the whole climb. Each step at this point had to be carefully secured. The strictest perseverance might not be enough. We needed the help of the Sage for every step.

I saw the support group that had made the climb possible, and how final success really depended on being exactly correct. I saw how high and far we had climbed—up to 31,000 feet. I saw how I must maintain my will to go on, for now the danger was greatest because of wanting to be home free.

On the conscious level this meditation seems almost cruelly ironic since I related being home free to saving our marriage. On the inner plane, however, the images indicated a type of preparation needed for getting past the most hazardous part of my journey. If I could remain persevering through his leaving and later through divorce, I would have made it past the worst of the difficulties I would have to face. This proved to be true in all respects.

Quite often meditations which foretell the future are confusing as to the time frame in which the situations happen. The following meditation confirmed an intuition I had that I would not always be engaged in my current business. I greeted this confirmation from the Cosmos eagerly.

Closing Down My Business 1981

I saw that my business had reached the end of a rainbow-shaped trajectory. This image made me realize that I would soon be freed of this difficult responsibility. Immediately I began making plans either to sell the business or close it down. But then my *I Ching* counsel told me it was not yet time to do this. I was not meant to rush its demise, but to allow things to happen organically. This prediction was not to be fulfilled for two more years. If I had not followed my *I Ching* counsel and had gone ahead to close down the business right then, I would have suffered considerable financial losses. Allowing it to wind down naturally permitted all loose ends to be dispensed with in an orderly way.

Through meditations and dreams, I have been blessed with foreknowledge of and preparation for events whenever I needed such foreknowledge and preparation. These meditations happened of their own accord, except in the case of my friend, when I meditated specifically with her problem in mind. Generally, I have not sought to know the future, nor have I been curious about it. These meditations were simply gifts from the Higher Power.

12.

Meditations on Spiritual Matters

A number of meditations centered on questions of a spiritual nature: the hereafter, reincarnation, the significance of the inner world, the Sage, the way we are meant to live our lives, and attitudes which block our inner growth and inhibit the development of inner power.

Some of these meditations were realizations that dawned on me. Some were involved and complicated. The meditation I next relate was a vision—an overall view of what my life would be, what I would be doing, in inner world terms, and where I would be going. This vision was distinguished both by the brilliance of everything I saw, and by the high sense of reality it conveyed, as if everything in it was much more real than life.

Vision   November 18, 1972

Meditation began abruptly as a clear vision, more lucid than reality. I was on the shore of a small, deep, clear, and utterly placid lake in the mountains. I had entered the lake in a life raft, and I had been traveling down a narrow, swift river which emptied into this lake. Still in the life raft, in a deep sleep, was my husband.

Although I did not look at Him, someone stood beside me. I knew that it the Sage, my teacher of the *I Ching*. I noticed how beautiful and calm the lake was, especially in comparison to the perilous and difficult river that had led here. I did not look backward at what we had traversed; I was simply filled with gratitude to be here, safe.

Then the Sage led me to the edge of the lake, from where I looked down upon a grand, encompassing scene. Below was an enormous and beautiful lake into which the river leading from this lake eventually emptied. My attention was drawn to the shores of that farther, beautiful lake.

There I saw the home that eventually would belong to my husband and me. It was explained that we would stay on the smaller lake for a while. We would not know when we would have to make the descent, but that we should be prepared for it at any time. Meanwhile, we should prepare ourselves and rest. Then the Sage warned me that we should not grow lax in our attitudes because of the pleasantness of life on the lake, for the journey down the river was exceedingly difficult. While my husband had come this far without his inner consent being necessary, his full cooperation would be essential to make it safely down the river.

The Sage directed my view to the river by which we were to descend. Because I could see for over a hundred miles the river looked like a small brook, but I realized it was a mighty white-water river. For the greater part of its length it was precipitous, but nearer the larger lake it meandered slowly.

Then I saw a tiny black figure beside a narrow part of the river just before it emptied into the large lake. Immediately, it became magnified, as if I were seeing it through a telescope. The figure was a black angel about fifty feet tall, armed with a bow and arrow. As it stood guarding the entrance to the lake, I realized its business was to shoot anyone it saw trying to pass by. The figure was dressed all in black except for his face, which was white. His eyes were extremely alert, unblinking, and watchful. I knew nothing could pass by him without being seen, and that his shot was unerring.

I then asked the Sage how it would be possible to pass by this figure. He replied that it would be similar to having come into the lake where we now were. Only by becoming completely free of selfishness could we become invisible to his eyes, for he was set there to guard the passage against all unworthiness.

I then wondered how we had made it into this lake. The Sage explained that because I had allowed myself to be led blindly and to trust him implicitly, he had led me here. Through not giving up on my husband I had brought him here, though unconscious.

Later on in the day an image of the Black Angel flashed once more before my eyes. This time I saw him from my position in the life raft, floating by in the channel. I was in awe and admiration of his stature, keen-eyed purity, and dedication. He did not look in our direction or seem to know we were there. I understood this to be a premonition of things to come, and confidence on the part of the Sage that eventually we would attain freedom from selfishness.

My Husband in the Bottom of the Lifeboat
November 23, 1972

I noted that the business at hand was my husband, still lying asleep in the bottom of the boat where he was the other day. The Sage said the problem was that of awakening his spiritual nature. The first sign of this awakening would be the opening of his eyes (here in the invisible world). At that point the Sage went over and touched his eyes and they opened. My husband appeared as one awakening from sleep—looking around but not really focussing on what he saw.

Little by little, in his isolation, the Sage said, he will see things as they really are, and focus his views. The Sage then said, "Now that his eyes have been opened it is only a matter of time to make actual what is potential. It may be soon or late, it all depends." (Here He made no further explanation).

I consider the next meditation to have been a great gift. It told me why our spiritual development is so important, and showed me how the Creative is at work in the world in a dynamic way to solve the difficult problems of our times.

Change Equals Time Squared / The Tent Pole Meditation
May 22, 1973

I saw a lump of fissionable material and I realized that it had radioactive energies which would take millions of years to decay if left to do so naturally.

I next saw the lump placed in a special circumstance in

149

which the radioactive energies were discharged all at once, creating an Atom Bomb.

Then I understood that for anything to develop great power, a special circumstance has to be brought about.

Next I saw just such a special circumstance as thousands of people scattered around the world. Though separate and alone, each was centrally balanced and correct within himself. From a height they looked like tent poles in a tobacco field, spaced apart to hold up the tobacco cloth.

These people were all linked together by a giant net which covered the field, and in this linkage they created a great energy field. Being centrally balanced and pure within, they had the ability, in their totality, to accelerate time so that changes which otherwise would take generations to accomplish could be accomplished quickly. Creating a supercharged atmosphere, they were able to intercept ideas from the Cosmos and serve as conductors of those ideas. The ideas, in turn, were transferred to those around them as if by osmosis. By their self-discipline and selflessness they achieved what could not be achieved by the most contrived or organized efforts.

I also saw that the outflow of such energy could not be stopped by anyone, or contorted to wrong means by any faction, or put to any private purpose. It was simply a massive upwelling of truth, the benefit of which was to flow to all life.

Then I heard the statement: "The Tao of the times is full of energy; time is being compressed to renew, correct, and heal on a grand scale." Then I understood that because the Creative is at work, we have nothing to fear from the way things are going. Things will fulfill themselves if we but allow ourselves to be used. The Cosmic power is at work in the world during our lifetime.

This meditation also explained the meaning of the Creative as being full of power. When the Creative becomes activated, time compresses. As a force that works for good, it cannot be resisted.

Every person who allows himself to be trained and used by the Cosmos becomes a tent-pole, and though he limits himself to his own small field of action by rescuing those who are linked to him by inner ties, his sacrifices and travails make him an integral part of the Creative force itself, dynamic in the larger field of action.

Self-Development a Do-It-Yourself Enterprise
June 1, 1973

I saw a raw, dressed chicken.

Next I saw a stairway which, although wide at the bottom, narrowed sharply to be just big enough for one person to pass at the top.

To my left I saw a light in the shape of a hand. It crossed to the right so fast I thought it might be lightning.

After a while these diverse images began to emerge as related thought. The raw, dressed chicken, being ready for cooking, symbolized potential nourishment. Nourishment, in *I Ching* terms, is what we have to offer others from our experience in self-development. That the chicken is uncooked means that it is up to the individual who is offered nourishment to cook and eat the chicken. At least this much effort must be made by those who come, otherwise the food cannot be absorbed, or properly understood.

The stairway, being wide at the bottom, symbolized the broad tolerance the Sage has towards those who come, accepting them as they are. The successive narrowing of the steps, however, represents the limitations that the student must place upon himself if he is to climb higher, and the necessity to strip off all that encumbers his higher nature. The climb upwards indicates the effort which must be made. Reaching the top indicates that he has become his true self. The height represents all that has been achieved.

The hand of light that crossed my plane of vision is the helpful hand offered—the help granted by the light of insight that flashes from time to time, as needed.

The more I learned of the Cosmic Laws, the more I became aware of the decadence and self-destructive nature of many widely-held ideas. Finding them so hard to eradicate in myself, I wondered if it might not be too late for a broad and general correction of the problems of our day.

151

The following meditation provided the answer.

The New Age   November 11, 1973

I saw my inferiors and heard them saying plaintively, "How are society's troubles—decadence, crime, drugs, and other such problems—to be corrected?"

Then I saw how mothers give their children dolls or blankets, or toys to pacify them when they feel insecure. I saw that beliefs are kinds of dolls which we cling to because they give us a sense of comfort and security.

Considering this, I thought perhaps that my question "How?" was only a search for some sort of doll, so I presumed it would not be answered by the Sage.

Then I saw a theater with an empty stage and a full audience. The stage, it was revealed, represented life, while the audience represented everyone.

From the left side of the stage an invisible force blew through an opening that seemed to have broken through the wall. The invisible force entered as though it were enclosed in its own transparent container; it did not mix with the atmosphere that preceded it, but rather displaced it entirely. As soon it occupied the entire theater, the people began breathing this new air, which was pervaded with light, so that they began to think and feel differently about everything. They began to seek truth and want to improve themselves.

Later in the day I thought about the different feelings during different periods in history. Sometimes these were bright and hopeful, moving people towards renewal; sometimes they were tense and dark, moving them towards war, or revolution. Each atmosphere seemed to displace the previous one. This meditation reassured me that a great new age is dawning, when we will correct our current self-destructive attitudes.

The next meditations concerned my insecurity.

The Safe   November 22, 1973

I was flying in a cargo plane. Near the cargo door was a

safe for keeping valuables. As I looked at it, it blew up. Seeing its pieces lying about, I pushed them out the opened cargo door and watched them fall to earth.

As I wondered about the meaning of this image, the explanation came to me that the safe represented my need for security. Then I saw that the safe had contained all the beliefs I held which neatly and completely explained everything I tended to worry about, including those beliefs I held in reserve, in case the first ones fell short. I also saw that having the safe made me feel secure, enabling me to think I could always do things my way if the path of the good and the true did not work out.

Then I realized that the safe, with all its contents of ideas and beliefs, were really hedges in my trust of the Unknown.

I grew aware that the airplane represented my spiritual nature, and that it was inappropriate to carry a heavy safe around in one. Once I had understood how my hedging was inhibiting my development, the safe had blown up. Throwing the pieces out and letting them fall to earth enabled the plane to fly freely and effortlessly.

It was clear that once I committed myself to trusting the Unknown, to allowing myself to be led, and to allowing events to show the way, my progress would be light and easy.

As for the false self-confidence that accompanied my feeling of security in "having a safe," it was only a delusion. It had tricked me into thinking that I could go outside my natural limits of conduct without suffering any consequences.

More Earthbound Matter   November 26, 1973

I was once again in my cargo plane with the door open, cleaning out more earthbound matter, when I smelled something foul. Searching for the cause, I saw something furry. I was about to pet, or comb it, when I realized with a shock that it was a dead rat. I instantly threw it out the door.

At that moment, a bad opinion I had had of someone replayed in my mind. It made me aware that the rotten smell was related to the "rotten" thing he had done to me, and hence to my bad opinion of him. I realized that holding on to this bad memory was like keeping a dead rat around, as if it were a pet. Then I noticed that although I had got rid of the rat, its smell lingered. I had to sweep the air out of the plane as well.

Later in the day, when I saw the person about whom I had the bad opinion, I made a slightly negative remark, which immediately had a bad effect. I then realized that though we may rid ourself of a bad memory or opinion, it may nevertheless appear for a time afterwards, until its smell wears out. We are not immediately free of the effects of a bad thought, even after giving it up. It passes away gradually, just as the odor of a dead thing does, after we have got rid of it. If we are aware of this, we will guard our speech and actions for a time, so as to avoid saying or doing harmful things inadvertently.

We are not just influenced by our own stored-up opinions. The following meditation showed me that we are influenced by the spirits of people who have lived before us. These influences may be good or bad. To be free of bad influences, we must decide not to allow ourselves to be influenced by them. Once we make up our minds to be firm and persevering in resisting them, we receive help from hidden friends.

The Dank Green Air   November 25, 1973

I heard low moaning voices saying such things as, "You can't make it. No one ever does." Then I saw Odysseus passing by the Sirens. The low moaning voices returned, and I noticed that they had a compelling quality that drew me, just as the Sirens undoubtedly drew Odysseus. I now saw that the voices emanated from the stagnant layer of green air, and seemed to be contained in it, moaning away their discouragement and despair.

I perceived that these voices came from all those spirits of people who have passed through life and never persevered on their true paths. They were spirits caught in their own despair.

Then a fresh breeze came up and blew off the dank air. A whole different mood began to prevail, and all the doubt passed away. I saw the image of a friend's dead brother who had come to her, taken her hand, and said, "Hold on, don't give up." Unlike the spirits of the dank air, he was "one of those who have gone before" on the spiritual path (see *Preponderance of the Great*, Hexagram 26.) and therefore was able to hold out his hand to help us and reinforce our perseverance.

Being Rescued by the Sage   December 3, 1973

I was attacked incessantly all week by inferior thoughts which tempted me to abandon my path. Finally, however, I summoned strength to meditate in an effort to get free of them.

As I came into meditation I saw myself clasping a hand that reached down to me from above, pulling me up from the dark place where I had been, onto a plain that was in complete daylight.

I realized that I had got off the path and fallen over the edge of a cliff. My situation had been more desperate than I had thought. I had been clinging with both hands to a slippery rock, ready to drop thousands of feet into a deep canyon. Obviously the Sage's helping hand had prevented disaster. Had I persisted in deviating from the correct path, I would have joined the voices who cried in the green air, "It's hopeless."

This meditation made me see that whatever good we achieve in life is owed to the help we receive. The final step of perseverance in every difficult situation is made with the help of the Sage. So it has been with all who trod this path before, those whom the *I Ching* calls the Ancestors. I was to remember from this meditation that all our achievements are made in partnership with the Sage. We therefore need to keep our humility when we think of our successes, and not allow our ego to appropriate them to itself.

As time went by, my curiosity nagged, "Who is the Sage?"

Was He the spirit of a historical person like Christ? Was He Lao Tzu? Why was the figure always faceless? Why did He never identify himself? He even seemed to resist being identified. Also, my husband had seen the Sage as a female in one of his meditations.

Perhaps because of my Christian background I wanted him to be Christ. I wanted Him to feel familiar, and comfortable. I had also wondered and worried from time to time if using the *I Ching* was "against Christ." Whenever I would ask the *I Ching* about it I would get *Biting Through*, Hexagram 21, which inferred that the truth had been covered up by slanderous tradition. All these questions were resolved by the following meditation.

The Identity of the Sage, or Invisible Teacher   about 1973

As soon as I entered meditation I saw a somewhat fat Chinese mandarin sitting in a yoga position. My reaction was, "Surely this is not the Sage!" Everything about him looked plastic except his eyes, which, curiously, were very sharp and alive. Then this image disappeared.

Next came a somewhat "blubbery" middle-aged Westerner who might have the qualities of a Sage, except for that troublesome blubbery look. Nevertheless, the eyes, like those of the Mandarin's, were exceptionally sharp and alive looking.

This image was replaced by a figure who looked like the traditional Sunday School portrait of Jesus Christ standing by a stream with hand outstretched. Surely this is the Sage, I thought, as I rushed to clasp him by the knees in worship. To my keen disappointment the image proved to be nothing but air. I had noticed, however, that his eyes, like the others, had been penetrating and alive.

Then I realized that the eyes in all three faces had been the same. Immediately, my vision was completely filled with a huge ball of light which began receding away from me. Slowly it receded upwards, becoming smaller and smaller, until it took its place as the most brilliant star in a night sky full of stars.

Puzzled about the meaning of these images, I sat waiting. Then the meaning was explained. We need images, I was told, to be able to handle the concept of a higher being. The mandarin, the Western man, and Jesus were all such images, but none were correct. The most correct one was the ball of light, which represented a highly-developed being—bright among the millions of people who have fulfilled their higher natures, here represented by the millions of stars.

This meditation destroyed forever the limited concept I had that only four or five people have ever developed themselves—Gandhi, Christ, Confucius, Buddha, Lao Tzu. Worse, this concept leads one to think a high development of self is probably impossible, so why try.

Perfection, in fact, is not the goal; only the ego envisions "perfection," and is entangled with the idea of becoming a hero. Humility is the goal.

The Printing Press, or Meaning of Grace   June 8, 1974

I saw a printing press that seemed to work only in fits and starts. In spite of this it printed perfectly neat blocks of currency, which, on closer examination proved to be U. S. dollars.

Wondering what message might be connected with this image, it came to me that the machine represented society and its workings. The currency represented the customs and values of a given society: To get along in a society, we must use the currency of that society; in other words, we must work within the given social norms. For example, just as we cannot superimpose Chinese customs upon Western society, we cannot create personal social forms, which would be like printing counterfeit money. To do so exposes us to penalties.

We cannot use U. S. money in France or Germany, or vice versa. Moreover, all these currencies fluctuate in value, depending on the times and circumstances within each country. The only value they have at any given time is the value society gives them at that time. In every real sense they have no value in themselves.

Then I saw on my right hand gold coins showering down

from above. They glinted brightly as they reflected the sun's rays and I knew they were made of the purest metal, and that no matter whose face was imprinted upon them, their value endured and fluctuated very little. Although the workings of custom, time, or circumstance affect the gold's demand, they do not greatly affect the coins' value. They are usable currency for all societies and remain interchangeable and convertible. Then I realized that the gold coins symbolized Universal Truth.

Then I saw these images in relation to the Hexagram *Grace,* Hexagram 22. The customs, or forms, of society were here symbolized by the paper currency. While customs and social forms beautify and enhance life in the given society, their values fluctuate, depending on how society regards them, and they lack intrinsic value. While this beautification and enhancement is important for life to have harmony and order, they are not the main thing. When they become important as things in themselves, they lose their purpose to beautify and create order, and instead create rigidity and enslavement and thus make up the trivial and the vain.

As the hexagram says, there are times in life when even beauty of form must be sacrificed. Customs do not answer our needs in the great controversies or in times of great stress. We must seek the pure gold coin of Universal Truth, for ultimately only those principles which are based the very foundations of human existence endure through time. We must look into our hearts for what the Sage would say, and follow what is essential and correct.

The Question of Reincarnation   about 1975

During an *I Ching* group meeting, some of those attending brought up the subjects of reincarnation, karma, and the influence of possible past lives in our present lifetime. They wondered what the *I Ching* viewpoint might be on these subjects. On throwing the coins the answer was clear that we are not meant to concern ourselves with such things, and that the task before us to is to deal with this lifetime. We were to concern ourselves with what is essential, and not get caught up in "diversions," and that it is the ego which involves us in these side paths.

Having received such a definite answer, I thought no more on the subject. In putting together this book, however, I have noticed that a number of meditations touch upon this question.

The first of these occurred only a year or so after I began to meditate. The preceding night I had been at a friend's house for dinner where I got into a discussion on metaphysics and had stated the *I Ching's* point of view that we should never give up on anyone. "What about Hitler?" one of those present demanded. "Hitler too," I said. The fact that my statement created instant hostility in that man caused me to doubt myself and the *I Ching's* teachings. As usual, meditation resolved the matter.

The Mountain Path   about 1975

In the next morning's meditation I saw myself halfway up a mountain path. The mountainside was bare of trees, as if it had been grazed over by sheep. I could see the path wind up from the bottom of the mountain, past me, to go on farther than I could see. From where I stood I had an excellent view of the surrounding countryside and hills, but my attention was drawn to the fact that the path was lined with people climbing. The line was so dense we almost touched each other. On one side the line extended up and beyond my view; on the other it extended down into the valley where people, who appeared to be the size of ants, were getting on the path. All of us were clad in white garments from neck to toe, and I immediately understood that this was a metaphor for the spiritual journey each of us was completing through the life process.

I heard myself describing to someone farther down the path, who had not yet reached my location, things that could be seen only from where I was. Then I realized that in spite of my efforts, he was unable to imagine or understand what I saw.

I then heard someone ahead of me trying to tell me what he saw, and I realized I could not really visualize it. It seemed remarkable how each of us was stuck within the limits of what we had experienced in climbing.

Then I was guided to look back at the beginning. There, enlarged, as if someone had put a magnifying glass over part of the scene, I saw that one of the tiny, ant-like people getting on the path was Hitler, to begin again his climb towards self-understanding and growth.

In addition to pointing out that life's purpose is to complete a course of self-development and spiritual understanding, this meditation indicated that those who have failed in developing themselves are fated to return and start all over again—a specific kind of reincarnation and karma.

On "Being Saved"   about 1975

Many times in consulting the *I Ching* I was counseled not to give up on others. The point was made that saving myself gave me an obligation to rescue the others to whom I had inner ties.

One day it came to me that what the *I Ching* meant by this was not what religions commonly mean by being saved. Rescuing others means that through believing in them we aid them in recovering and establishing their essential selves. To save ourself means that though we lose the path many times, we keep returning to following the high and the good within ourself.

It also occurred to me that following the path of the true and the good is quite different from the self-oriented goal to be saved in the Biblical sense of "getting into heaven," or to be accepted in God's kingdom.

The goal in following the good and the true is to divest ourselves of all selfish purpose, and to learn to follow the good only because it is good, not to follow it through fear of damnation, or because we hope for reward either now or in the hereafter. In simply following good without purpose, we fulfill our nature and establish our existence in the beyond. Thus, ironically, by not pursuing the goal to be saved, we are saved, in the sense meant by religions, and we do win acceptance in the beyond.

The Goal   April 28, 1979

This meditation began by my remembering the many
other meditations in which I had seen myself traveling
along a road. It now occurred to me that I had never seen
where the road went. As the railroad track disappeared
over a crest, and the mountain path around a curve, I
always felt I was proceeding towards a goal.

I remembered the many times I had been counseled by
the *I Ching* not to be goal-oriented, and I realized something in me was always in a hurry to get "there," but where
was there?

Then I saw myself on top a mountain like Mt. Everest. I
was looking back over the path I had followed to get to this
high place. Down below, the path had led me over sea and
land, over streams, across chasms, and up and down
mountains of great size. The winding trail seemed endless.
Then I turned around to see where the path went. There
before me it went, down, around, up, over streams, past
precipices, as before. What! I thought in dismay, for I had
expected it to lead to a place, a particular place where I
could get off and relax. Then the voice came, "The path is
the goal. How you walk it is what counts, not where it goes.
The path is the goal."

Gifts From the Teacher

Throughout my development I have received gifts from
the Sage. I have already mentioned some of the more
helpful gifts—the laser ruby which helped me regain my
inner balance, the altar of sacrifice, and the Cosmic Vacuum Cleaner. The following are some of the others which
came in meditation.

The Opaque Mirror   April 4, 1979

After becoming painfully aware that I had indulged in
several follies, I found myself standing before a large bright
mirror in a Victorian house. Looking at the mirror, I
became aware that in this rather dark house the mirror

161

was a thing apart, almost alive. My first thought was that mirrors were connected to vanity and ought to be destroyed, but I was held back by the awareness that this mirror was different, and probably could not be broken. I noticed that when I looked in it for vain reflections, its brightness clouded over and the mirror became opaque. I also noticed that merely by passing by it, without looking into it directly, it vividly reflected my follies. Moreover, it hung in a hallway where I would pass it frequently. Then I realized it was a gift from the Sage, to help me see myself truly. How useful, in the quest for growth, not to be able to deceive ourself for long! I also saw that I must forgive myself for my momentary back-slidings and deviations, and go on.

The Royal Visit   May 19, 1983

I had been going through a minor illness for the past three days, one which I felt sure was related to an inner metamorphosis now occurring. For the past several months I had felt dissatisfied with people around me who were making no progress. I became aware this morning that this was the reason I received *Darkening of the Light*, Hexagram 36, Line 4, last night. It indicated that my dissatisfaction with others was at the heart of the darkening of my inner light.

As I sat down to meditate I was in search of the correct perspective towards these people, or at least one which would enable me to stop being impatient. I was aware that my critical attitude was inhibiting them from returning to the correct course within themselves. I was measuring their progress, and looking at them expectantly.

The first thing I did was to take the whole cloud of ill feelings, alienation, and hopelessness, and place it on my alter of sacrifice. Hearing my ego protest for an instant, I saw its hand in this problem. I caught it and put it, too, on the heap.

Then I saw that I was not at my usual sacrifice place, but at the foot of the most handsome and kind-looking king (who I also realized was the Sage). He bade me kneel and then knighted me with the tip of his sword. Then I saw myself beautifully robed and honored, and said to myself, "what could I have done to deserve this? I merely put that cloud of ill-feelings upon the sacrifice place."

Then the king noted that my sacrifice was purely self-less. Always before I had perhaps some inner purpose connected with sacrificing. This time my act had been purpose-less. Immediately I felt a feeling of love so strong that I wept tears of joy. Only an hour before I had noted that the Sage treats all people like "straw-dogs," as Lao Tzu had put it. Feeling this great love, I wanted to stay in this place as long as possible.

Then the king explained. Surely the Sage, our teacher, must treat all of us as straw dogs, wholly impersonally, so that we learn what goodness is in our hearts. When we are able to develop the good in ourselves purely for the sake of goodness, then the love of the Sage can flow freely, because the goodness is our own doing.

Everyone is born free to move towards degradation or towards self-development. The Sage is capable of teaching each and every person by whatever means it takes. We need have no fear about this. Then, when we do mount the heights, it is truly a great achievement, for we do it ourselves, without anyone in the world understanding what we are doing. Because the steps are difficult and slippery, the dangers manifold, and the trail long and plodding, the rewards are what they ought to be.

Although our self-development is connected to the development of those around us, freedom is still of the essence. We need to be patient and tolerant of their slow, even halting, growth. We need to control ambition with understanding. That is the only way to help others. We need to keep our minds open about them, and about the creative process and the way it works.

Concerning those with whom I had been impatient, I was reminded that a good deal of growth had already occurred. I saw that I needed to be content with this.

In a number of meditations I found myself in the Sage's garden, which I have described earlier in the meditation entitled *Crutches*. The Sage's garden was always a pleasant setting, and just imagining myself there transported me quickly into the meditation state. The following two were the first and last meditations of many which occurred in this setting.

The Sage's Garden   about 1982

The first time I was here I found myself sitting opposite the Sage, who appeared only as an indistinct and faceless Presence. I immediately knelt, as I thought I should, before a higher being. No sooner had I done this, however, than the Sage gently took my hands and bade me stand up. "Do not kneel before me," he said, "nor before anyone. Do not compromise your dignity, which is sacred."

This experience made me aware that my dignity was a sacred gift of God. I was not meant to place myself in suppliance before anyone, even the Sage, who respected this sacred gift within me. I have since realized that every life form has been given this gift. It is to be respected, for it is the way God manifests Himself in all life forms. Regardless of how our dignity may have been degraded, it is still there, and can be revived.

The Atomic Cloud—Sage Within   May, 1983
(The End of the Sage's Garden)

I saw a fire within myself expand until it became an Atomic Cloud, rising high and visible from a very great distance. It destroyed within me everything that was left of my personal self, down to the last shadow. Then the Sage got up from his seat in the garden and instead of going somewhere, as I expected he was about to do, he came straight toward me and passed into me, or at least into the space I had inhabited.

When this happened I knew that the garden of the Sage would no longer be there for me to visit. I would no longer be able to look outside myself, or indeed anywhere else to see the Sage; henceforth he would be an invisible presence within me.

At first this seemed flattering, and I wondered if I had done something deserving. This, however, was not the message. I was made aware that I (or rather my ego) had begun to attach myself to the comfort of the idea of being in the company of the Sage. I realized that attachment to any such idea or images, or to a sense of comfort, was incorrect. The meditation was a kind and gentle way of correcting my attachment to images.

We soon learn that the job of rescuing people is not what we think it is. Most of the time we cannot intervene in a direct way to stop people from doing destructive things. We give them space to go their own way, without giving up on them. This was the subject of the following meditation.

Fate in the Department Store   September 16, 1981
(On How Much We Can Help People)

I saw that the shoe department of a large store was recessed down a few steps from the main level. I was about to enter this department, though I hesitated on the top step.

Then I saw the manager of the department looking at me with the most impersonal and detached blank look, as if to say, "What are you doing, entering this department?" That was warning enough. I recognized him as "Fate," and knew that if I entered his department I would encounter something unpleasant. Clearly, I should not intrude in his department. It was a setup for those who were bound, by their fixed ideas, to go there.

This was a message that I should recognize my boundaries, and not chase after people who insisted on going the wrong way. In trying to help them I should not go too far, but let them go into Fate's Department if they were bent upon doing so.

In the Eastern Bazaar   about 1985

I was invited to a house-warming by some friends who were followers of a well known guru. In dedicating their

house, they had everyone participate in a religious ceremony, after which the leader of the local ashram spoke.
Then we were asked to meditate. As I began, the thought
came to me, "What should I think about the question of
having a guru, which the ashram leader was recommend-
ing?" Almost immediately I saw myself walking in a
middle-eastern bazaar. There were dozens of stalls, each
filled with wares of different sorts, and people milling
about. Wondering what this scene represented, the answer
came, "You don't have to buy any of the goods for sale."

Finding the Middle Way   January 1, 1982

I realized that to relate properly to a certain problem I
needed to become neutral, so that I neither believed nor
disbelieved in the people involved. In meditation I saw this
middle ground as a razor's edge, an impossibly fine line.

Then I saw myself stretching out the fine line, as might
happen if we were to draw a line on a balloon and then blow
the balloon up. The balloon in this meditation was giant-
sized; when it was blown up, the thin line became the size
of the path that goes down the Grand Canyon—about four
feet wide. Then I realized that by the same process the line
could be made as wide as a field, and I would have no
problem following it. But then the question arose—How
was this to be accomplished?

I saw that the more I shrank myself—that is, my self-
image—and all the ideas of how other people should be, the
wider the line became. If we relinquished our sense of
demand altogether—all demand that relates to our self
image—the line became as wide as a field. Then we would
be able to let people go, accepting where they were in their
state of development, without losing our own sense of
values and standards. Gaining such equanimity, we would
be like the Sage, who is never sad, and never disturbed.

Being Below Rather Than Above   January 16, 1982

The first thing I saw when I opened the curtains one
morning, on a visit to my mother, and looked out, was the

sun coming through the trees. I thought with surprise that the sun appeared to be below the horizon, but then I realized that I was seeing the sun as it was reflected in a small pond off in the woods. The sun was actually higher, behind the trees where I could not see it.

In my meditation, this view returned, and with it the realization that in trying to influence my mother I was trying to shine like the sun, from above. I was standing in the place of the sun, the truth, while all I could ever really do was reflect it.

I saw that everyone is surrounded by defenses which act as curtains that they open to look out upon the world. When they look out, they do not look up at the sun, but down at things on which the sun shines. If truth is not self-evident in all that we do, we will not appear below where they can see us. To reflect truth we need to be below, and keep still as a mirror formed by pond water. This is the image of acceptance. Only then will we be able to have a true and correct influence; our modesty and perseverance will provide the view that they see.

The following was not a meditation, but a spontaneous outpouring of realizations that occurred during a talk I gave on the *I Ching*.

The Props of our Lives   March 18, 1988

While I was in the process of describing the yang/yin circle as symbolizing a sort of wheel of change, a lady in the audience asked me if the wheel moved to the right or to the left.

I replied that it doesn't matter which way the circle moves. The movement could be one way or another, or one way then another; it could contract or expand, or it could move in a circle, or in a spiral, or in a linear way. All these visualizations, I explained, merely attempt to deal with something we are not able to place entirely within our understanding—the Tao—the way of the Universe.

Such questions invariably make me aware of our human tendency to want to pin things down so that we feel we know, thereby no longer feel painfully exposed to not knowing, and to the constant ambiguity that resides in the Unknown. Our search for knowledge, to a great extent, is driven by our insecurity, our need to make things more predictable. Once predictable, we feel we can relax and be comfortable. This desire creates strange paradoxes. For example, because we know an earthquake is going to happen along the San Andreas Fault within a reasonable time, we feel more comfortable!

What we are trying to do is make life a pre-written script so that we can shut out the Unknown and no longer be bothered by it. The fact remains, we are not authors of the script of life.

When we live life without a script of our making, we allow ourselves to be guided. In accepting and trusting the Unknown, we experience the most marvellous script written by the Higher Power.

I mentioned to my audience Pirandello's play *Enrico IV*, the story of an Italian aristocrat who fell off his horse at a costume party. When he came out of his coma he thought he was Enrico IV, the Thirteenth Century king he had portrayed at the party. His wealthy family humored him by recreating the court of that king, and the history of the time, which the aristocrat knew precisely. For many years afterwards hired actors re-enacted the historic incidents of Enrico IV's life, in order to allow the aristocrat to "live" his role.

As the play progresses the audience gradually becomes aware that Enrico has been sane for the last dozen years. He has only pretended to be Enrico because, on returning to his senses, he had found it safer and easier to live a pre-written script than to go back into the uncertainties of real life which had changed while he was in his altered state. Eventually, however, he grows tired of "knowing the outcome."

Through our belief systems, our maps of the afterlife, our fixation on diagrams and explanations of reality, through our science and engineering, we attempt to fix life and feel comfortable, but in every way that we become comfortable with our fixation, the Cosmos acts to blow our explanations apart.

On the way home from this lecture I saw how, as Piran-dello pointed out, our houses, our choices of furniture, our clothes, all are props on our particular stages. We imagine that these props define our lives and establish who we are. The way we arrange our particular stage, however, has nothing to do with who we really are, or the reality that exists independently of our contrived settings. We are simply trying to write the script of our life.

There is nothing wrong in building a house, or a theory, so long as we do not mistake it for the greater reality, which is always unknowable. There is no harm so long as we do not get habituated to our security blankets. Such activities come from the ego, in building the delusion of self-impor-tance. These delusions are the source of all the imbalances and injustices of life.

Genius Is God Shining Through   March 17, 1989

An older Christian friend once expressed fear for one of her sons, who seemed to her to "be lost." He told her many times that he did not believe, causing her to despair and to say that if only something could be done about this, she could die in peace.

I was thinking about her fears and worries one night as I went to bed. I was nearly asleep when I was awakened suddenly by the following thought: "Genius is God shining through."

Then I thought of her son. All his life he has stood in awe of the genius of things: a brilliant architectural design, a culinary masterpiece, a great play, an opera, or a sea creature discovered while scuba diving. As a mountain climber he stands in awe of the high peak, as a traveler he stands in awe of a rift valley, and can point out from an airplane the geological features of the land below, or some-thing unique about a forest or the plain. He is in love with beauty and truth, and seeks them everywhere. Certainly he is not what we might call spiritual, but it seemed clear to me that one day it would surface in his consciousness that all these things were God manifesting Himself.

A few meditations were about the Tao—the way things work in the Cosmos. It is said that the Tao can be perceived, but it cannot be known. I became aware that the Cosmos has a direction, and that to disregard that direction can create an adverse personal fate, which may also affect all those with whom we have inner ties.

Life—A Trip into the Sun   October 13, 1974

From a window in a space ship I momentarily saw the sun before the view became black once more. I had been trying to steer the ship in such a way as to keep the sun in view, but every time I steered the ship one way, inertia kept it going that way so that by the time I saw the sun, it was too late to put on the brake, so to speak, and hold it in the right direction. Steering it back the other way, the same problem occurred, but in reverse. The sun would come into view, only to go past, as my ship revolved on its own axis.

Then it occurred to me that all this trouble resulted from trying to steer the ship myself, so I decided to turn on my auto pilot. Immediately, the ship headed in the right direction so that the sun came into view and the light began to stream consistently into the cabin.

Then outside my window I could see other space ships which, similarly, were trying to head into the sun. The people in those ships, too, had been over-steering, therefore wandering here and there. They were spending all their energies compensating for wrong turns.

I realized that when we cease striving we turn on the auto pilot. Because our natural direction is toward the light, we begin to flow in the direction meant for us.

Then I saw that heading toward the sun was symbolic of life's journey—a trip into the sun, a re-unification with the light source. To get there we need only let ourself be pulled.

The Dragon Force   February 15, 1975

I saw certain relatives arranging their wills and creating trusts so that one child, who was deemed careless with money, could not use it all up; another, whose spouse they did not like, could not benefit from it; and so on. It came to me that this was the dragon force.

Then I saw that almost every situation involves some aspect of the Dragon Force—a force which exists only by the negative energy it arouses in those who connect with it and are bothered by it. The dragon force lives only so long as this negative energy is sustained. The effort to fight it actively always fails, and just adds to its ability to endure. Abandoning it utterly deprives it of energy, and it dies.

The next two meditations concern our personal destiny to rescue those to whom we have inner ties.

The Wall to Be Scaled, and Where the Path Leads
June 17, 1974

I saw a young man at the bottom of a rock wall that was quite high. He was trying to figure out how to use his new climbing gear to scale the wall. Part of the gear was in his hands, part at his feet. He also had an instruction manual which showed how to use the special equipment, but this too lay on the ground and was practically covered up by the other paraphernalia. Although he had been informed that the book contained instructions on how to use the gear and climb the wall, he disregarded it because he had decided he could figure things out for himself.

Then I realized that the wall surrounded a magic city, and that the wall also had a doorway which contained a magic lock. I then saw that the instruction book at his feet also contained the whereabouts of the magic key, and that although this man could stand at the base of the wall for the rest of his life, unless he inquired into the book, his scaling equipment could not be made to work for him, nor would he find the key.

Then I saw dozens of paths which led to similar doorways. Each of these doorways represented entrances to people's hearts. I saw that people's hearts are all magic cities, and that to gain entry we may not resort to stratagem or device. We must have either the magic key, a knowledge of how to scale the wall with the equipment, or divine help. Then I saw that when I follow my inner path, which has always led straight ahead, only to disappear over the horizon or around a bend further on, it leads straight into people's hearts. The magic key that enables us to enter the hearts of others is to be straight and true within ourselves, regardless of what they do or think.

The Obstructing Mountains and the Hidden Passes
June 27, 1974

I saw myself confronted by mountains that I recognized were barriers to people's hearts. These mountains seemed nearly insurmountable because they were high, heavily wooded, and steep. These were the Massanuttens on the east side of the Shenandoah Valley of Virginia. As my brother and I had driven north on route U. S. 81, I had pointed out the obscure pass through which Stonewall Jackson had moved his army to surprise the Union Army at Front Royal. When the pass came into view, I realized that whether the mountains are high or low, if you are back far enough you can see where the passes are.

Then I realized that when we are preoccupied with emotions, it is like being too close to the mountains to see the passes. Retreating and disengaging is like getting back far enough for the passes to become visible.

Then I saw that these passes represent obscure places in each of us through which our essential selves may be reached. For one person it might be flower gardening, for another it might be painting, for another it might be compassion reserved for working with the handicapped, or with children, or with animals. To find these passes, through which another's capacity for sincerity and love may be touched, we must become objective, detached, and completely free of our egos. Only in this way can the obstructing mountains be passed.

Something Sweet and Delicious   May 12, 1981
(Searching for One Thing and Getting Something Else)

I saw something that closed off and opened up the light

before my eyes, as if a set of windshield wipers were connected to curtains which opened and closed towards each other. But then I saw that the curtains were connected to the antennae of a bug. In fact, as it became more focussed, I could see that the bug was a cockroach! It soon became apparent that it was interfering in this strange way with my access to the light.

Then I saw another image: light coming through a tube, but being partially obstructed by something in the tube.

I remembered an incident from my youth in which I was sitting at a table with friends at my home town drug store, sipping a milkshake through a straw. I drew very hard at the straw because it seemed the milkshake was too thick to come through it. Then something else came through the straw—a cockroach!

Suddenly I realized the irony of the situation: while seeking something "sweet and delicious", a milkshake, I got instead a cockroach. This incident had made me cautious ever after as to what might be coming through straws. In fact, I have carried this hesitation forward into many areas of my life, even to working with the *I Ching*, although I have never received anything but true and pure nourishment from it.

Then I realized that it is a general principle in life that if we go in search of something sweet and delicious we might get a cockroach, whereas if we go in search of the truth we invariably get something sweet and delicious.

We never need hesitate in searching for the truth. Even though we may expect to get something surprising, it will never be a cockroach, or something bitter.

I had the next meditation after I had observed how hard a certain person worked, contriving and striving to accomplish this and that, all with workaholic zeal. It reminded me of myself at an earlier time in my life.

Swimming Over the Ocean (On the Easy and the Hard)
1984

In meditation I saw myself in a boat, and the person I had

been thinking about was swimming over the ocean. .

Someone in the boat with me threw the person a life ring to which he could cling, but he was so intent on his swimming that he did not notice the help offered. I thought that he could ride with us in our nice power boat, but though several of us called to him, he was deaf to our cries. We were powerless to help him.

I then realized that the degree to which a person is open to being helped determines the help he receives, or whether he receives any help at all. If he is open to it, he can ride effortlessly all the way across the ocean of life.

Dim View   March 10, 1987

Our ego is responsible for the dim view of God we occasionally adopt. In the musical *Fiddler on the Roof* Tevye says something like this to God: "What new wars, floods, catastrophes do you have in mind to bring us closer to you?" Occasionally, we say such things to ourselves in a fit of doubt, and even though we do not wholly believe them, a childish part of us does. Even harboring a small bit of doubt about the goodness of God creates a barrier between ourselves and God.

I remembered an early meditation in which I had seen imprinted in the face of the Sage all the suffering of the ages. Seeing this indescribably sad face made me realize that the Sage had nothing to do with human suffering. All suffering arises from human indifference, which we have the power to correct within ourselves. Even the smallest correction ends some small suffering somewhere, both now and in the future.

The Cost of Defective Attitudes   1988

Once, in a facetitious mood, I made a list of the cost of certain attitudes which break the Cosmic Laws. Although the cost is not always in terms of money, it sometimes is. The cost may not be evident for a long time, while we are testing life's trampoline, nor may we be required to pay up right away, but the day does come when it must be paid.

Attitude	*Cost*
Titanic ambition	$100,000 to our life
Vindictiveness	$50,000 to $1 million
Desire for more than we need	$20,000 to $100,000
Carelessness	Loss of friendships to physical injury
Abandoning our responsibilities	Being abandoned
Following someone who is incorrect	Being defeated
Buying into things we don't understand	Embarassing obligations that last for years
Obstinacy	Being broken

The following was an insight into a theme implied throughout the *I Ching,* but which struck me particularly when I read the *Bhagavad-gita* and one of its small essays on the "Pull of the World."

The Pull of the World   1988

The *Bhagavad-gita* said that the world has such a pull on us that, even though we have experienced the inner reality, we easily forget it.

In meditation I saw the affairs of the outer world as symbolized by Uncle Remus's tar baby, with the realization that if we allow ourselves to become too involved in them, we get stuck in the tar, so to speak, and have difficulty extricating ourselves. They have an enchanting, dominating quality that tends to exclude the inner life, and we soon question whether our perception of the inner world was not just some trick of the mind.

Even if we have had many inner world experiences but cease practicing meditation, it soon becomes difficult to reestablish our connection with the inner life. It is as if the door develops rusty hinges and may only be reopened through persevering effort.

175

It is my view that we are meant to become aware of the drawing power of the outer world, so that we will see the importance of keeping our connection with the inner world strong through daily meditation.

We are meant to become so thoroughly aware that we include the Higher Power in everything we do. We remain alert to our duty to serve the good and the true by our example in all things, even in our inmost thoughts.

13.

Meditations on Business Relationships

Owning and running a business was the source of many *I Ching* lessons. I had run this business for four years before beginning my studies with the *I Ching*. From that time and for the next ten years my business problems seemed designed to teach me lessons. For a long time I did not apply *I Ching* principles to my business, since I was preoccupied with family problems. In time, however, the *I Ching* counseled me to extend these principles to all aspects of my life. Through meditating I learned how these principles could be applied. In most cases the questions were on my mind when I began meditating.

The nature of my business required dealing with the general public through contract arrangements. Problems often involved what to me were large sums of money, so that failure to resolve the problems was costly. Often I had to learn a particular principle before a given problem could be resolved. Every lesson cost money or placed what I owned at risk. The sooner I related correctly to the problem, the less it cost. A few cases dragged on for months.

These learning experiences generally taught me to be more firm and correct in my attitude, more reserved with clients, and more cautious in entering arrangements. I learned to combine inner firmness with patience and gentleness. In making contracts I became meticulous, disregarding what others might think about my petty regard for the details of arrangements. I learned not to be intimidated out of following what I saw as essential and correct. This did not make me generally assertive. I was assertive when it was absolutely necessary to say what had to be said. I learned to take the time and trouble to establish relationships on correct terms in the beginning, to avoid later problems from the customer. When I neglected to follow these guidelines, trouble invariably followed.

Above all, and perhaps hardest for me to learn and accept, was the Cosmic principle that the way we solve problems is more important than the fact that they get solved. Once I accepted this principle, problems got solved. Until then, the problems remained obdurate.

I learned that some things which I thought I was obligated to do were wrong. One of these was the idea that if the customer met my normal terms, I was obligated to do business with him. There is no such obligation. In fact, I learned that if I was warned by my inner feelings that the deal would turn out badly, I had to, and could, say no, even if there was no supporting reason. Curiously, once I made up my mind to follow this rule, I never again experienced a time when I had to say no.

I learned that while good manners are important, there is a danger in the attitude that we must "be nice." Danger lies in the attitude that we must "be" anything, as in "being tough," "being firm," "being polite," "being attractive," "being truthful," etc. All such self-images are defenses, and as such are traps which set us up for problematical situations. Invariably, people sense the weaknesses implied by our need for these defensive postures. Invariably, they engage us in these areas of vulnerability because the weaknesses act like magnets which draw the problems.

I learned how to make myself invisible to people. Times occur in everyone's life when we are exposed to people who are dangerous because of pre-existing conditions within them. In my business this occurred two times in the 14 years I ran it. My inner voice told me these people were dangerous, and in listening to it, I learned how to remain outside their consciousness.

We get the impression, in following the *I Ching*, that it is a wholly passive way of life. This is not true. There are times when initiative action is appropriate and necessary. However, we must approach initiative action in a particular way, otherwise we exceed our Cosmic limits and invite a rebound. Initiative action is a very particular thing.

Since I was the owner of the business and it was my sole means of livelihood, each difficult experience jeopardized me emotionally, sometimes to my limits of exasperation.

Threats did not always come from the customer; sometimes they came from insurance companies, or others with whom I had regular relationships. In nearly every case I was forced to recognize that I needed help from the Higher Power. Generally, this help came only when I relinquished all my old ways of doing things to allow myself to be led. A few times help came in the form of people with a particular expertise who came along at the right time, and who happened to be willing and able to help me.

The fact that each lesson cost something made me aware that a certain cost is always involved in self-development, and that the cost is necessary and just. I have since wondered why there is a conventional belief that spiritual lessons and help ought to be free. If they do not cost money, they cost physical or emotional pain and suffering. For a long time I begrudged this fact. One of my lessons and meditations was about being willing to go through these experiences. Once I became willing to do so, the deficit I incurred was made up in some way.

I learned the meaning of waiting in a correct attitude. Through waiting I learned that time is the vehicle of the Creative; we need only allow time to fulfill itself. Time takes us on a zig-zag journey, but it gets us there—to real and enduring results. The straight line so desired by our ego is far more costly in the end, and it fails to achieve what we really seek.

Being constantly at risk taught me to approach each difficult situation one day at a time. I was forced to see that secure situations are illusions. We are all at risk all the time, whether we know it or not. Moreover, we are dependent on the Higher Power in all situations.

My business, as well as everything else, has been a device to teach me Cosmic lessons. The following meditation came as I was reflecting on this. I had become tired of being fully at risk, and of facing difficult situations and being emotionally jeopardized. Until now I had awaited, and undergone, these learning experiences with dread. Now, I was to learn their meaning and necessity, and to accept them willingly.

This meditation came on the eve of starting my book

publishing business and publishing my first book, *A Guide to the I Ching*. To a certain extent it dealt with fears of exposing myself to the public in this new way. It also delineated in what ways I had chosen my "fate," and in what ways Fate had chosen me.

On My Fate to Serve the Higher Power   January 9, 1980

A procession of ideas started with the observation that during turbulent times trinkets made of precious metals such as gold and silver are collected and melted down.

I saw inside an Egyptian tomb, such as King Tut's, where such trinkets (and a fair share of precious metals) were buried with their owners. I noticed that none of the kings or personages embalmed were fat. This seemed to point out that kings, as chief warriors and leaders of their realm, kept fit.

Then I saw a king instruct an aide to raise his son not to be afraid to fight. The aide, an old warrior and comrade-in-arms, was to accomplish this in whatever way he chose, so long as he did not subject the Prince to real harm.

Then I saw the aide fencing with the son, exposing him to his weaknesses, and making him conquer them. He put him in situations which made him deal with his fears and learn to become unafraid. I saw that the essence of leadership was mental toughness and integrity.

This scene showed me that I was being exposed to my fears and required to overcome them as part of my training to serve the Sage. Many of these fears had to do with time—that I would not be able to accomplish my goals within the necessary time, before my death.

The images of the meditation confirmed that the Sage has come to help the world in its difficulty. First, however, He collects trinkets containing precious metal (people like myself) and melts them down (by training them) to refine them into precious pure metal (helpers chosen to work for the good). Like the king's son they are trained to become leaders by dealing with their fears. In the meantime they may not, like other people, do what they want to do, nor may they indulge in selfish pursuits. They must attend strictly to their duties.

A New Source of Danger   June 10, 1981

My *I Ching* reading began the night before with *The Abysmal/Danger*, Hexagram 29. In my experiences with the *I Ching* I soon learned that danger nearly always refers to threats to our will to go on. The threat usually is caused by ambition and effort; when we think that effort produces no progress, our will is threatened. In this case, however, danger came from a different source.

When I had finished dealing with a most difficult money question the day before, I found it hard to disengage from the feeling that my possessions had been at risk. I began an inner quarrel with the *I Ching* over what "ought" to be mine, and about my "rights." I also concluded that I would like a pause from problems that concerned my possessions. It seemed that to be subjected constantly to threats and risks was like being on a dangerous train. It did not occur to me immediately that these thoughts, which I had indulged in early the previous morning, would become the subject of danger by the end of the day.

In the next morning's meditation I saw myself on the train, looking for ways to get off. It seemed clear that my anxiety to get off, by nearly any means, had become a problem. First, wanting to get off a moving train is dangerous. If I did not injure myself, I would in get off in the wrong place. It was important that I continue, even though the train was careening here and there. I did not trust the Sage to lead me in a manner that was correct. I worried about being subjected to more than I could bear.

As I continued to meditate, I saw myself climbing over a precipice onto flat ground. Then I saw that I had climbed straight up the El Capitan mountain in Yosemite Valley. I was conscious of just barely having a place to hang on with fingers and toes, and that throughout the climb, an inch-by-inch care had been required.

Lao Tzu has mentioned "prizing calamity." He knew that when calamity strikes, growth and enlightenment result; he knew it so deeply and completely that he could prize the experience. I seemed infinitely far from welcoming whatever comes.

Climbing a mountain such as El Capitan must strain the climber's every resource and ability. It is no less difficult to maintain our spiritual integrity during difficult learning experiences. Like the climber who climbs ever so carefully and deliberately, straining every muscle, the follower of the invisible Sage has no time to look ahead or look back. He must attend strictly to the thing at hand. In this way he, like the climber, accomplishes something that otherwise would have been impossible.

Being firm in our willingness to grow, instead of being hesitant and resistant, is part of the power of truth. Our willingness to undergo whatever comes, and to allow ourself be guided, engages the great power of the Creative Force.

On Being Willing   June 26, 1982

Looking down, as if from an airplane, I saw long rows of mountains. It looked like the Appalachians as you first see them on a flight westward from Washington, D. C. I remembered that crossing them on the ground west of Charlottesville, Virginia, they are steep and full of hairpin curves and switchbacks. When I used to cross them to visit my parents in West Virginia, they were true obstacles, requiring good horsepower and brakes from my car, and care from me. I remembered a time when it had begun to sleet and the car in front of me began spinning around. It spun three times before it careened into the embankment. I remembered other times, on other mountains, when cars had gone off over the side. Now, in meditation, these mountains, with their threats, struck me as hurdles we might cross in a race, and that the whole point is our willingness to accept them as challenges. Life presents us with challenges in many forms.

The night before, I had received *Possession in Great Measure*, Hexagram 14, Line 3. This counseled me to put whatever I possessed at the disposal of the Sage so that it could be useful to the people at large. The image of the hurdles made me realize that I was to accept being challenged in matters that had to do with my possessions.

Sooner or later we are tested as to the degree to which we are willing to allow ourselves to be used by the Sage for His purposes. Situations occur in which people use us badly. They cheat, or fail to return property. We are asked, in effect, to sacrifice our defensiveness and possessiveness to the benefit of the Higher Power. We acknowledge what is happening, but disengage from our feelings of grievance. In so doing, we allow the Creative Power to teach us how to deal with the situation correctly. These challenges give us the opportunity to meet and conquer our fears. By being willing to be put through these experiences, we place everything we possess at the disposal of the ruler. In following this path we find that in the end we suffer no loss.

I was not meant, as I suspected at first, to sacrifice my possessions by abandoning them to those who were not living up to their contract obligations. I was meant to learn the *I Ching* way of solving problems: Chief in the hierarchy of considerations is *how* the problem is solved, not *whether* it is solved.

Beyond my business affairs, I was to accept whatever came in life—sickness, apparent bad luck in the form of accidents, apparent losses, threats to what I "owned" or whatever Fate wished to put before me in the form of obstructions and difficulty—in the spirit of "Well, let's see if I can find the correct solution to this puzzle."

In our training with the *I Ching* we are called upon to accept adversity as essential to self-development. Sometimes adversity requires us to endure a mounting crescendo of tension which concludes in everyone's learning a number of important spiritual truths, truths that cannot be learned in any other way.

A part of my problem at this time was saying "I want out," and "I don't want any more challenges or threats to what I own." I came to realize that our challenges come only in areas of attachment and insecurity, where our fears lie, for these are the fears that separate us from the Sage, isolate us from help, and prevent us from growing. If these fears are not aroused by threats to our defenses, they remain below the surface, where they influence us from our subconscious.

The Cosmos is not unkind. The Sage is not insensitive to our feelings. It is simply that if we are not jeopardized in the areas that involve our fears, we will not reach them, or be able to deal with them. Where else are we going to learn meaningful lessons? What good is it to say, "I want my lessons to concern only those areas of my life that I don't care about." Swimming means taking our feet off the bottom; flying means learning to stall and spin. Because things have gone awry does not mean that we should close ourselves off to experience, and say to the Sage, "you may not teach me by that means again, for I am going to safeguard myself from you by not jeopardizing what I own."

During many of these experiences I felt heavy resistance to what was happening, but when I could sacrifice this resistance, along with my feeling of rights, the situation began to be resolved in amazing ways. The problem seemed to be put before me for my learning. Once I learned its meaning, the problem was resolved and I never again was faced with that kind of problem.

Accepting adversity does not mean that we expose ourselves to unnecessary risks, or invite Fate to deliver us a blow. We do not stand out in the lightning holding a lightning rod. We do our best, and use caution and common sense. We follow wise policies that do not jeopardize us, but when these fail to protect us, we allow ourselves to go through the experience willingly. We try to deal with the situation in a sincere and conscientious manner. If we cannot find the correct solution, we wait for it to emerge. We do not settle for quick fixes, comprehensive solutions, diversions, or anything less than what we perceive through insight to be truly correct.

Another misconception which became the subject of a series of learning experiences was the idea that I had to treat people in a certain way. To get business I had to "be nice," to get things done I had to "be tough," or "be efficient," or "be current and remember everything properly." I learned that any fixed attitude of that sort is incorrect. All we need to be is balanced, and in tune with ourselves. We need to have an inner firmness about what is correct, but inner firmness must not be rigidity. We are to be open-minded towards the customer, but reserved. The following experience pointed out the value of being open-minded but firm in attitude.

The Man Who Didn't Cheat Me   about 1976

While in business I had a repeat customer with whom I had a good relationship. I realized that a certain discipline had to be maintained with this customer, to make sure he kept his accounts paid. I managed to keep that discipline with him. About two years after he left our area I had a call from a competitor who asked me if I had done business with him. I said that I had.

"Did he ever cheat you?" The competitor asked.

"No," I replied.

"Well," the competitor said, "You are the only one around here he didn't cheat." (This man had called all the others in our line of business.)

I could credit this fact only to having kept a correct balance with my customer at all times, and otherwise to having been open-minded towards him.

Why I was successful in keeping the correct balance with him and not with others I do not know. I was unprepared to deal with the problems associated with customers who are more friendly than usual. I was to find that some such customers have learned to "lean" on their charm by allowing payments to slide until they become too burdensome to pay. I had three such customers. It was not that they set out to cheat me, but that they had developed an easy and careless attitude because people always treated them leniently and did not require them to do what was correct.

In the case of my customers, they had been customers on other occasions and had paid their bills, though always a little late. On the last occasion they had slipped behind further and further. Since they had a history of paying eventually, I failed to send them bills, thinking, "They'll come to pay," or, "I hate to make them think I don't trust them," and, "They're such nice people." The fact was, I really did not know how to deal with them. Their friendliness intimidated me, and it seemed wrong to be strict with them. Searching for the answer, I meditated.

On Being Nice   Spring of 1982

I saw myself playing a role of "being nice" to these customers as if I had an obligation to be nice to people. I then saw that they were people I could not "handle." I did not know how to relate to them to get them to live up to their contracts.

Then I saw that my idea that they had to be "handled" contained a certain arrogance. It was an old point of view I had absorbed from other business people I knew. These people shared the view that you have to "be tough" with difficult customers. Being tough, however, was not my way, so I had fallen back on the weak approach of being nice in the hope that they would be nice back. While being nice worked with disciplined customers it did not work with these people.

Several misconceptions began to emerge: (1) that they had to be handled (which I was unable to do), (2) that I had to "be" something special to relate to them, and (3) that such situations can be handled at all. My *I Ching* hexagrams had mentioned the folly of having "a contrived approach," and that some situations required help that could come only from the Higher Power. I must ask for that help, but I must have no barriers of my own set up in the form of techniques, such as intimidation, being nice, or being firm. I could see that inner firmness was necessary, but that "being firm" was like wearing a suit of armour— heavy, cumbersome, and ineffective. After all, these customers were not adversaries, they were merely indolent, and took advantage of my confusion. They intuitively understood that I was being nice from weakness.

Firmness, I began to understand, was not a matter of hardening myself up from within, or wearing a certain expression, or staying continually on guard against someone.

Firmness comes from erasing any feelings of leniency on our part, any softness, or any feeling that, "Oh well, maybe they can't pay." I also needed to shed desire, or wanting them to pay, because this too was based on inner knowledge of my weak position, and on background fears that I would not get paid at all, and that the situation would not work out even if I did relate correctly to it.

Once I corrected these aspects of my attitude, it was necessary to wait and be guided to the next step in solving the problem. I learned that there were times when I could and should take initiative action.

After more than ten years of consulting the *I Ching* I had only experienced its passive ways of dealing with problems, so I could easily conclude from this that the *I Ching* was totally passive. This is not so. We act constantly on the initiative. We make agreements, go on trips, see friends, and buy things without thought of consulting the *I Ching*, because we do not even think to do so. Initiating action becomes a problem only when we have some emotional involvement in the situation, when fears and doubts have been awakened. Then the *I Ching* counsels non-action and disengagement, to deal with the emotions, doubts, and fears which prevent clarity of mind. When we become free of these elements in our attitude, the correct response is able to break through. Then, initiative action, if it is necessary, is able to be taken. As *The Receptive,* Hexagram 2, Line 2, indicates, we need not plan what to do; the situation holds all the ingredients for its own solution. We need only wait for the right moment for these means to become visible. I learned about initiative action in connection with the problems I had with these friendly customers.

The following meditations occurred over several months. They defined initiative action and helped me understand its limits before I used it. In following this guidance, I found that my problems with these customers were successfully resolved.

Initiative Action   May 7, 1982

In meditation I was brought back to the subject of

initiative action. Up to now I have been warned against taking action, however, I noted that each time I have wished to act, it has been from some level of frustration or feelings of hopelessness. Now it occurred to me that if our attitude is proper, initiative action may be the correct response. Lately, I have received the hexagram *Revolution*, Hexagram 49, many times, with lines indicating that initiative action may be taken, if certain essential conditions precede it.

Chief among these conditions is that we first must have "tried in every way to bring about reforms," without having had success. "Trying in every way," it must be noted, does not mean as determined by our impatient or vindictive inferiors. Any hint of impatience or vindictiveness in our attitude would countermand initiative action. I saw that initiative action is permissible only when there is some degree of receptivity in the other party, otherwise our action is mistimed and we throw ourselves away.

I had also received the second line of *The Receptive*, Hexagram 2, telling me that what I was to do or say must meet the requirements: "Straight, square, great," and, as it is put in *Revolution*, what we do "must correspond with a higher truth and must not spring from arbitrary or petty motives." If, it said, a revolution is not founded on inner truth, it has no success; people will support only that which they feel instinctively to be just. I realized that, after ascertaining that what we require is universally and timelessly true, we must adhere to it with the utmost firmness. If, in the back of our minds we hedge, by holding to the idea that we can always resort to powerful means (leverage, threats of lawsuit, etc.), we lose the way.

Then I saw that initiative action was like walking on the high wire. To keep balanced within we stay close to the sound of our inner voice, listening for when to advance and when to retreat, and how far to go. We keep aware that whenever we move, the dark force is close by, and the ego is ever ready to take over, to press forward ambitiously, to assert itself, and to gloat.

Then I realized that initiative action can never be ideal, for ideal action is arrived at spontaneously, when we are totally detached, yet in harmony with the truth. Then we are surprised by what we say and do, yet in retrospect see that our actions were appropriate.

In order to put myself in position to use initiative action, I first had to become free inside. The following meditation produced the insight that true freedom is to be free of envy—the envy that arises from anger at others' wrong-doings, the envy that arises on perceiving others' easy successes, and the envy that arises because we see others in a better position than ourselves.

On Being Free Inside   May 23, 1982

In meditation I saw feet doing ballet steps, clumsily, because they were clad in steel armour. I saw that if in my heart I were barricaded against other people because of their wrong-doings, I would be unable to move agilely, with the steps of a truly free person.

I saw that the source of my hardness was anger. After freeing my inner gaze from watching three of my customers fail to do what they should have done, I gained the inner freedom to be able to take initiative action and call each of them. On all three occasions I kept tuned to my inner voice, and allowed myself to be guided. What I said was correct, and exactly fit the needs of the moment. Because I was correct, my customers were receptive. Each moved to solve his respective problem. Although the money owing me was not paid in its entirety, most of it was. I chalked up the remainder to the cost of my education.

Dealing With Our Concerns   June 16, 1982

As long as we hold onto concerns, they are burdens. If we can bring ourselves to hand them over to the Higher Power, a solution becomes possible. We turn them over, not because we do not care, but because we care so much, and because we need superior help to deal with them.

Handing them over is the first necessary step to their solution, for so long as we carry the burdens alone, we remain in the vortex of the dark force, where all is struggle and obstruction. We remain trapped in the pattern of hostile events.

Handing them over means we relinquish them totally. If we were to have a mental image, it would be of handing direction of the entire course of events over to the great light, with an acknowledgment that we need help.

Having done this, we wait until it becomes clear what is to be done next. This is only the first step; there are many other steps to take in solving the problem. Each step becomes a vehicle for learning. While we are waiting for these steps to show themselves, we avoid indulging in idle diversions, or listening to temptations to forget the entire thing. By handing over our concerns, we clean the slate. We discard all plans, anxieties, desires, and fears. With the slate cleared, we then come to the barest essentials of what is correct and just .

Having determined what is just and correct, we move forward cautiously as the openings allow. We back up whenever we feel resistance, but without wavering in what we see as essential. Then, we wait with an open mind. We should take care not to allow firmness to become hardness. The war is mainly that of keeping our inferiors dispersed, that we may disperse theirs, and gain their willing assent to do what is right.

Dealing with the public, I was occasionally cheated intentionally. The next meditation concerned leaning on policies to protect myself from being cheated. Normally, before entering a contract with a customer, I had him fill out forms which indicated his financial ability and readiness to enter a contract. If a customer met the terms, it was my policy to sign the contract. The object of the forms was to discover any reason not to do business with that person. While this procedure worked most of the time, relying on it, and similar policies turned out to be unwise. It was not until I learned to rely on the "vibes" people gave off that I ceased having problems with cheaters. Of course, this is hardly a rational policy, but it worked. We cannot say what it is about a person who intends to cheat; we can only say that there is something, and that it is perceptible.

The Woman Who Cheated Me   about 1982

For several days I had been receiving calls from a woman who was a potential customer. Something in her voice and manner on the telephone translated into "bad vibes," both to me, and independently to my son, who happened to answer one of her calls when I was not there.

Having policies, however, I felt I should follow them, even though I had these bad vibes. I felt that if she could meet our terms, I would not turn her down, even though I wanted to.

Filling out the forms, this customer met my policy requirements, but as she left my place of business, I had the sinking feeling that she was stealing my property. That, in fact, was the case. All her documentation turned out to be false.

This experience taught me once and for all to listen to my "vibes," and to go with them, regardless of policies. I made up my mind that henceforth I would turn down anyone, for no reason at all, if necessary, if I felt bad vibes. Once I became firm in my attitude in this way, I was never again cheated by customers.

Determining the Price   about 1978

For a long time I used to dread raising the price of our products and services, even though our costs demanded it.

Every time I raised the price I would have a period of self-doubt over whether or not I had done the right thing, despite the fact that if I failed to raise the price I would be out of business anyway.

I noticed during these periods of conflict that prospective customers often said, "What! That's too high a price," even though competitors would not have such low prices. I consulted the *I Ching* about this, and I was told that my doubt and self-conflict raised doubts in the customers; they were merely responding to these doubts. This proved to be true, for once I ceased doubting my convictions I heard no more such comments. I needed only to set the price at what I needed it to be, then let go of the matter.

On Being Invisible   about 1978

Three young men, prospective customers, came into my office one day inquiring about my business. One of them had a rather engaging personality. The second joined in the conversation some, the third not at all. After they left I was astonished to realize that while I remembered the first and second men, I had not the slightest memory of the third. This was curious, as I usually tried to be aware of people. It occurred to me that some people have a way about them, either consciously or unconsciously, that makes them slip entirely from memory, and so are invisible to us in a manner of speaking.

A week later a regular customer brought his client in to do business with me. There was something ominous about this man. In the ten years I had been running this business I felt he was perhaps the most ominous person I had encountered. My inner voice immediately said quite audibly, "Be quiet. Keep from thinking, say only what business requires, and be neutral. Then he will forget all about you when he leaves." I followed these instructions to the letter. After he left I began to realize that in following these instructions I had become invisible to him just as the third man of the previous week had been invisible to me. This ominous customer would forget about me immediately on leaving.

A short time later I told my daughter about these experiences and about how to be invisible when danger is present. About a week later she told me that on leaving a night class at the University, she was going down a rather dark street to her car when she heard three people running up behind her. Her immediate thought was that they were purse thieves. She remembered what I had told her and decided to be neutral. The first of these young men knocked her purse out of her hand, but halted, as if something were wrong. He then looked up at her and handed her back her purse. The three then ran on. From their looks and shouts to each other she felt sure they had originally intended to keep her purse.

The following meditation was similar in nature.

The Hunter and the Prey   April 27, 1974

I saw a hunter walking along, looking for small animal quarry. Then I saw a rabbit which, on perceiving the hunter, was startled for a moment, but then sat as still as possible. I realized that in being startled for just that moment, it drew attention to itself, but through being as still as possible, it allowed the hunter's attention to be drawn to something else.

Then it came to me that because we follow the way of the Sage, we do not defend ourselves. Therefore, we are sometimes like small animals exposed to hunters. In this case the hunter symbolizes another's ego, which by nature is predatory, seeking to dominate, manipulate, or unbalance us. The only means of protection is to respond by recognizing this fact and not allowing ourselves to be intimidated by it. This is made possible if we keep still inwardly. Even if we so much as anticipate with dread, or become uneasy, we alert the other, just as the rabbit alerted the hunter by being startled. If, however, we continue keeping still, their attention will soon be diverted to something more interesting, and the testing and probing will cease. By not engaging their egos, we may influence them for the good.

Near the end of my first *I Ching* group, which lasted five years, I began to notice that many of those attending had become comfortable, and that the meeting had become a sort of picnicing on the river bank, more about fun than about the *I Ching*.

In the intervening years I had been collecting my occasional insights into the hexagrams and lines of the *I Ching*. Gradually, the collection—kept in a card file with 64 sections—became fairly complete. Friends who were using the *I Ching* began to ask to see my notes, and I could see that their value was not limited just to me. At this point I had the following meditation.

The Out-of-the-Way Train Station   about 1978

I saw that I was holding my *I Ching* group in an old railway station on an abandoned spur of track. The message came, "No one goes there anymore."

This imagery made me realize that running the group was not putting my energies to the best use, and that it was appropriate for me to withdraw. The implication was that I should seek the place where the main railway ran. But where was that? The answer came a few months later in the following meditation:

Grand Central Station   about 1978

I saw Grand Central Station in New York City, filled with people walking to and from all the trains coming from everywhere, and going to everywhere, as in the old days. A magazine stand and book shop were in the center of the station. It came to me that here passers-by could come in and by chance find my collected notes, published as a book.

This meditation made it clear that I must compile my notes into a book and get them into the bookstores.

The Newspaper Center Fold   July 15, 1979

Having been provided with my direction and goal, I began to be attacked by myriad doubts. Should I seek a publisher or publish it myself? If I were to approach a publisher I would need someone—an expert—to vouch for me, to say I knew what I was talking about. Not only did I not read Chinese, I was not a Chinese scholar. Moreover, my approach to the *I Ching* was novel. From all I had read of Chinese commentaries on the *I Ching*, there was nothing like it, nor would there be, since my interpretations were based on my meditations. As for publishing it myself, this seemed to be an enormous undertaking. It would require not only that I put it together and edit it, but that I do all the business of a publishing house, selling and distributing it myself. It began to be apparent from consulting the *I Ching* that this was to be my path, and that one by one the problems would be solved.

In the meanwhile, I must continue to run my regular business to meet the needs of my family.

Time was scarce, so that the final editing was constantly interrupted, and I was plagued with doubts, such as "Assuming I could get the book into bookstores, would anyone buy it?" The *I Ching*, as usual, counseled me not to look ahead, but to continue with the work at hand—to compile the book.

The job proved to be harder than I had anticipated. I seemed to have a continuing battle with the English language. At times the whole prospect seemed impossible.

Finally, one day in meditation, I saw myself opening up a newspaper to the center fold. There, written in large bold letters across the two pages were the words, "YOU CAN DO IT!" This meditation resolved, once and for all, my major doubts about this project. I was simply to take it one step at a time, and not think ahead.

Several years later I happened to be shown the cockpit of a Lear Jet. Looking at the array of instruments, I asked the pilot, "How do you manage all these instruments and switches?" He replied, "You only use one of them at a time." This is always how the impossible is accomplished.

The Gold Bricks   June 1, 1980

After I had received and stored in my garage the first 10,000 copies of *A Guide to the I Ching*, I had the terrible thought, "How will I ever get rid of all these books?" Immediately my consultations with the *I Ching* spoke of keeping company with wrong thoughts. I did not relate these messages to "getting rid" of all those books until I had the following meditation.

I saw myself inside a well-guarded compound which contained a massive building with no windows. Outside and all around were guards. Being permitted to see inside the building, I saw it was full of gold bricks. Indeed, this place was Fort Knox!

Wondering for an instant what this scene meant, it came to me that the gold bricks were my books. They were not something to be got rid of, or given away, but they were my security and blessing, and that I must view them accordingly. From that time on, when I called on book buyers at bookstores I had this point of view.

On Selling My Books (The Princess of Nobodies)
January 9, 1981

In selling my books I did not always maintain the inner independence granted when I remembered the gold bricks. New doubts invariably arose, especially when I experienced a rebuff. After such setbacks I realized in meditation that one of the reasons I sometimes dreaded going out to meet people to sell my book was that I thought I must defend myself in some way. I saw that if I became "nobody" in my own mind, that is, if I detached from any feelings of identity, there was nobody to defend. Then, who was I? Suddenly, I saw myself as the Princess of Nobodies. This struck me with great amusement.

If I am nobody, I will need no defense.

Shall I remember it?

Before I had the following dream, I had momentarily become enthusiastic about creating an Eastern U. S. small press distributing company, because of the difficulty I was having reaching some Eastern markets.

Getting Caught by Diversions   May 13, 1981
(On Distributing My Books)

In the dream, I was walking along a path with my dog Sasha, a Cairn Terrier. Suddenly she ran onto someone's property and got into in a fight. Running to her rescue and grabbing her, my right arm was seized by one of her adversaries, a moray eel, while my left arm was seized by the other, a wildcat. I was immobilized.

I noted that I was not hurt unless I tried to deal with the problem forcefully. I also realized that so long as I held

Sasha, nothing could be done, for she was not free to defend herself. Certainly, with both these predators after her she had little chance, but if I let her go, she could attack one while I dealt with the other. Deciding that was the answer, the dream ended.

When I meditated the dream arose as the subject of meditation. I realized that Sasha symbolized some inferiors to which I am attached as "favorites," which have the tendency to wander off onto by-ways and into other people's yards. That is, they get interested in problems I am not meant to solve. A number of these have cropped up in my thoughts; being connected to them has interfered with my meditating.

For instance, I see a "great" business opportunity that would insure better distribution of my books. Each time I think of this, however, I get entangled in its varied aspects and ignore the fact that a good book is going to get around anyway. All I need do is give it adequate time. My job is to publish really good books. This, more than anything, will insure their distribution. The business idea, I realized, is just a distraction, a side-road into someone else's territory. Obviously, in pursuing this favorite scheme I would get both my hands tied, not to mention wasting time.

In addition to representing my inferiors, Sasha also symbolized my books, which, if left to their own devices, are capable of "biting through" any obstruction they meet as they go out into the world. I need only trust them to handle themselves.

Getting off onto side-roads exists on many levels. I can best succeed by limiting myself to what I can do best, and by not getting involved in so many things. Whenever I feel I am getting enthusiastic about side-schemes, it is time to quit, let go, and return to the path. [Within a year, by the way, a distributor fitting my needs set up shop in Connecticut.]

On Not Fearing Others' Fears   1987

Occasionally I have been asked to do *I Ching* counseling on a regular basis for pay. This has mostly consisted of interpreting the hexagrams received on the client's subject of concern.

On one occasion I saw that the client had some preconceived views that blocked him from understanding his problem, but which I thought would be difficult to bring into the open, both because of his attachment to them and because they concerned a number of fears that seemed to be hidden from him. I was at once concerned about how much I could say.

Consulting the *I Ching* about it and meditating the next morning, I realized I was getting caught up in fearing what my client feared, and that doing this would cause me to condition everything I sid; I would be of no use at all. I needed to remain unstructured and open-minded, cautious and hesitant, but not fearful.

I was also reminded of the *I Ching* principle of "not slaughtering all"; when, during conversation, we uncover an evil element, we should not make it an excuse to discuss other inferior elements. To bring out these other things is to "slaughter all."

The Principle of the Hidden Door   May 20, 1983

I saw myself facing a tall stone wall and understood it to be a wall of obstruction. Wondering about the meaning, I suddenly noticed the outline of a camoflauged doorway in the wall; I realized that I could have passed by it many times without noticing it.

Pondering the presence of this hidden doorway, I realized that our way of viewing things is so habitually logical that we fail to see the principle of the hidden door.

I saw that in looking at those around me, I have judged this person as "habitually improvident," that person as "having a blind spot," another as "too involved in seeing negatives," another as "too parsimonious," and another as "too set in his ways to ever change," and so on. What I fail to do in all this activity is to see the operation of the hidden door, the one factor that often makes a thing possible that otherwise seems unlikely.

The principle of the hidden door is constantly in operation, upsetting our best assessments and preparations. We may think we have everything mapped-out, and well-planned, while in fact, the unexpected controls everything. Good sense and hard work can succeed, but there is no guarantee of this. The most unlikely people turn out to be successful in their work, and people to whom we attach great expectation often fail.

All things being put together correctly, the chances are good for success, but these chances are greatly enhanced if the person putting them together is consistently open-minded about the possibilities of the unlikely. Such an attitude is in harmony with events, for there is always a hidden doorway through difficult situations. Looking for this hidden doorway is like looking at a picture that has another picture hidden within it. The harder we try, the more difficult it is to see it. As for the unlikely, we have to wait until it shows itself to us. It does so obliquely, as it were, rather than directly, happening when we are are not watching for it, but are in an alert and ready state of mind.

The reason things sometimes do not work out as we expect is that we have stopped the hidden door principle by presuming that because some particular outcome is un-likely, it won't happen. It is easy to assume that a 10% likelihood, for example, is really a 0% likelihood. An unas-suming attitude, however, makes it possible for things to work out, in spite of appearances to the contrary. Our attitude creates the possibility, for Fate mocks our atti-tude. The surest way to guarantee ourselves failure is to have the Titanic Complex: to be firmly confident that we have figured out, and accounted for, everything.

Only when we have a free, open, and unassuming mind does the hidden picture appear, the hidden door open. The hidden door holds all the creative potentials in any given situation.

The next meditation occurred several months after I dis-banded my regular business to devote all my time to publishing. After selling my inventory, I invested some money in stocks, not knowing much about the stock mar-ket.

The Pet Snake, a Dream and Meditation October 5, 1983
(A lecture to myself)

My meditation followed a dream in which I had had a pet spotted snake that had turned on me, and in fact, had proved to be dangerous. In meditation I realized that the snake represented my current pet idea that I could somehow figure out a system for investing in the stock market, based on the fact that things work in cycles.

After several experiments and minor successes, my stock broker called to say everyone in his office thought I must have a crystal ball. From that day on I began to lose. My system (pet snake) had proved to be dangerous after all. I had momentarily lost contact with the realization that we need the help of the Higher Power in everything we do. It is arrogant to rely on bright ideas. If I were truly to do well in the stock market, I would have to put in the years of study that every good stockbroker puts in, and develop the experience to sense when it was right to invest and when right to sell; by paying our dues, we also attain the help of the Sage.

It must certainly be a Cosmic rule that nothing comes from nothing. We must put in our time and work. Putting time and work into studying stocks was something I had no inclination to do. Purely and simply I had been gambling, and hoping that because I was trying to do the right thing in general, it would somehow pay off in terms of money. Wrong.

14.

Meditation-Dreams

What I call meditation-dreams are those occasionally vivid and even disturbing dreams I have that seem to press themselves on my attention. Often, on meditating after having such dreams, the meditations explained them. I have already mentioned a few of these dreams in preceding chapters. I have included others in this chapter, along with four dreams by a friend; I consider these last "classic," in the sense that their symbolism is both universal and apparent.

A Friend's Four Dreams

All her life, my friend told me, she loved to dream. Lately, however, her dreams seemed to have turned against her. They had become grotesque, waking her up rudely. One such dream, which was often repeated, was of someone knocking loudly.

The instant I heard this I felt it was a classic "wake up" dream, calling her to wake up to the inner life, and to examine the meaning of life. The urgency comes from the unconscious trying to break through barriers erected by the ego in its confirmed view of reality. The unconscious is trying to say "hear me, listen to your inner voice." Most of us have had variations of this dream.

In another wake up dream she was riding in the open top of a tour bus through Paris, her "favorite city." The trouble was that she could hardly keep awake. She yawned and yawned and had trouble paying attention. Finally, the faceless tour guide came back and said, "If you don't wake up soon you will have missed the whole trip."

The faceless tour guide was, of course, the Sage who appears in dreams as a teacher, wise friend, doctor, background helper, and so on.

For any variety of reasons we may remain somnolent

throughout life and fail to wake up, as the tour guide put it. For instance, we may focus too keenly on the external world as the "only reality," or we may be too intent on pursuing self-affirmation, or recognition by the external world. The pursuit of pleasure, sensuality, diversion, or vanity can effectively block us from the inner life. Similar blocks can be the steady use of tranquillizers, alcohol, or pain-inhibiting drugs, all of which inhibit inner awareness.

In the third dream my friend found herself on the stage, rehearsing the lead role in a play. The problem was that she had been given no script. As she stood waiting to be given her lines, the faceless director insisted that she begin.

"But I don't have any lines," she protested.

"You live every day of your life without any lines," he retorted, "why should you need any now?"

In this dream the director was encouraging her to live her life, to risk going without a script, to react innocently to the day-to-day events without knowing what to say and without planning what to do. He was admonishing her to take a chance, open herself up to the Unknown. This is a great general message all of us receive in dreams.

The fourth dream was more complex, though equally remarkable. In it my friend was riding on a Fifth Avenue bus in New York City when the man sitting next to her began to talk to her, much to her annoyance. He spoke of the wonderful restaurants in New York and their specialty dishes. Because he seemed to be such an authority on the subject, and because the subject particularly interested her, her resistance to hearing him was soon overcome. However, it made her a little envious to discover that when he spoke of French restaurants he spoke in French, and when he spoke of Italian restaurants he spoke in Italian. In fact, it was soon evident that no matter what sort of restaurant he mentioned, he could discuss it in the corresponding language.

Then he asked if he could take her to lunch at a particularly fine restaurant. At first she declined, but thinking of what a great experience it might be, she agreed to go. Getting up to leave the bus, however, she noticed he was wearing high-heeled women's shoes, and was wobbling and turning his ankles as he walked, as if he weren't accustomed to them.

This was too much, she decided, so once off the bus she ran to the corner and crossed over into Central Park where she hid behind a bush. Hobbling clumsily after her, he finally crossed over, but once there did not pursue her. He simply began digging up all the bushes. Thus the dream ended.

Immediately I thought the odd man to be the Sage, since in dreams the Sage is usually an expert, or someone most knowledgeable. His wearing inappropriate shoes symbolized the irony that really good things come in strange and unaccustomed forms. It was clearly his intention to introduce her to some particularly fine food, but in being put off by his unconventionality, she withdrew her trust and decided to hide from him. His pulling up bushes was a statement both that sooner or later the places behind which we can hide from the greater truths of life will all be pulled up, and also that one day she would understand, even though for now she might have resistance to what could lead her to understanding.

His unlikely shoes reminded me of the *I Ching*, which many distrust because it requires being consulted by pennies or yarrow stalks.

I had a number of dreams about tornadoes passing nearby. All seemed to indicate the threat posed by destructive attitudes which had been accepted into the social fabric. I give the following meditation to illustrate how doubt becomes a vortex. I then describe one of my more vivid dreams of a tornado, which showed how individual doubts can sweep destructively through an entire society.

Doubt as Vortex   May 1, 1983

I saw my emotions flowing along as if they were a breeze. Watching, I saw that the breeze, in a moment of hesitation, turned and said, "I must not be going in the right direction, because such and such is not happening?" It looked around to see if what was hoped for was visible. It was not. Then, the breeze seemed to feel depressed, as if it had no cause to continue. Failing to continue forward, the rest of the breeze that followed crowded in upon it, so that the whole became a whirlwind. Swiftly everything got out of control. There were angry threats of executions.

The Tornado Dream July 2, 1973

In this dream several of us (my husband and myself, and two other married couples we had met on the way) were hiking in the mountains and came to an old Victorian-style inn nestled between two ridges near the top of a mountain.

After settling in at the inn for the night we sat on the front porch talking in the afternoon sun. Then I noticed, beyond the nearby ridge in the valley below, three indistinct tornado funnels sweeping up the valley. At their focus on the ground, fire was burning, as if everything they touched was destroyed.

I was quite surprised to see these funnels on such a clear and tranquil day, and I tried to call the others' attention to them. But they were busy in gay conversation, and could not bring themselves to notice some indistinct and improbable thing far off over the hill.

As the afternoon wore on I looked up and saw three enormous funnels coming across the immediate ridge before us. I called to the others to climb under the tables on the porch since it was too late to run for shelter. Everyone did as I suggested and we simply left ourselves in the hands of fate. The funnels passed by, skipping the little ravine in which our inn was located.

The danger past, it became night time. As we all sat wondering what might happen next I noticed, just above the porch roof, two voices and two small pocket flashlights hovering about 30 feet up in the air, as if they were on silent flying discs. One said to the other, "We missed this place."

I then realized that these voices were instigators of the funnels. They now seemed to be planning to start another here where we were. As they left I felt they would be back soon with an apparatus of destruction.

I then asked whether there might be a large culvert nearby and was told there was one about a hundred yards down near a fork in the road. I told everyone we ought to hide there, which we did.

Looking out of the end of the culvert I saw three funnels coming up out of the hotel. It had been destroyed right after we left. Although everyone felt a sense of peril, I felt calm and watchful.

Then I saw an army truck drive up near our culvert. The two people who had started the tornadoes got out and stood planning where they would start the next funnels. When they went off down the fork in the road, I went to the truck and removed the key, then returned to the culvert. When they returned and could not find the key, they panicked and ran off down the road to try to escape the effects of their own misdeeds. Once they were out of sight, we got into the truck, and drove down into the valley where the tornadoes had already been. This was the end of the dream.

In meditation the images of the dream returned. As the meaning unfolded, I wrote it down with a minimum of activity so as not to disturb the meditation process.

The hotel represented our lives in a state of transition. The three couples represented marriages in transition. The number three represented many marriages.

The tables under which we hid symbolized protection granted by trusting the Unknown.

The tornadoes symbolized the destructive effect of having allowed decadent ideas into the social fabric, ideas which particularly threatened marriages.

The culvert was shelter and concealment, through holding our own by keeping still, we stayed out of the tornadoes' paths.

The two instigators with their devices were vindictiveness and insensitivity (moral indifference). The destruction levied was divorce.

Through patience and waiting we were able to capture the key of the vehicle (understand what was happening and correct it in ourselves), and were thus able to leave at the right time and return to our homeland in the valley. Obviously, however, our homes would need rebuilding.

The instigators, being deprived of their vehicle (misunderstanding) were caught up in the destructive force of their own vengeance.

The Dresser in the Wood's House   March 23, 1980

This dream occurred at a time when I thought I should give up on my goal to rescue my marriage. It was now four years after our divorce; I thought I must have misinterpreted the *I Ching* on this issue.

In the dream a friend was cooking dinner for a large number of people. She lacked some ingredient and I said I would go get it for her. This involved going over a hill to another place. As I went along a path I came upon small brush fires starting in three or four spots. I thought they had started because it was so dry. At first I thought, "Oh, they are such small fires, they're insignificant." But then I thought they really should be put out, and began stamping on them and smothering them with sawdust that lay in a pile nearby. In the most active fire I saw a still-burning cigarette and realized the fire had been started by someone's carelessness.

I proceeded on my way, only to find an abandoned building shaded by saplings that had grown up around it since it was last used. It was well-built and still in good shape. Obviously it had stood in a sunlit clearing, but now the saplings were beginning to shade it. If they were not cleared away soon, the building would begin to rot and fall in.

I could see this was a good utility building, like a miller's, for storing grain. Walking through it I saw it was empty, except for an object on the upper floor that was covered with a mover's blanket. Obviously something had been moved into the building for storage. Pulling the blanket off, I uncovered the most beautiful chest of drawers. Made of curly maple, it was fit for a museum collection. Then I realized how important it had been that I had put out the fire. I had not only saved this good building, but the priceless chest of drawers it contained.

I realized right away that the building had to do with my

relationship with my former husband. The chest of drawers was something beautiful and valuable he had within him which he had left behind in this building. The destructive fires were the emotions that eat away our inner perseverance. They are ignited by the doubt that invades when there is no visible progress. Through judging things only on the basis of what we see externally, our perception of the inner reality suffers. To have let the building and chest of drawers perish through leaving my path would have been a shame. Had I done so, my former husband would not be able at some later time to recover that valuable something within himself that he had once developed and left behind here in the wood's house.

The Gold Coins   January 22, 1981

In this dream I was hiking in the Swiss countryside. Suddenly I saw some pennies and a nickel glinting in the sand, so I stopped to pick them up. Then my foot hit something in the sand. Pulling the sand aside, I discovered a metal chest which I opened. It was full of gold coins.

It occurred to me that if I used this newly acquired treasure to luxuriate in a big way, I might get into trouble for not reporting to the authorities that I had found buried treasure. If, however, I spent the coins a few at a time, modestly, I would receive all the benefits of having discovered them.

Contemplating this dream and my strange desire to evade the authorities, I realized that the authorities represented the fate I could incur if I did not respond appropriately. The gold represented the universal truths I had discovered in the *I Ching*.

There was implied a danger in treating the treasure I had found in the *I Ching* with the enthusiasm we feel on discovering riches, or from luxuriating in the riches through becoming self-important and egoistic. A certain modesty and caution was required. If I remained modest and attuned to my inner voice, I would be able to enjoy the benefits of possessing the treasure indefinitely.

This dream reminded me that there is a cosmic rule

against luxuriating.

The Dream of the Little Green Snake   December 20, 1981

As this dream began I was taming a small green snake. At the moment I held the snake by the back of its head. It kept opening its jaws to grab me, but I simply held it firmly out in front of me, rendering it harmless. As I waited patiently, it gradually became quiet and docile. In the meantime I had to pay constant attention to it.

Then I seemed to be coming back from somewhere. I was aware that while I was gone, the snake, which by now had become tame, had been keeping the mouse population down, and was eating black widow spiders, tarantulas, scorpions, and other dangerous things. As I approached the house I called the snake. It came slithering across the grass, just as a dog would. When it got close it jumped up onto my arm as if it were a friend. I did not have to hold it.

After waking I realized that taming the green snake was a metaphor for taming an aspect of my ego. It had now been rendered harmless. The dream had made it clear: if certain aspects of our ego are kept strictly under control, they act as a balancing agent, keeping other, more evil aspects (here pictured as mice and tarantulas) in check.

My first thought on waking, however, was that it was better to endure the threats caused by the other evil things than endure this unpleasant green snake. I would rather be without it!

On the other hand, it seemed important to be aware that I had a green snake, and that I had to discipline and tame it, and then keep on guard so as not to allow it to get out of hand. Once disciplined, it could even be useful. The snake was not poisonous, but a garden type of snake. Also, it was more visible than other, more concealed and evil aspects of the ego, like the black widow spider, the tarantula, and the scorpion.

The Dream of the Smouldering Volcano   December, 1981

The scene was a tropical island. I, and a blond, handsome man about my age, as scout leaders, were leading a troop of small children, showing them the scenery and sights. We were following a well-worn trail constructed for sight-seeing and foot traffic. The trail gradually wound up around a mountain. The incline was slight and the trail short, so the mountain could not have been more than 500 feet high. Shortly, we came upon a ramp that seemed once to have been a corridor. Parts of it were richly decorated, as if it had been a sumptuous older hotel. Then we came to a stairwell which led up a number of flights to another corridor without a ceiling. This part was more like a carpenter's scaffolding that goes around a building, but I could see, still, that it was a ruined corridor.

Then we came to a place where we could look down into what had been the center of a building. It was a smouldering ruin which gave off a stench. Immediately I recognized the stench as sulfur, and I saw with alarm that we were looking down at the center of a volcano that was only momentarily quiet. We had been walking upon the ruined outer walls of the building that had been here before the volcano erupted. Obviously, this was the curiosity, the sight everyone had come to see.

I alone seemed to recognize that our situation was precarious, and the folly of leading all those children to this site. Although I wished to leave at once, the other leader seemed unconcerned and eager to continue. He seemed unwilling to consider that it posed a danger. Obviously he did not think, as I did, that it was irresponsible to continue leading the children on the tour. I therefore presented my view of the danger to the group, and when none took my advice, I retraced my steps and left them all.

After getting back to the point at which we had started in the dream, I found a narrow, rather treacherous path that led away from the scene, and followed it up a ravine, across a small stream that was crystal clear, past some brightly colored rocks (vermillion, pink, and green) that jutted up sharply, so that I could not climb upon them without great difficulty. There also was a question of barracudas being in the stream. This was a treacherous trail, it was impressed upon me.

Making it to the other side of the stream I got my first clear view of the mountain I had left behind. On a far side lava had streamed down to the level of the stream-bed. What at close range seemed to be only a small hazard, in this overall view, appeared to be a much bigger, a monumental hazard. The building which had straddled the site, and upon which everyone was walking, was ready to cave in at any moment.

The meaning of these images began to come to me on my waking. The volcano represented unknown aspects of our natures that can erupt at any time, causing a big stir within our personality. These unknown aspects are powerful, once disturbed. On the move they are dangerous.

For a long time we (we, meaning the superior and inferior aspects of our personality, and the inferior man) feel that we can dally and play with things that might grossly unbalance us. We fail to see the possibilities because we lack an overall view. The other leader of our group represented our Inferior Man, who takes no heed as he leads us to the edge of losing ourselves. He does so even while appearing to be innocent and guiltless (symbolized by his fair-haired, handsome qualities, and by his position as scout-leader).

Having obtained an overall view, I realized that it was necessary to stop dallying around, to stop following the well-traveled roads of consensus and do what "everyone else" did. We need to make the lonely, difficult, even treacherous journey that leads to an overall view. This is, as I am already aware, a road of discipline and self-denial, a road that has dangers which can only be overcome by sincerity.

Leprechaun Dream   April, 1984

While in the hospital recovering from appendicitis, I dreamed I saw freshly-painted rooms with neat, clean woodwork. The walls were brightly colored. One was yellow, another green.

Next, my eye focused into a sighting device with cross-hairs. I found that I was looking through someone else's eye, seeing what it was he had trained the cross-hairs on. No sooner did I look than a bolt shot down the line of sight from a crossbow, hitting the leprechaun, or pixie-like man I had seen in an earlier meditation—the one with black lederhosen, white shirt, and shiny black shoes. He was instantly shot through the chest and killed. At the moment he was shot he appeared to be darting through a doorway out of sight. I barely saw him, but obviously the one handling the bow had seen him, and was fast.

This person, I then saw, was the Black Angel of my first Vision.

I found all this puzzling. When I had seen the leprechaun earlier, it had represented Fate. Moreover, the Black Angel could only see and shoot where selfishness existed. It had not occurred to me that Fate was selfish, although it certainly could be mischievous.

I did not understand at first. Later, when I was talking about it with a friend, clarity began to emerge.

At the time I had the dream, I felt its significance lay in the implication that the mischievous figure would no longer be able to inflict injury on me.

All this, of course, was symbolic. The leprechaun represented Fate's tendency to play tricks, especially when we are leaning on wrong things. Whatever we lean on—plans, strategies, defenses against fate—whatever we are attached to, these are the stools that Fate pulls out from under us.

Some of these defenses have to do with feeling that we must have answers. Then I suddenly realized: we do not have to know. Sometimes we think we must worry about money, to make our money affairs work. The thinking that it is necessary to worry is another of these stools. When we think we must contend, or strive to make others understand—these also are stools. Thinking we must be tough, hostile, alienated, or even good, easy going, nice—all these are secret defensive postures we adopt to protect or advance ourselves, and thus are stools on which we lean.

Where, then, is the heart of our disbelief? In thinking we have to do something—anything. In recognizing that I had been leaning on these things, and that they were at the very heart of my disbelief, Fate, in the form of a leprechaun, had been caught and killed. In removing the heart of my disbelief—the stools on which I leaned—I had killed that aspect of Fate in my life. There would no longer be a leprechaun to pull stools out from under me. The black angel had removed that aspect of threat from my life, and had allowed me to see and understand how it had happened.

On Not Letting Others Off the Hook   about 1984

In this dream I was in a village at the base of a small mountain about a thousand feet tall, that went straight up to a peak and was bare of trees.

Then I saw myself at the window of a house, looking down from the top of the mountain. This seemed strange, because from the village, I had not seen a house. I now looked at the sides of my house, and I could see that it had been carved out of the rock, and that it blended perfectly into its surroundings.

Down in the village, an entire caravan of citizens led by a police car, was making its way up to my house on a little-used road. They seem to know the house was here. Just then a friend came in, asking me to hide him in my house. The police and crowd were trailing him up the mountain.

This friend had grown up with my older son and was like one of my family. I was torn as to whether I should hide him. The crowd climbing the mountain looked angry and determined.

My friend was out of sight and seemed to be in hiding when the crowd arrived with the chief-of-police at its head. When the police chief asked if I were hiding anyone, I replied with a question: "What is the penalty for hiding fugitives?"

Thinking the penalty would probably be insignificant, I was shocked to hear him reply nonchalantly, "Oh, you'll only get life imprisonment."

That was the end of the dream.

I was quite puzzled by this dream, except that it was clear to me that I should not interfere to help others evade the fate they had made for themselves.

That very afternoon I was visited by this friend, who asked for guidance. I had not seen him in months, though I knew he had been going through a crisis. The dream was a warning that while I might help him, I should not lighten his predicament, try to lessen his suffering, or in any way let him off the hook. His suffering was an important pressure necessary to his learning, and to his remaining open-minded.

Ever since this dream I have felt a certain caution about interfering in what other's might be going through. We must be careful *how* we help.

Dream: The Lion   January 4, 1986

I dreamed I went into a small church where I joined a friend. I had no sense of the denomination of this church except that it resembled the country Baptist church I once visited with my country cousins.

I began chatting with my friend, but then I noticed that I was standing in her line of vision with the minister in the pulpit. I stood aside and glanced at him, and I saw that his lips were pursed in annoyance at my interruption. Then I sat down, feeling apologetic for being so unaware and rude.

As the sermon proceeded, I glanced up at the balcony. In one corner crouched a lion, watching everything below. I called to everyone in the church to look up, there was a lion loose up there. As everyone's attention was drawn to the lion, some men got up and went out the back door; I had the impression they were going to shut doors to contain it, but then it disappeared, only to reappear on the main floor.

To my astonishment the lion came straight toward me. At first I thought it was going to attack because it grabbed my hand, but it held onto me, not biting; it let go when I tried to pull my hand free. It took hold of my sleeve, but let go again when I resisted. It seemed to be reassuring me that it intended no harm. Once again it put its paws up and stretched out its claws, then tucked them away again, proving that it was docile and friendly. I distinctly felt, however, that it was entirely wild and free, not a tame lion.

It only became friendly with me because it had decided to. This fact seemed to protect the entire congregation from harm. The lion and I left the church as people kept their distance. The dream ended.

In meditation my attention was drawn to the men who went out the back door. I noticed there was an elaborate ironwork gate and porch there, just outside the main room. It seemed clear that they had intended to close the gate and cage the lion within.

Then it came to me that the lion represented the Creative Spirit and Truth as a wild and totally free thing. Once I pointed out its presence in the church, people were afraid, and tried to cage it in, or institutionalize it, however, we left the church.

I realized that the dream was saying that the lion can be caged, but the spirit of the lion cannot. When the lion gets free we have growth and a return to the Cosmic Order. When the lion gets caged, we see regression into rigidity and the comfort of thinking we know, which only keeps us from learning. We are lucky to be living in an era in which the lion has got free. We must keep the lion free.

Dreams, obviously, are capable of serving many purposes. It is my experience, however, that some dreams are more important than others; they convey to our conscious minds truths known only to our unconscious. They may also warn us of things to come and tell us where we stand in the Cosmos. Often they help us attain a higher viewpoint from which we can perceive the correct and safe path to follow. These unusual dreams are certainly deserving of our attention.

15.

Meditations on Refining Our Attitudes

A number of meditations seemed to have had the purpose of shaping my point of view. By removing small errors of perception, these new viewpoints either solved problems confronting me at the moment, or else helped me understand situations which had puzzled me. These errors in perception either blocked progress or inhibited others from cooperating with me.

First among these is a group of meditations which were on the subject of tolerance. As in all things connected with the *I Ching*, tolerance is taken in a particular context. We neither give up on people nor excuse them. We seek to understand them. We soon find that this involves dealing with intolerance in ourselves.

Extending Tolerance Outward (Or Inward)   about 1975

I saw an image of my oldest son doing something naughty when he was young. My immediate response was to excuse him by saying "He did that because of something that once happened to him."

Next I heard my mother saying something unkind. I noticed that I did not feel quite the same sense of tolerance for her that I had felt for my son.

Then I saw my grandmother doing something wrong and noted that I had even less tolerance for her errors. After all, she should know better.

Next I recalled a time from my youth when I saw a boy stealing my bicycle. How extremely angry and intolerant I felt.

Then I noticed that as my kinship with the wrongdoer decreased, my intolerance increased. Then the thought came, "If you can extend to those furthermost away the tolerance you feel for those closest you, then you will have developed true tolerance."

215

I related this meditation once in a lecture, only to have one of the audience tell me that it was easier for her to be tolerant to those furthest away than to those closest her. She said she was much less tolerant of her children's mistakes than those of strangers. Extending tolerance either outward or inward will suffice.

Tolerance Is Seeing the Great Man in Others   June 3, 1973

I was presented with images of a number of people I knew whose faults inhibited them from having a true and open fellowship with others.

One person's fault was his tendency to regard friends as workers or errand boys for his personal projects; his friends felt like running when they saw him coming because he always had a job in store for them.

Another's fault was to use his friends as a test audience for his slide shows, or other presentations he constantly put together. Another saw her friends as potential contributors to her favorite charitable project. Another saw them as potential buyers for her books.

I realized that viewing our friends as "resources" is a decadent tradition that breeds all sorts of evils and shuts off true fellowship. The problem for me was my tendency to be oppressed by these people's faults, so that it was hard to remember their good qualities.

Then I realized that what I must do was search for that element in them by which they showed real concern for others, and hold that in my mind as a way of remembering and clinging to what was good and great in them. I saw that it is our capacity to recognize in others the very core of their real selves that comprises love. It is the only open door through which we can find them, and it is the only means by which we can support and nourish the good and great in them.

On Achieving a Moderate and Just View of Others
November 22, 1973

It came to me today that in a purely objective sense,

people are only as good as they are capable of being at any given moment. If a person's worst self is the only thing that shows at a given time, subconscious forces (often fears adopted in childhood) are at work, making him less than his true self. Remaining undeveloped, he lacks the means to perceive and deal with these forces. If we are to be truly objective in viewing others' deficiencies and mistakes, we must be patient.

We often see our parents as the cause of our problems, as if they should have had the perception and resources to do better. The fact is, they acted or reacted to the best of their abilities. If they had achieved the correct viewpoint, they would have done better.

Moral deficiencies are always traceable to degraded attitudes, which have their roots in fear and doubt. In Taoism it is said, "a lie is the truth to the liar." If the liar could see things differently, he would not need to lie. All errors of perception are caused by misunderstanding the way things really work. Seeing the truth with clarity is the only thing that gives us strength over our fears and doubts.

Ambition was a frequent subject of my *I Ching* consultations and meditations.

It may be said to be our nature to work towards progress, much as it is in the nature of the child to learn to sit up and walk. Problems beget solutions.

Ambition, however, goes beyond our natural tendency to learn, grow, and find solutions for our problems. Too often, because one is goal-oriented, ambition involves us in a wrong use of power. Being too focussed on the goal, we forget the *I Ching* principle that *how we achieve things is more important than whether we achieve them.*

The following meditations and short essay concern some of the more subtle aspects of ambition. The remedy for every sort of ambition is the same—perseverance when losing, perseverance when winning.

Climbing Mt. Monadnock   February 12, 1974

I saw scenes from long ago when I had climbed Mt.

217

Monadnock, in New Hampshire, with some older friends. As we climbed slowly we were passed frequently by young climbers who were heading straight for the top. I noticed that as they climbed, these young climbers tended to focus on getting to the top of the mountain as soon as possible. My older friends, by contrast, ambled along, stopped to look at a certain family of plants, stopped at a lookout to appreciate the scenery, stopped to sit on a rock or simply breathe in the mountain air, and so on, all the way up the mountain. After getting up the difficult places they stopped to rest for a few moments to renew themselves. When they got to the top their muscles were relaxed and they were in condition for descending, whereas those who had rushed up might have trouble with their muscles for the first few hundred feet of descent.

I saw that this scene symbolized a lifetime. It was a statement that time is the vehicle by which we make progress in our lives and create changes for the good. However, if we are too ambitious, we rush up the mountain as fast as possible and miss the whole point.

By going along patiently and steadily we negotiate the rough places without too much difficulty. We avoid becoming discouraged, and discover something new and different at each turn. We fully appreciate the beautiful views seldom seen.I realized that being too ambitious not only blinds us to great and wonderful things we might see, it wears us out and deprives us of savoring the best parts of life.

Ambition—A Fishlike Blob   February 27, 1974

I saw ambition as a fishlike blob that eats its way in a straight line. Turn its nose in any direction and it goes off that way, eating. It sees nothing, it simply munches as it goes.

I saw it munching its way towards me. I suddenly realized it was going to devour me! At the last second I turned it around and away it munched. I turned it towards the left and saw it munch its way out of sight.

The Wheelchair   February, 1974

I entered the ancient Greek amphitheater I had seen in meditation only a day or so earlier. Its circular stage of black onyx was like a mirror. On the far side the curbing surrounding the circle was interrupted. Investigating, I found a tarpaulin draped over something. When I pulled it off, I saw myself in a wheelchair.

I remembered that on the previous day someone had criticized my way of speaking. To get this person to stop criticizing me, I had made up a story that as a child I had been dyslexic, giving this as a reason for not always expressing myself clearly. To get along I had presented myself as handicapped—a wheelchair case, as the image indicated.

Looking at myself sitting in this wheelchair, however, I realized that this was the wrong way to deal with the problem. I must not sacrifice my integrity or dignity just to get along with people.

Ambition was also the subject of the following meditation, except that in this case ambition exposed me to danger.

Tying My Ship Up on the Beach   December 4, 1973

After a long ocean crossing, I spotted land. Then I saw my ship being tied up to two pylons which jutted out of the beach sand. It struck me that there was something wrong with tying up on an exposed location such as a beach. Even when the Pilgrims landed at Plimouth Rock, they were protected by the great hook of land which comprises Cape Cod. Here, my ship was not protected by land, but was exposed to the relentless pounding of the surf on the open ocean.

However unpleasant it was to think of getting back in the ship and sailing on until a safe harbor could be found, I had to do so.

The message of this meditation was that although land had been found and the ocean crossed, I could not just tie my ship up anywhere. Plenty of dangers still existed, and

I had to continue being cautious and circumspect until conditions were safe and correct. I could not let myself be deluded by desire and ambition to reach the goal.

The Problem With Ambition (An Essay)   April 28, 1989

As I sought more clarity to a question that had been put to me by an *I Ching* follower, an insight followed reading several *I Ching* lines.

The question the man had asked was: "I am out of work and the *I Ching* seems to be telling me not to seek a job. Am I interpreting this correctly?"

It is my experience that often, when a person is seeking to reach an objective—find a job, collect money owed, sell his products, change a price, or ask his superior (parent, teacher, boss, person giving a referral, etc.) for something, he receives warnings from the *I Ching* not to act. We question, does it really mean we are not meant to get a job, not meant to ask the boss, not meant to go out and sell that day?

Usually, the *I Ching* is drawing our attention to the attitude with which we approach doing the thing in question. Before we can be successful our attitude must be correct.

Generally the problem lies in the way we focus on the objective. We have attached ourselves to attaining what we want, the way a child becomes focussed on getting candy, or the alcoholic on getting alcohol. It is constantly in the back of our minds, pushing us on in some way. We may be blaming God for our difficulties, entertaining the thought that God (or Fate, or even an evil spirit) is in some way blocking us. Such contests between our ego and God bring all progress to a halt. Total acceptance is required.

The person approaching an objective needs first to remove it as an objective, much as we approach getting out of bed in the morning as a non-objective: we simply get out of bed. We walk, we answer the telephone, we do whatever is necessary to get on with things without thinking of them as objectives. Before we can get a job or do the thing which has begun to obsess us, we need to make it a non-objective.

Obviously, the physical therapist sets out with the objective of restoring as much movement to a damaged limb as possible. He does not know precisely how much can be accomplished, nor does he focus on that aspect of things. He simply sets out to achieve something, however small, so that even the tiniest improvement is a victory. Thus, by achieving tiny improvements in tiny steps, he often is able to restore more functions than even he thought possible. Above all he de-activates the patient's despair and hopelessness about ever being able to do the big things again.

So it is with getting a job, asking for a leave, selling merchandise, or whatever. The mind must be kept open and unfocussed. There is a general objective, but we condition our mind in such a way that we remain open-minded, both about what is to be obtained, and how it is to be obtained. We allow the Unknown to write the script, and we follow along and deal with each thing that presents itself, with an open mind. This is true modesty.

By concentrating on how to relate to the moment, we allow the bigger problem to be resolved in the uniquely beneficial way of the Creative. If the expected thing does not happen, we do not quit, or come to the grand conclusion that we are a personal failure. We simply go back to the drawing board and look at the situation again. We may then ask if we are allowing ourself to be led. Are we making demands on the Cosmos? Is our pride engaged? Are we angry or frustrated?

We need to be led forward the way a hunter follows a rabbit by catching glimpses of it. We do not know where the path leads, we only know that we are able to follow it.

To a certain extent we act like water flowing on almost flat ground; we flow into a small depression here, fill it up, then flow off wherever the ground dips slightly. We follow the terrain. This total inner independence and openness to flowing wherever resistance gives way, is *the way*.

On Our Ambition to Rescue Others   June 15, 1989

In answer to a question put to me by *I Ching* students, *What does it mean to rescue another?*, a series of hexagrams and a subsequent meditation led me to the following observations:

Rescuing another refers to influencing him to see the light for himself. To see the light means to lift the veil from his eyes, and see things as they really are. This is to achieve enlightenment and understanding.

How do we go about this? Certainly not with ambition. We learn quickly that we are not meant to use power. We must not verbally harangue others, preach to them, or otherwise stand between them and the Sage, blocking the light.

Rescuing another requires that we stand in an invisible position. We do not try to draw attention to ourself. We help by acting and reacting correctly to everything that happens, even though our actions and reactions may be misinterpreted and misunderstood.

This does not mean that we do not say anything. When people are open to us we may state our point of view, but when they are closed, we withdraw. By focusing only on being correct within ourselves, the right things come to us to say.

The fact that we seem to have little chance to interact with another means nothing. We interact with people to whom we have inner ties whether they are near or far, because they are tuned to our innermost thoughts. Seen in meditation these connections appear as buried cables, like telephone cables. If we are clear-minded and correct, they know that, too. If we have doubts, they know that. If we intentionally try to influence them it is only an inner statement of our doubt, which they intuitively understand.

Our effort should be only to keep our thoughts innocent and firmly correct, the way the Sage is firmly correct, but open-minded about us. Little by little, as we find and rid ourselves of obstructions and slipshod elements in our attitude, the other is liberated to be his true self, free of suspicion and distrust. Some of these negative elements include residual annoyances, grievances, fixed definitions of people that imprison them in their bad habits of mind, impatience, loose morality, and selfishness. As long as we have such elements in our attitude, and we lack firmness in our principles, others' suspicion and distrust is warranted. By relating properly, and by selflessly serving the good and the true, we rescue others. Without doing anything on the outer plane, we achieve everything through inner truth. We never allow ambition or other ego elements to influence the situation. This is what it is to be a true servant of the good.

Another group of meditations helped me deal with fear. I saw the origins of fear in experiences from my childhood. I saw how I had been imprisoned by fear in its many guises: doubts, obsessions, defenses, flattery, anticipation. I also saw how fear kept ensnaring me.

Dante's Inferno, or Learning to Endure the Ambiguous
May 4, 1978

I saw the ghost of Hamlet's father; I remembered how Hamlet had felt a chill in the air when he saw it.

Then I saw a scene from my youth, in which an older teenager asked an eight-year-old, "Aren't you afraid?" The eight-year-old looked puzzled and shrugged his shoulders, not knowing what he was supposed to be afraid of. The older one said, "Well, you ought to be afraid, otherwise something might happen to you," as if the younger needed fear to make his perspective correct.

I remembered how others had said such things to me, and I in turn had said such things to others. I remembered feeling intensely that if the younger children lacked the proper amount of fear they would not be cautious and would therefore get hurt.

Then I saw how, in a more ideal culture, an adult might guide a child to be cautious rather than fearful; the child would also be encouraged to keep an open mind. Then, the correct reaction would come to him.

I remembered a time when I was a teenager. A man grabbed my wrist, intending to molest me. I immediately recognized the danger, but was not terrorized by fear. Instead, I spoke to him with firmness, telling him that if he failed to let go immediately, I would call for help. Studying

223

my expression only for an instant, he let go and left. Afterwards I felt sure that because I had not feared him and was extremely firm in my resolve to stop him, he had backed off.

Then a third image came: jagged, yellow sulphur rocks in some inner part of a mountain, like Dante's inferno. I was seeing the lowest level of our minds, in which the most primitive fears, held since childhood, are stored. This tortured part of ourselves continually expresses itself to others in warnings such as, "If you do this, something bad will happen: you will fail in business, have a car accident, fall off a cliff, go to hell," all in an unreasoning way. These fears are a sort of purgatory of the mind in which we are trapped on our road to self-development. Sometimes we are trapped there for a long time. Each fear is a separate trap from which we can be released only by cleaning it out of our inner spaces. Often this requires that we perceive the original image which gave rise to the fear, then come to understand that the fear is really harmless, after all.

Sitting in the Center of One's Chief Fear   June 26, 1978

I saw myself sitting in a semi-circular enclosure. Looking at the floor more closely, I was astonished to see that it was live tissue, as the tissue in a mouth. Then I saw that this tissue was surrounded by a double ring of fine, pointed teeth which slanted backwards towards the rear.

Just as I realized I was sitting inside the opened mouth of a giant reptile, I was suddenly catapulted out of it. Although my instant response was alarm, shock, and repulsion, I was amazed to think I did not feel terror.

I had been in a reptile's mouth, one with jaws about twelve feet wide. At first I thought it was a dragon, but I had not felt hot breath, or been drenched with acidic saliva. I could now see it was a giant snake. I realized, on seeing its languorous eyes, that it was dying.

Then I realized I had been sitting in the center of my foremost fear. Since I had stayed put and quiet, it had been unable to devour me, and therefore it had begun to die. The fear—my chief fear—had been met, understood, and overcome.

The Smiling Face   May 30, 1981

I woke up at 3 A. M., full of ideas about how to accomplish a difficult public task I had accepted. The assembled committee, which was to be my support, had asked, "Now what do we do?"

Off the cuff I had thought of and propounded a preliminary list of things to do. It had been several years since I had done this sort of work; once I was back at home, I began to recall other important things that should have been on my list. Then I began to worry that I might leave out some essential step in the process. My worry continued in a background way for several days.

Now, at 3 A. M., missing steps and procedures came to me in such a clear way that there was nothing to do but get up and write them down. As I returned to bed and began to relax, I remembered other important steps; once more, I got up and wrote them down. When this happened twice more, I began to feel frustrated, so I decided to meditate. I realized that although I was getting the help I needed, there was something strange about the ideas coming to me in this manner.

In meditation I saw a cloud which shaped itself into a face, then smiled the most ironic smile. As I realized it was the Sage smiling wryly at me, I also understood that because I had entertained the fear that I would not get the help I needed in time, the Sage had awakened me in the middle of the night to give me the answers. If I had trusted, the answers would have come to mind as I needed them, without any further problem. Being distrustful and impatient, I was awakened to receive them forthwith.

I could not complain, because the joke was on me. I had asked for this interruption in my sleep.

On Being Obsessed With Chores   March 4, 1973

I saw two engines lined up, one opposite each of my ears. Each was saying, in a robot voice, "Must watch over this,"

"Must clean the floor," "Must paint the ceiling," and similar compulsive phrases.

Then I caught a glimpse of a black thing retreating to hide in a cage. I instantly shot it with an arrow, realizing it had been the one which had set these work engines in motion to drive me compulsively.

Then I understood that the chores would be better done if I just got to them when I could. As for giving them a specific order, what should be done at a given time would come to me at that time. I need not press or harass myself, exhausting my energies in worry and anxiety.

The Fortified Gun Position   about 1976

This meditation came after some adverse experiences had made me defensive: I saw myself standing in a fortified trench behind a machine gun, waiting for the next "enemy" to approach.

Then the authoritative voice I knew to be the Sage said, "Get out of the trench, and abandon the defenses." This command made me apprehensive since I imagined how, if I stood out, I would be exposed and no doubt shot. Nevertheless, I did as I was bid. To my surprise, after standing out in an exposed position for an entire minute, I had not been shot.

Then the Sage said, "As long as you defend yourself, you cannot be defended. If you will abandon your defenses, I will defend you."

Flattering Elements Hindering Deliverance
March 12, 1974

This meditation was in response to an *I Ching* reading, *Deliverance*, Hexagram 40, Line 3, counseling me to find the "flattering foxes hindering deliverance." Then I heard the words, "Why bother, you won't succeed anyway." I took this oppressed thought to be one of the flattering elements, although I did not understand how and why an oppressed thought such as this should be flattering.

Then I saw that I stood behind a rusted trap door that

opened into a tube. The tube was suspended in the air ready to be connected with a similar tube which was being extended towards it. These tubes reminded me of the way two airplanes meet to transfer fuel during flight. But then the door which opened into my tube closed.

I saw that the whole apparatus symbolized two people extending themselves tentatively towards each other to make connection. Then the words came, "Even a small connection is better than none."

Then I remembered my *I Ching* counsel to remain open and accessible to others, in order to accomplish something. The door from my apparatus had closed just at the point of making a connection, after I heard the words "Why bother?" I then saw that doubt had given me an excuse to avoid the risk of being open-minded; I could relax back into a comfortable indolence in which the Unknown was no longer a threat. This doubt had been a flattering element, securing me from risk.

Then I saw that connected to this doubt was another flattering element—pride. Pride had caused me to remember all the other person's transgressions that had led to my saying, "Why Bother?"

Meditation on Anticipating   January 9, 1981

This meditation preceded a lecture I was to give on the *I Ching,* and had to do with the dread and anticipation I had built up.

In meditation I saw the sun low on the horizon, as if on an arctic landscape, except that there were telephone poles, which showed that normally the place had a temperate climate. The wind was blowing up mounds of snow. I thought of the sun rising higher in the sky day by day as spring approached, and of the returning power of the warm light force overcoming the cold dark force. This, I saw, was also how the power of truth and light steadily and slowly rise to overcome the dark, icy power of falsehood and fear.

Then I saw myself at the top of a mountain, about to ski down. Not being a good skier, I usually gasp in anticipation. The bottom of the mountain represents safety to me.

227

Then it came to me that the skier's mogols are like steps down the mountain, and that while I had been looking at skiing as a flight down the mountain, full of risks, the skier does not look at it that way. Each turn or diagonal is a step which enables him to break and control his speed. He does not focus on anything but the step at hand.

I remembered when I was young, living in a town where nobody skied. One Christmas, my older brother got skis. As soon as it snowed he went to the top of "playground hill," which was very steep, and skied straight down. That became my image of skiing, and I now realized that this conception was wrong. Skiers stair-step down a mountain rather than flying straight down.

Then I saw myself at the bottom, looking back at the mountain after having stair-stepped all the way down. An expert skier sped by me heading straight for the lift. Having completed his descent, he did not even look back at the feat overcome; he headed back to do it again. Obviously my outlook was all wrong about this.

Then I saw myself at the head of a room, giving my lecture. I had the same sense of being at the top of the mountain, gasping in anticipation at what lay ahead, with the end as a place of safety. Then I realized that if I ceased looking at it in its totality and saw it, instead, as stair-stepping from one set of essential points to another, all would progress harmoniously.

Doubt—the Dark Force   about 1975

It came to me one day in an astonishingly simple and straightforward way that doubt is an active rather than a passive force, and that once engaged, doubt acts as a vortex. Once we touch its outer rim, we are swiftly pulled into its whirling center.

We cannot miss this effect when we play a tennis match. A bad shot or error can spark doubt. Within moments confidence is shaken. As we anxiously seek to re-establish our shots, our whole game crumbles.

When we listen to a seedling of doubt it swiftly grows into a jack-in-the-beanstalk, opening upon dangerous new worlds overnight. Despair and doubt of our children sends them reeling in confusion and endless self-examination. This does not mean that we should have unfounded confidence in them, or in ourselves, or our situation; rather, it is important to deprive doubt of its destructive energy. We do this by being neutral.

Doubt is an active, destructive force that obtains its energy from the credence we give it when it first enters our minds. When we resist doubt and resolutely fight it, we deprive it of its destructive power.

The following meditations concern the way emotions keep us from seeing things from the Cosmic perspective, how they collapse our will to go on by erecting obstacles in our relationships with the Sage and with other people, and how they decrease our inner strength and power. Chief among problem emotions are nostalgia, letting loose our temper, pride, wanting, and all forms of inner dependency.

On Being Dominated by Memories   February 27, 1974

I saw a fenced enclosure in which a Shetland colt had worn a path all along the fence line. He had eaten all the grass on each side of this path but because he kept looking at the grass outside the fence, he failed to notice that the center of the pasture was full of grass. I saw that something in his point of view gave him this limited perspective, and shrank his possibilities.

I saw that this was an analogy for what happens to all of us. Our perspective either opens up possibilities or shuts them off. Pictures in our minds define what is possible or not possible to do. To a great extent these pictures create our reality.

We may have in our minds a veritable scrapbook of negative experiences from the past which no longer apply, but which, because we have never gotten rid of them, dominate our point of view. Valid or not, we need to clean them out. They clutter our inner spaces and keep us from seeing things from a fresh perspective, and they keep us from seeing others' potential for good. By imprisoning us in negative attitudes that affect our physical, mental, and spiritual well-being, they spoil our enjoyment of life.

On Losing One's Temper   June 27, 1984

When we lose our temper with another person we give them power over us. In evaluating the situation we should not overlook the possibility that the other person may have sensed the issues on which we are vulnerable to losing our tempers, and have brought them up so as to gain the upper hand. We can recover from such losses if we relate properly to the situation.

We lose inner power whenever we disappoint ourselves, for this kind of disappointment creates self doubt. Also, failure to maintain emotional independence makes us uncomfortable, so that we strive to restore the losses incurred. The *I Ching* counsels us to be content with slow progress, and to be free of ambition to restore lost comforts or lost positions of strength and influence. By remaining indifferent to the uncomfortable situation, we will see it straighten out by itself, and we will regain our inner independence and inner power.

Wanting, How it Leads to Pride   July 9, 1983

My lesson of the past days had been on pride which, like a Trojan Horse, enters softly by way of wanting, to become a full-fledged tyrant. I saw that the mechanism of pride is subtle and starts with wanting.

The first consequence of wanting is ambition to acquire the thing wanted. The second consequence is that our wanting is perceived by others on the inner plane for what it is, a loss of inner independence and weakness. Losing inner independence, we also lose our influence on others, therefore progress halts. The disappointment we feel on seeing that things are regressing is soon transformed into hurt pride because we see that what we want is not yet attainable. Hurt pride further isolates us, since others feel our growing disappointment, and our resulting hardness and vindictiveness. Because we think we have been pursuing what is right, we become angry at the Cosmos for not cooperating. This isolates us from Cosmic help. Because we feel vindictive about the Cosmos, our pride prevents us from asking the Unknown for help.

To return to the path it is necessary to give up pride and anger. Clarity is to see that *wanting* is the culprit that led to pride, then anger, then giving up. In such circumstances the only thing to do is to hold to the power of truth and ask for help. Sacrificing anger and pride is essential. Then clarity will come. The next thing is to be on guard against more wanting.

We also need to be aware that we often get into such situations through being tested by others who are envious of our inner independence. Their testing may take the form of bad behavior. If we allow ourselves to be disturbed by their testing, or if we are tempted to give up on them as hopeless, we become entangled. The remedy is to let them go, and rid ourselves of any wanting which would damage our inner independence. Inner independence is all-important to making progress in our relationships with others.

More on Wanting   July 15, 1983

In connection with my lesson on wanting, the following experience made me see that wanting begins with "looking aside," "looking ahead," or "sizing up the situation."

I was picking wild black raspberries. As an experienced berry picker, I like to think I can recognize the difference between "just berries" and those special few which are tremendously sweet and delicious.

Every time I spotted one of these exceptional berries I noticed my interest quicken, but that day it was my luck that the berry in question would fall into the deep grass, or into the poison ivy. Every one seemed to escape.

Since I was losing only the special berries I began to realize that I was being taught a Cosmic lesson. My particular brand of avarice was turned on by the merest hint of something I had sorted out as particularly desirable. To cure my wanting I needed to deal with this sense of the particular, and turn it back into "just another berry," to keep from being drawn off balance. Certainly, many things are special to me, but it is my *attachment* to their being special that pulls me off course.

Even More On Wanting   September 7, 1983

It occurs to me that we must be terribly resolute against wanting. This powerful emotion is always ready to insinuate itself into our thinking and rob us of our inner independence. Even when we think it is not there, we need to assume it is lurking in the shadows.

If we find ourselves snapping at people, impatient, or annoyed, wanting is probably the hidden cause. We want someone to "be better," so he will relate better to us. When he is not, our disappointment surfaces as annoyance or impatience. Worse, we may give up on him, becoming hard as nails because our pride is activated. We then may vehemently deny having wanted, or having believed in the other. Vehemence betrays our desire.

Wanting is perhaps the most natural human emotion. It seems to be in our nature to want things such as human companionship and comradeship. People, however, will prove difficult, not ready for a free and open friendship. We must therefore resign ourselves to walking the lonely path, and thus deal with our inevitable wanting. If we are to have freedom from regret, we must learn to bear with people even though we may not join them in a free and open fellowship until they relate properly to us.

Still More On Wanting   November 22, 1988

Wanting sometimes is so elusive it may take weeks of introspection to detect. I have just discovered that wanting things for my granddaughter—a good education, good habits, a good life—is a problem because it is a form of doubt of her. She already is what she needs to be within herself if I will just open my eyes to that fact. My wanting is also a form of doubt of the Cosmos—that the right things will happen for her.

My doubt resulted in an anxious supervision and in anxious urgings, rather than a calm acceptance of her, and a calm confidence in her natural propensities. As a consequence, I was having the opposite effect to what I sought, and I was forcing her away from her natural ability to point towards the good and the true. How subtle is wanting, and its destructive effects.

Wanting as a Negative Principle   September 8, 1983

Oppressed in a golden carriage, a line from *Oppression (Exhaustion)*, Hexagram 47, means to be imprisoned in the inner workings of a negative principle: in this case, wanting. We cannot get free of wanting until we realize with clarity that like hope and fear, which produce each other, wanting and doubt produce each other, and keep each other activated.

When we have done everything we think we ought to do and what we want is not forthcoming, wanting activates doubt. Doubt, in turn, intensifies wanting. As these two attitudes chase each other our view becomes narrower and narrower until we can see nothing but the hopelessness of the situation.

Intuitively we understand that doubt and impatience prevent success, but because of the strength of wanting, we continue to strive, push, and contrive. When we fail, we feel pride and anger—the more dangerous operations of vanity. What a villain is wanting!

To free ourselves from the oppression caused by wanting it is necessary to return to acceptance and dependence on the Unknown, and to give up inner resistance. To disengage, it may be necessary to ask for help from the Higher Power. Often we need to realize that having the subjective feeling of being helpless against the power of our emotions is the work of our ego. We need to let the ego know that we are resolute to carry on.

On Controlling Our Heart   1988

If we can control our hearts, we can control our world. The emanations of our heart influence all those with whom we have inner connections.

People are able to take advantage of us and abuse us if we depend on their having good will towards us. They intuitively recognize our dependency and exploit it; it is important to reach and maintain inner independence. We need to shun the weakness of needing another's good will. If we can keep disconnected and independent, not caring for their good will unless it be based on truth and justice, then our feelings will begin to mean something to them. By being too free and easy with them, instead of reserved and disinterested, we foster insolence and injustice. We can give of ourself freely only to those who are honest and just with us, and who meet us halfway.

Several of the following meditations concerned nourishment in the sense of the ideas we entertain. Of particular concern are thoughts which lead to the danger of giving up our path—wanting, wondering, and worrying.

Winged Seeds (Developing Ourself is Our Destiny)
January 18, 1974

We are like a matrix, upon which ideas and images, like winged seeds, light and take root. Whether they do so is a matter of choice.

Within the matrix of self lies dormant an idea that was always there, waiting to be given birth. So long as the matrix of self is occupied with images received from the outside, the one image that is distinctly ours cannot develop.

When we clear the matrix of self of all the extraneous ideas received from without—images of what we are, or what we ought to be—the Cosmic image of us is able to flourish.

What We Feed the Pig (Nourishment)   May 23, 1974

I saw a bucket of swill being poured into a trough. Then I saw a pig with a voracious appetite eating nearly anything set before it, including half-rotted garbage.

I saw other images of pigs—contented pigs lying lazily in mud, pigs rooting among the leaves in the forest. Then I remembered the terrible smell of the pig farm in the nearby town. I remembered that a woman who knew something about pigs had said that pigs which are fed good food do not have a bad odor, and pigs which are kept in good conditions are not dirty. How pigs are depends on the people keeping them, and what their keepers give them to eat. I remembered Iowa farms where pigs were kept in large open places and fed corn; the meat from these animals was far superior to the greasy pork produced by swill feeding.

As I wondered about the significance of these images, it came to me that human beings, unlike pigs, have a choice of what they take in as nourishment. They also have a choice in how they keep themselves. I saw a huge garbage pile of decadent traditions and ideas, and people carting this material home and surrounding themselves with it, like rats at the dump. I saw that I must be cautious and thoughtful about what ideas and images I allow in as inner nourishment. I must make sure that this nourishment is always wholesome and good, and that I accept nothing from the garbage pile of decadent, flattering, and seductive ideas.

Looking at Hurtful Things   June, 1977

In meditation I saw that looking at evil was like looking directly at the sun; it is too bright, and it damages the eyes. Similarly, looking at something hurtful damages the spirit and our way of seeing things.

I then saw a curtain coming up over the scene, closing it off. I perceived that the curtain was a sort of inner eyelid, like those that reptiles have. These inner eyelids separate the reptile from the outer world and allow them to sleep, yet also to awaken when things move.

While it is necessary to acknowledge bad things that happen, it is necessary, afterwards, to close off viewing them with our inner eye. In this way we avoid the harm that comes of dwelling on others' bad behavior. Acknowledgement, combined with disengagement, enables us to keep our inner equilibrium, and to respond appropriately to events.

Do It Yourself   July, 1978

It is a flattery (*Deliverance*, Hexagram 40, 2nd Line) to think that someone else is going to develop us. We can skip no steps in this work. No one will do it for us, not even God. We must undertake the discipline of correcting ourselves. To think otherwise is as the first line of *Enthusiasm*, Hexagram 16, puts it, "to boast of aristocratic connections."

A Sealed Hull   December 1, 1979

I saw myself in a ship in which water was pouring through gaping holes in the hull. Then I saw that the negatives of doubt and uncertainty are like an ocean, and that focussing on them as if they were a primal concern, in order to be prepared for things to come, is like having holes in your ship—you are open to their negative effects. Not focussing on them is like having a sealed hull that rides on top the waves.

It is dangerous to our inner independence and stability to focus on bad news—the ups and downs of the stock market, events in the Middle East, the nation's capitol, or whatever, in an effort to anticipate every turn and twist of Fate. Without scrutinizing the negative things which happen in the world, we inevitably become aware of them in this age.

The best defense against whatever Fate has to offer is a strong, cheerful, persevering, and determined attitude. Maintaining such an attitude, we are guided past dangerous reefs and shoals by the unseen hand of our Cosmic friend, the Sage.

Wanting Approval of Our Family and Siblings
December, 1980

This meditation explained why I wanted my relative's approval of my book, *A Guide to the I Ching,* which was published that year.

I saw a monkey on my back. Like the slang expression, the monkey on my back clung tenaciously in spite of my trying to free myself. When it wasn't clinging, it was flying through the trees in great sweeps and leaps, showing off its wonderful skills and daring. I realized that the monkey symbolized my childish need for approval from my peers.

Seeing that wanting others' approval was like a drug addiction helped free me of "the monkey's" tenacious clinging.

Perseverance and maintaining our inner independence are keystone principles of the *I Ching*. These two attitudes, more than any others, engage the helpful power of the Creative.

Once we have engaged the Creative we need to realize that time is the means by which it accomplishes things. To benefit all, the solutions often follow a convoluted course, requiring one thing to be accomplished before another. In the meantime we must adapt ourselves by learning to wait, free of doubt and desire, in total inner independence. Waiting correctly is the meaning of perseverance.

The following meditations helped me understand the meaning of persevering, and maintaining our inner independence.

On Countering Oppression   May 6, 1976

I saw parts of meditations in the past which reminded me that if I left matters to my inferiors, my inner organization would soon be in disarray, and my work would fail.

I saw General Kotusov of the Russian Army, fighting Napoleon. He was in hiding, waiting for the forces of nature to turn the war in his favor. I was reminded of his dispirited men who had just lost the battle of Borodino, and that it had been necessary to leave Moscow to the enemy.

I saw General Washington, whose ragged troops had neither money, nor food, nor decent clothing. In spite of all difficulties, they did not give up.

Then I saw that at the low moment in any struggle the

cause must seem hopeless, but that times change, always in favor of those who persevere in a just cause.

It became clear that attaining a broader and longer view of things frees us from the despair that arises in the dark moments of our journey, when our task seems virtually hopeless.

Timing Is Everything   January 23, 1979

I saw a field of ice about two inches thick, nearly impossible to break up with an ice chipper. Then I saw myself and my son painstakingly breaking off little sections. Precisely when the temperature reached 33 degrees F, the ice began to soften and break off in large sections. The message became clear that a little chipping at the right time has a big effect, whereas a wholesale assault on the problem, when the conditions are unsuitable, has very little effect.

This meditation was a warning to work with the conditions and concentrate only on the essence of the problem at hand.

I also got the fourth line in *Limitation*, Hexagram 60, which counsels not to strive against the object, but to work with it, as for example, "the limitation by which water flows only downhill."

On Not Presuming On Your Luck   July 24, 1979

I saw myself entering a run-down place in a depressed part of New York City. I went upstairs into a room that might have been used for meetings. It had little furniture and no comforts. It seemed I might be living there. It was quite depressing.

Then I saw myself in a small garden in a courtyard outside this building. The garden was lovely, with many strange and colorful plants. It was a surprising contrast to the area.

Then the meaning came that we should not expect things to remain the same, or to take for granted what we now have. We should not expect good things to happen, or that things will happen the way we want them to. We may work hard, have luck, or fail to have it. We must always be ready for changes, either for the worse or for the better. Then our character has meaning.

I also realized that the garden was a message: no matter what happens, I carry my own inner garden within me.

The Booby Trap   January 26, 1981

Last night I watched a television show: in it the hero's job was to defuse various types of bombs which had fallen on Britain during World War II. In the latest episode a new type of bomb had been booby-trapped so that it could not be taken apart without killing the person attempting to defuse it. By a slim chance, however, one bomb, in falling, had broken apart without exploding. This enabled the British to discover the nature of the booby-trap.

In meditation I saw myself trying to defuse this bomb and figure out how to take it apart.

Then I remembered that the day before I inadvertently had been drawn into a negative situation in which I failed to remain disengaged, and that I had been disappointed with myself.

I then realized that whenever any challenging situation arises, it is by nature a booby-trap which we simply cannot figure out intellectually. Only by the merest chance can we discover the secret by which that given situation is rigged. Even then it is dangerous to handle. The only way through such a situation is to keep still within and listen. If this does not appear to work we should not stop listening, but accept each twist and turn of the situation, greeting the ups and downs with acceptance, while keeping alert and detached. In this way we will find our way through the maze and surmount the difficulties.

How we see things very much influences our ability to wait in the correct attitude. The next two meditations concern the effects of seeing things from a dark point of view, and the way indolence traps us in "standstill," the state of "no progress."

On Not Taking Someone's Advice to Give Up the I Ching
February, 1981

I perceived myself taking a dim view of people, their prospects, and their paths. I also saw that I tend to take a dim view of events when I listen too much to the radio or become too involved with what I read in the newspapers. I saw these dim views as black photo-negatives. I saw that mentally I could rinse the photo-negatives in a rinsing solution that returned the film to clear, so I took all the dim views of people I could think of and put them into this solution.

Then I thought of a dim view another had of me. A member of my family had asked me to "give up the *I Ching* for a month or two." The implication had been that it influenced me too much. I thought of Confucius's comment near the end of his life: if he had twenty more years to live, he would spend it studying the *I Ching*, "so as not to make many mistakes." I thought of the *I Ching*, a book that in its potential for good balances all the poor and bad books of the world with all their potential for evil. I felt lucky to be influenced by it. To extend tolerance to the person who had suggested I give it up, I washed his negative point of view in the rinsing solution.

The Indolence of Disbelief (Meditation and Essay)
January 30, 1981

At the opening of a computer museum a professor-inventor demonstrated a "turtle," a device he had programmed to roam around within stated borders, creating paintings. It had been given all the "knowledge" of color design principles, along with certain random qualities so that it created a totally new painting each time it was set to work. This demonstration very much interested the engineers and scientists present, as an advancement in what they then knew of robotics.

Entering meditation I saw this turtle roaming around, making paintings. Then I saw a miniaturized robot about half the size of a mouse traveling down an esophagus, into

240

a stomach to "look at," diagnose, anesthetize, cut out, suture, and otherwise treat an ulcer. I saw it then proceed down the length of the intestine, giving a running account of every defect it "saw." It came to me that one day robotics would be part of the medicine of the future, and be used in many other technologies as well.

Just as I thought how wonderful, indeed, are such products of the intellect, I realized they were but shadows of the ability and power of the Creative (Sage), which has means far more subtle and powerful to heal, create changes in conditions, and correct injustices, if we will but see from the perspective of the higher self instead of from the perspective of the intellect alone. I saw that the difference between these two perspectives was that the higher self solves problems by modifying behavior, while the intellect solves problems by using devices, inventions, and remedies by which things are made to work together.

From birth we are trained to contrive solutions. We ignore and deny the ability of our higher self to gain access to the Creative power. Nevertheless, this ability is certainly the source of our really great advances, which usually occur by chance, when all other methods and means have failed.

Because we do not usually have a steady way to gain access to the Creative, we tend to see breakthroughs as a fickle sort of luck, too unreliable to wait for, or depend upon. That we are capable, time and again, of connecting with this luck through keeping ourselves empty, is too simple, and eludes most people. As a result, we tend to settle for manipulations and contrivances. Thus, devices such as robots may do in medicine, for instance, what we could do through meditation, without striving at all. This tendency to settle for less came to me as *the indolence of disbelief.*

The tendency to approach life as something to be "overcome," a battle to be fought, a race to be run, is to be caught in the indolence of disbelief. This indolence is based on accepting the dark view. So long as we accept this view, it has an inertia that seems impossible to overcome. Held in its grip, we cannot see other possibilities.

The ingeniousness of the intellect is like the light of the

moon when compared to the greater light of the sun. The bright viewpoint of the higher self begins when we start to exclude and suspend all forms of doubt. This view enables us to perceive the myriad possibilities that lie beyond the fantasies and contrivings of intellect. To connect with it we need first to disengage from the dark view in which we have become submerged. We have to break out of the indolence caused by disbelief.

Consider the nature of disbelief. We look at and listen to every sort of dark observation in our media. The way we use language reflects these dark views. Thus, the man who commits murder is not described as one who murders, he is presumed to *be* a murderer, as if murdering is inherent in him. Similarly, the person who lies *is* a liar, and receives the sentence of hopelessness that goes with this identification. The alcoholic is, in the words of Alcoholics Anonymous, "always an alcoholic," as if once inflicted, his condition is hopeless. In the dark view people are incapable of change; at best they can only contain or control their behavior.

In the smaller affairs of private life we look at people as rude, selfish, perpetual complainers, or gossips. In labelling them we place barriers between ourselves and them. To hold our minds open requires a certain effort to break through the contentment we have in viewing people darkly. This contentment is the essence of the indolence of disbelief.

To see from a light perspective means that we stop seeing from a dark perspective. We become aware of the negativism of seeing things as fixed, hopeless, and irreparable.

We can test this for ourself. The next time we suffer internal pain, instead of seeing a "problem" in our kidney, for example, we look at our kidney, or the affected area, with light. We let the light of our looking flood out all negative, dark images. Gradually, we will experience a cessation of pain.

On noticing people behaving negatively, we should look at them with light. This creates an empty space into which creative possibilities can pour. Once we are free of negatives we act as a mirror of inner truth, enabling others to see themselves as they really are, not just as their egos trump themselves up to be. Initiating the Creative power, we also become its instrument. Then what we say and do is totally spontaneous, and suitable to the situation.

Similarly, instead of thinking about the high price of oil, or taxes, we can flood out these impressions with light. It is one thing to notice the high price of oil, or taxes, it is another to allow our inner light to be dimmed by the inertia of disbelief. It is important to notice wrong things, then to sacrifice our wounded responses, then to take the remedial action of flooding the scene with light.

There is such a thing as attracting and keeping luck. In the dark view there is no such thing as luck. So long as this view prevails these things are true. Indeed, luck cannot be attracted or harnessed by our intellect. Through calculating we cannot attract it; by measuring the amount of good gained by luxuriating in luck's benefits, and expecting it to continue, we cannot hold onto it. Selfish aims always thwart it. It is truly a free spirit that comes only on very specific terms, for it follows the way of the Cosmos. Luck is drawn by a humble, accepting, and persevering attitude. It really does come when we least expect it; that is, when we are free of expectation.

In the light view the right things will come at the right time. If we are in the middle of a shocking situation, the dark view pronounces it to be a bad or tragic circumstance, or a loss that cannot be recovered. In the light view it is seen as the only means by which we can learn something, or become freed of an obstruction to receive something of enormous value. In the light view everything is as it needs to be.

To see a thing as bad is to be mired down in the dark view (see *Shock*, Hexagram 51, Line 4). If nothing is happening, we need to be alert and open-minded to what will come. It is the dark view to be either apprehensive or over-confident. These attitudes make us too unstable to see creative opportunities until it is too late. If we are trapped in indolence, we remain afraid of taking the risks that accompany opportunities. If we keep the bright view, the difficulties that exist in every new beginning will clear away, and luck will bless our efforts. If we stop to luxuriate, indolence sets in again. When things go well the intellect steps in to say, "I did it." This arrogance chases luck away.

Luck is also chased away when disbelief returns in the form of not wanting to expose ourselves to any further risks. We chase after security, and thus keep real security at a distance. Indolence causes us to hedge against the Unknown, yet so long as we remain open-minded, luck comes again and again.

The power of the Creative is such that human beings are in the most dangerous spot when they think they have perfected their security. We need only remember the Titanic; it was titanic ambition and titanic presumption that sank it. To think that the engineers could outwit chance elements and the powers of the Unknown! No doubt similar realizations caused Lao Tzu to write:

> As for holding to fullness,
> Far better were it to stop in time!
> Keep on beating and sharpening a sword
> And the edge cannot be preserved for long.
> Fill your house with gold and jade
> And it can no longer be guarded.
> Set store by your riches and honor,
> And you will only reap a crop of Calamities.
> Here is the Way of Heaven:
> When you have done your work, retire!

When we attain true acceptance and freedom from the indolence of disbelief, risk no longer appears as risk, uncertainty as uncertainty. The light view obscures and finally obliterates risk and uncertainty. When we have perfected the light view of life, our view coincides with the Cosmic Will. Without effort, all we do is in harmony with the Creative and the good. Life is then what it is meant to be, and this life of light will endure even beyond life.

The following two meditations did not exactly fit into any clear category. The first seemed to be about a number of seemingly unrelated issues, each of which was based on the same habit of mind, and which had the same solution. The second explained what every student of the *I Ching* wonders: why it is necessary to go through so many difficult and painful experiences to learn the higher truths.

A Meditation About SeveralThings   January 7, 1979
(My Comrades Are Envious)
(Talking Indiscriminately)
(We are Not Obligated to Answer Envious Curiosity)

Before meditating I had received hexagrams indicating that I had dangerous habits of mind, and also a line from *The Ting,* Hexagram 50, Line 2, which said "my comrades are envious, but they cannot harm me."

Meditation began with perceiving that I was talking indiscriminately, answering questions that should not be answered, saying things I really ought not say, and talking about things on which I had intended to be discreet.

Why, I wondered, do I seem unable to have the degree of reserve and hesitation I know to be wise. A part of my problem, I realized, came from my old habit of thinking I ought to be outgoing; another came from feeling intimidated by people's wrong questions.

Then I thought about the line mentioning envy. I seemed to be intimidated by people who asked questions of envious curiosity, as when they asked how much inventory I had.

Then I remembered a lesson I had had about "playing down" to another player in tennis because she had not yet put her game together. The *I Ching* had called my attitude "magnificent," implying that I was arrogantly playing God by sparing her the cost of learning through her own efforts, and by assuming she could not do better.

Then I saw myself sitting in meditation, trying to reach the light, which for a time was obscured by clouds; gradually, the clouds cleared and the light appeared. revealing the Sage on a little hillock sitting on a throne. At his feet were three pots of gold coins, which I understood were for me. (The coins symbolized wisdom, each one being the fruit of an *I Ching* lesson.) Then I understood that the gold, like knowledge perceived intellectually, had no meaning or use until I put the lessons into practice. Then I would have the joy of possessing them.

Then the question of talking indiscriminately came to mind. The Sage, I realized, does not talk indiscriminately to me. Indeed, no words were spoken. I saw and understood, as if I had been spoken to.

I then remembered the light being obscured at the beginning of meditation. Just as it takes effort to acquire the help of the Sage in meditation, the same effort should be required by those who seek information of a valuable nature. People do not automatically deserve a reply. If a question comes from the wrong motive, such as envy, we are obligated by our service to the truth not to answer it.

Then I saw that my fault of indiscriminate talking was only a fault and not a real evil. It was, however, worth getting rid of.

The Goldfish Bowl
February 28, 1981

I saw an image of the sun being obscured by layers of clouds. In spite of this, its disk was bright and discernible. Then a butterfly flew across my vision, followed by a scene in which a fish slowly swam about in a fishbowl.

Then a line moved back and forth across my vision as if windshield wipers were operating. As this went on, each layer of clouds was removed until at last I saw the sun appear bright and clear.

I saw a figure placing fan-shaped objects over my eyes, the way an optometrist shifts lenses for us to look through. Then the relationships between all these images emerged.

The butterfly moved freely in nature, subject to all the risks of being free in the open. The fish in the fishbowl, however, was protected from all the normal risks of life, so it swam about in a bored and lifeless manner.

I then realized that the objects that were shifted over my eyes were all the experiences to which I have been subjected in my learning process. Going through these experiences and being subjected to risks gradually brightens my ability to see the meaning in things. Each experience seems to grant a better lens through which to see. By allowing myself to take the risks of learning, I am able to perceive the greater glory of everything in its totality, symbolized by the sun emerging from the clouds.

On Having Enough   February 10, 1990

I was reminded in meditation of a lesson of great importance to me, which, until now, I forgot to include in this book.

For a number of years now, I have found that my annual income has almost matched my expenses to the dollar.

Even during years when I had extraordinary expenses, I received money from an unexpected source that made up the difference.

In spite of all, I felt frustrated, since I wanted to put something aside for the future.

Then in meditation I saw that the Sage means for us to be content that the amount received is enough.

The Way of the Cosmos works.

16.

Following the Path

In naming this book *The Other Way* I indicated that a specific path exists. The path is that part on the medieval map which begins at the edge of the known, and is indicated by a blank.

It is a path that reminds me of the frontiers of science, where a new insight, like that of relativity, puts a whole new perspective on all the scientific knowledge that has been gathered before. It also reminds me of the highest level of religion, where after studying all the books and rituals, everything with which we have become acquainted is suddenly bypassed by realizations which provide an entirely new focus. Such a new focus led Zen monks, over a thousand years ago to say, "Burn the sutras" (the classic Buddhist texts). It is the same with studying the *I Ching*, or meditating. We must be willing to go beyond the known, and to penetrate the deeper meanings in things.

Groping my way along this path I engaged in a number of misguided "enthusiasms." When I first began to experience the liberating truths of the *I Ching*, I thought I should do all I could to share them with others. I was to learn, in the following meditation, that this was not the way of the Sage.

The Bird's Eye View   March 25, 1973

Before me there gradually emerged the image of a mountain. At first it simply looked like a vague hump with something rough all over it until I realized that I was soaring about it like a condor, and had a bird's eye view of it. From my height the forest looked like a beard on a chin rather than like trees on a mountain after the leaves have fallen. As I soared the thought came—"inside the mountain is a treasure." This caused me to envision a cache holding gold and silver. Then I saw the mountain containing rich

248

layers, seams of gold, coal, and other minerals. I realized that we would not know, just by looking at the mountain from the outside, that it contained all this wealth, and that if people did know it, they would be swarming all over it, to take everything away, for selfish purposes. A picture of a strip-mined mountain flashed in my mind.

Then I perceived that we should be like a mountain which contains hidden treasures. These treasures should not be advertised. Like the mountain we should be broad, tolerant, and still. That is the way of the Sage. We should not throw ourselves away on the world, and thus exhaust our energies, but give generously to those who come and who are sincere in their quest. Then our wealth is inexhaustible, and put to its intended use.

What the Goal is Not 1979

When in 1979 I was preparing to publish *A Guide to the I Ching*, I was attacked by a new enthusiasm. For a few days I indulged in a fantasy that I might be helping to generate a "new Taoism" in which thousands of people would be practicing *I Ching* principles. Indeed, the way of the *I Ching* would be the popular new wave of the future.

As usually happens when my ego gets involved, the *I Ching* brought me up short and made me back-pedal. I was counseled to sacrifice all attempts to achieve something tangible. Then in meditation I realized that to strive for fellowship in the name of an idea was misguided. True fellowship requires only that each person strive to end decadent traditions within himself. My job was to write only of the superior clarity of the *I Ching* principles.

For me the work of following the path often has been back-pedalling. Remaining modest requires unending vigilance.

By a Certain Magic November 18, 1989

In sending out this last of the three books I originally planned, to find its way in the world, I am reminded of a certain magic.

The great thing about a book is that as it resides in a bookstore, or on someone's bookshelf, without any fanfare or pushing, it finds its way into the right hands, at the right time. Having observed this magic at work since 1980, I am constantly amazed by it as yet another of the wonderful ways of the Creative.